GunDi

SHOOTER'S GUIDE to
COMPETITIVE
PISTOL SHOOTING

STEVE SIEBERTS

Published by

Gun Digest® Books, an imprint of F+W Media, Inc.
Krause Publications • 700 East State Street • Iola, WI 54990-0001
715-445-2214 • 888-457-2873
www.krausebooks.com

To order books or other products call toll-free 1-800-258-0929
or visit us online at www.gundigeststore.com

ISBN-13: 978-1-4402-4574-9
ISBN-10: 1-4402-4574-6

Cover Design by Kevin Ulrich
Designed by Sandi Carpenter
Edited by Corrina Peterson

Printed in USA

10 9 8 7 6 5 4 3 2 1

DEDICATION

No book of this nature would be possible without the influence and contributions of many people. Many authors dedicate their books to their parents or their teachers, and I'm no exception. My grandfather was an Army veteran and a doughboy in the War to End All Wars. He came through that war and the Great Depression, learned the values of hard work, humility and reverance, and passed those traits down to my dad. My dad was a Navy veteran of WWII and Korea, who, after WWII, worked in the aerospace industry for three decades, doing his part to help win the Space Race. They both had a work ethic and focus for the mission that was passed down to me.

I became involved in competitive shooting in the mid-70s when I joined the Southwest Pistol League, the precursor to the USPSA. I then became a paratrooper with the 82nd Airborne Division, later became involved with the U.S Army Marksmanship Unit, and eventually achieved the Distinguished Pistol Shot Badge, the President's Hundred Tab, and the NRA 2600 pin. I would like to think that the qualities of perseverance, hard work, dedication and focus that were traits of my dad and grandfather allowed me to achieve those shooting goals.

I also would not have achieved my shooting goals without the influence of two early coaches – M/Sgt Oscar Gomez of the Ft Bragg and XVIII Airborne Corps Shooting team, and SFC Ron Martere, Head Coach of the Army Marksmanship Unit – in the early 80s. M/Sgt Gomez taught me the importance of the fundamentals of pistol marksmanship, and how to apply those fundamentals in a consistent way in order to achieve winning results. He also taught me the importance of mental discipline and how that particular shooting fundamental becomes more critical as the shooter's skill progresses. SFC Martere gave me the opportunity to shoot with the Army team over the course of four seasons; he taught me how to compete at a high level, and how to overcome the anxiety known as Match Nerves. SFC Martere really ingrained in me the solid shooting fundamentals that I still carry and apply in shooting competitions today.

Finally, I would like to dedicate this book to my wife Lori, who has given me untold amounts of encouragement in my career over the years, and my two incredible kids, Kyle and Kelly, who have shown me what really matters in life, and constantly fill my wife and I with pride and amazement with their own accomplishments in sports and music.

PREFACE

Shooters new to competitive shooting sports may not have heard of Doug Koenig, but in the world of sport handgunning there is no bigger name.

According to Doug, "Traveling with a local group of guys to all of the matches was just like being at hunting camp every weekend."

If there is a good analogy to Doug's shooting accomplishments, it would have to be similar to what Peyton Manning has done in football and Arnold Palmer in professional golf. Doug holds more than 70 national and world pistol championships, including 16-time Bianchi Cup winner, 3-time World Speed Shooting Champion/Steel Challenge, and 10-time World Champion. He is widely considered to be the best all-around shooter in the world. Doug graciously spent a little time putting his thoughts together for the following contribution shortly after winning his latest Bianchi Cup Championship (2015). I asked Doug a few questions about competitive shooting and this is what he said:

1. Why did you become a competitive pistol shooter? I was drawn to competitive shooting because the hunting season was too short. I was looking for an alternative outlet that would give me the same level of excitement and adrenaline rush I experienced with hunting. Plus, I loved shooting in my back yard whenever the occasion arose.

2. How did you get started in competitive pistol shooting? There was a gun store nearby my home that my dad and I visited regularly. When I was 17, my dad accompanied me and I ordered my first handgun from Frank Behlert's store. Being anxious, I'd stop there every day to see if my pistol had arrived. Frank would show me USPSA and IPSC course books from recent matches he had competed in while explaining to me the different type of gear necessary to compete. Listening to him and asking questions got me super pumped up, so eventually Frank lent me some gear and invited me to a match in Ledgewood NJ in 1986.

Despite it being 17 degrees outside and snowing, I had the time of my life. It was a blast and I knew I was hooked. From then on all I wanted to do was to shoot, not to beat other competitors or become a professional, but just to shoot because I was having so much fun. Traveling with a local group of guys to all of the matches was just like being at hunting camp every weekend.

3. What makes competitive pistol shooting such a great sport? Simple, it's FUN! What makes competitive pistol shooting such a great sport is that you control the outcome of the matches and your score. You don't have to rely on anyone else or referees, you control and are responsible for your outcome. Competitive shooting also teaches you great mental and physical discipline. To be a top level performing shooting athlete, you must work hard to develop all of your skills – shooting, physical and mental. Even if you don't aspire to be great, you can still use the skill sets learned from shooting in your everyday life. Most importantly, be safe and have fun.

4. What advice would you give the new or upcoming competitive pistol shooter just getting started, or wanting to get started, regardless of what form of competitive shooting they wanted to get into? I think the best advice for a potential new shooter is to visit and attend several local matches, watch and talk to the shooters. Everyone is always eager to talk about their sport and they'll go out of their way to introduce someone to the shooting sports. It's a great way to look at the many different types of customized guns, while handling them in the safety areas. Pick the gun that best fits your hands and feels comfortable. A great online resource to check out is NSSF's website, **www.WheretoShoot.org**, you'll find a list of local clubs and what type of shooting discipline they offer. The NRA also has many helpful resources on their website that can steer a new shooter.

INTRODUCTION

The spirit of healthy competition is not unique to the shooting sports. Man versus Man competitions probably go back to when Grok the caveman challenged Hruk, his cave neighbor, to a rock-throwing contest. Mankind has been challenging each other in grueling, arduous and sometimes silly forms of competitions for millennia. The Olympics comprises 28 sports, 300 events and over 10,000 athletes. The shooting sports are represented in the Olympics with such events as the biathlon, which combines cross-country skiing and smallbore rifle shooting, and the handgun events are represented in free pistol, air pistol and rapid-fire pistol. Clearly, shooting, specifically handgun competition, is done at a very high level. What I find amazing is that the marksmanship fundamentals − sight alignment, trigger control and mental discipline − are the same whether employed by world-class athletes in an Olympic sport or the weekend bullseye shooter, casual plinker or 12-year-old junior shooter at a local USPSA match.

That's what makes the handgun sports so much fun; once you have learned basic marksmanship fundamentals, these skills can be applied to the wide range of handgun shooting sports available in the U.S. today. The good news is that these fundamentals are not hard to learn, are not complicated, and the equipment needed for many of the competitive events can be pretty basic. For many of the events outlined in this book, the shooter needs only a serviceable firearm in a minimum caliber, a good quality holster, quality ammunition, three to four reliable magazines or speedloaders for revolvers, and good eye and ear protection. Revolvers are not excluded from any of these events, and in fact, some types of competitive matches are revolver neutral, meaning that the shooter is not penalized for time for using a revolver, which is usually slower to reload. Also, some of the events are more fun and more challenging shooting with a revolver. Steel-type matches in particular are fun to shoot with a revolver.

The new shooter just has to pick one of the shooting events that appeals to him or her and get started. That's where this book comes in. Not only do we show what types of shooting sports are available, but we also discuss how to get started in the game, what equipment is needed, and more importantly, what is not needed. There is also a chapter on reloading and what types of ammunition are appropriate for each type of shooting sport. This book also covers marksmanship fundamentals specific to each game, some of which are unique to the individual game, and some fundamentals are applicable to all of the shooting games covered in the book. Finally, we cover what you need to take your game to the next level, once you have mastered the basics.

An important point to remember about handgun shooting is that is doesn't take great size, strength or power, as witnessed by the fact that some of the very best shooters in the world are women, and they deliver scores that soundly and routinely beat the men. Some of the shooting sports covered in the book do require a certain amount of athletic ability, for example, IPSC, and 3-gun matches that sometimes have the shooter run, jump over or maneuver around obstacles. On the other hand, IDPA, Bullseye and Steel-type matches are usually "stand and shoot," and require very little, if any, movement. In Bullseye, especially, the shooter stands with a solid stance, with no movement. Steel matches may have the shooter step from one box to another a short distance away so there is a little movement to break things up, and IDPA may have a stage where the shooter needs to move from one position to another, sometimes around barricades, or shooting through windows.

Accommodations are always made in the rules to allow the shooter to complete the stage in a fair manner, so people with physical conditions will always be able to compete. I've been to many matches when the rules are interpreted to allow a shooter with bad a bad back, for example, to shoot the stage from a kneeling position, when the stage stipulated firing from a prone position. What the handgun sports do require is a healthy spirit of competition, a desire to excel, dedication and, most importantly, a desire to have fun!

Junior shooters can also compete at a very high level, and I've seen teenage shooters outclass the older, more experienced shooters at matches on a regular basis. New shooters are also always welcomed at any of these events, and almost all matches have new shooter orientations before the shooter can compete. This is needed for safety reasons, but also helps alleviate the anxiety and intimidation factors that new shooters sometimes have, and provide for a welcoming environment that really helps new shooters into the game.

We hope you enjoy the book. We have tried to put as much good information into it as possible in order to get the new shooter, or the shooter who wants to expand to another shooting game, enough information to pique their interest and get them going in a safe and fun direction.

CHAPTER ONE

BULLSEYE COMPETITION

The Hi-Standard .22 LR was a pistol that was very popular for bullseye competition, and is still used today.

It's not by accident that the first chapter in this book is about bullseye pistol shooting. Competitive bullseye shooting in its current form goes back to the mid-20th century. Bullseye, also known as conventional pistol shooting or, in NRA parlance, precision shooting, was the original three-gun match. It combines the precision of a slow fire event, with the action of rapid fire shooting. The current form of the sport involves firing three matches of 90 rounds each, adding up to a 270-shot course of fire, with each shot being worth ten points.

The match is shot with three guns, the .22 rimfire, the centerfire, which is any pistol of .38 caliber or larger, and the .45 match, which is shot with a .45-caliber pistol. These days, the centerfire is often shot with the same gun used in the .45 match.

The three events are shot with 90 shots each, and are broken down with two, ten-round strings firing at a slow fire target at 50 yards.

The National Match Course is ten rounds slow fire with each gun, then ten shots of timed fire (two five round strings), in 20 sec-

The economical Ruger MkIII and MkIV can be effective at bullseye, even at Camp Perry up until the shooter gets to Sharpshooter level scores, and is a great way to get into the game.

This competitor uses the 7½-inch barreled S&W M41 with iron sights. This is the gold standard handgun for .22 LR pistols in bullseye competition. It combines an excellent trigger, outstanding ergonomics and match grade accuracy right out of the box.

This is an example of a classic bullseye wadcutter gun. This gun can be used to compete in the centerfire and .45 events. This gun could not be used to compete in the President's Hundred match or the Excellence-in-Competition match. This pistol is to be used only for light target wadcutter ammunition.

This shooter has attended the USAMU Small Arms firing School Clinic, and is using the Walther .22 LR pistol at the slow fire stage at the 50-yard target.

These shooters are replacing the 50-yard targets with the 25-yard targets. Camp Perry is one of the only bullseye ranges that has the competitor move their gear from the 25 to the 50-yard line and back. At most ranges the competitor sets up at the static firing line and the targets are set up at either the 25-yard berm or the 50-yard berm.

onds each at 25 yards; and rapid fire, which is two strings of five rounds at ten seconds each. Then two ten round strings of timed fire, and two ten round strings of rapid fire.

Short of competing in an Olympic shooting event, bullseye is arguably the most challenging handgun competition in the U.S. today. If you doubt this, take a paper plate, paint it black and staple it to a target. Now step back 50 yards, and with one hand holding either your .22 or .45-caliber pistol,

try to put one round into the plate. Now, try to put ten consecutive rounds into the plate within ten minutes. Next, take a smaller plate, around three inches in diameter, and place it at on a target at 25 yards. With one hand, try to put five rounds into the target within ten seconds. Now reload, and put five more rounds into the target in ten seconds. This is a brief representation of bullseye shooting.

It's fun, extremely challenging, and if you can do it well, you can apply those

This competitor is getting ready to fire the slow fire match. He is standing at the 50-yard line, and the targets can be seen in the background. Note how the shooter will place the pistol into his firing hand, using the non-firing hand in order to get a proper grip. This process can take several seconds before the shooter "feels" the grip on the pistol is just right.

fundamentals to virtually every other type of competitive pistol shooting. Some people may think bullseye is boring, but if you can do it well, it makes the action shooting games like USPSA much easier. Even though practical shooting games are slanted

USPSA: United States Practical Shooting Association
IPSC: International Practical Shooting Federation
IDPA: International Defensive Pistol Association

toward speed, there may still be a 60-yard shot on a target and this is where the skills like sight alignment and trigger control learned on the bullseye range really help out. If you can do it with one hand on a bullseye range, doing it with two hands on an IPSC range seems easy. IDPA becomes more fun, because while IDPA shooting is similar to USPSA, it is slanted more towards accuracy and not speed. Applying the fundamentals of sight alignment and trying to hit a three-inch circle at 25 yards with a .45 ACP using one hand, transferring that skill over to an IDPA target that has an eight-inch circle at eight yards, and firing with two hands seems almost too easy.

I first started my shooting career in the mid-70s with the Southwest Pistol League, but didn't really learn how to shoot until I became a member of the Ft Bragg Pistol Team in 1980, competing in bullseye matches, and then as a member of the Army Marksmanship Unit.

I believe bullseye competition is the best way to learn how to shoot a handgun, not only because it is so challenging to do well, but also because it really ingrains the funda-

Camp Perry instills competitive desire and dedication from many shooters. All competitors receive a blue cloth tab noting the year of the match. This competitor has continuously competed at Camp Perry every year since 1972.

During the Harry Reeves Memorial Revolver Match, competitors can fire revolvers with iron sights and with electronic dot sights.

Just another day at the National Championships at Camp Perry. The firing goes on, even in the hard wind and rain during a rapid fire string.

When in doubt, official NRA referees are asked to come in and find a shot if the scorer does not find ten holes on the target, or declare a shot value.

During the revolver matches, the iron sight firearms can compete right along with the electronic sights. Note the guns are the same, both are S&W 686 revolvers, one blued steel and one in stainless steel. Both are equally competitive.

mentals of pistol marksmanship.

Once these fundamentals are learned, it's much easier to apply them to other forms of competition. I would argue that it's easier to make a bullseye shooter into an excellent IPSC, IDPA or practical pistol shooter, than it is to make an action shooter into a bullseye shooter. Additionally, the slow fire stages of bullseye transfer very easily to silhouette competition.

The game is actually pretty simple, there are three courses of fire: slow fire, timed fire, and rapid fire. These are shot at 50 and 25 yards for an outdoor match. Indoor matches are usually shot exclusively at 25 yards with reduced targets used for the slow fire event. An example outdoor 900 match would include:

- Two strings of slow fire. Each string consists of 10 shots at 50 yards at a NRA B6 target.
- One National Match Course consisting of one 10-shot slow fire string at 50 yards, two 5-shot strings of timed fire at 25 yards, and two 5-shot strings of rapid fire at 25 yards.
- Four strings of timed fire. Each string consists of five shots in 20 seconds at 25 yards at a NRA B8 target.
- Four strings of rapid fire. Each string consists of 5 shots in 10 seconds at 25 yards at a NRA B8 target.

The First 900 Match is shot with .22 LR. The next 900 is a centerfire event, shot with .38-caliber or larger, and the last 900 event is

This competitor in the revolver match dons full rain gear and can keep shooting in relative comfort, even in the rain and wind.

This competitor is getting ready to fire a string of slow fire. The green 25-yard line benches and the white 50-yard line targets can be seen in the background. Getting ready to shoot a string of slow fire, the shooter needs to get a plan together in mind prior to firing a single shot. The mental game is critical to any shooting, but especially in slow fire in the bullseye game.

Camp Perry is an outdoor match, and with it comes the threat of rain and wind. Here a fairly large storm front moves in quickly during the rapid fire string, and the shooters must be ready to shoot under any weather condition.

shot with .45-caliber for a 2700 point course of fire.

The current record is 2680x159 Xs, shot by Herschel Anderson in 1974. There has never been a perfect score fired in bullseye.

The Small Arms Firing School is a clinic put on by the U.S. Army Marksmanship Unit. It allows civilian shooters the op-portunity to get the best coaching from the top shooters in the country. The classroom portion is followed up with a range portion. This is a great opportunity for civilians to receive tips from military competitors, who fire thousands of rounds each week and have a deep understanding of marksmanship fundamentals.

Target analysis is an important teaching tool at the Small Arms Firing School. Quite a bit can be learned by looking at the results on the target.

The Small Arms Firing School is broken down into Basic and Advanced schools, with a classroom portion and a range portion. The military provides the range expertise. Here is a young Marine showing a civilian shooter the finer points of sight alignment.

Target analysis and discussing the application of marksmanship fundamentals is an important aspect of the Small Arms Firing School, where military competitors offer helpful tips and coaching to civilian shooters on the range.

The Small Arms Firing School gets a huge group of shooters wanting to learn from the best of the best. The level of marksmanship instruction from the Service teams is the highest in the world.

This Marine at the Small Arms Firing School demonstrates to the new civilian shooter the finer points about placement of the trigger finger on the trigger, and how to press the trigger straight to the rear.

Under the watchful eye of their Marine instructors, these shooters can significantly increase their scores.

This Marine shows the competitor how to get a natural point of aim.

CAMP PERRY PHOTO GALLERY

The entrance to Camp Perry has been unchanged for decades.

The Civilian Marksmanship Program oversees the Distinguished Shooter Badges for rifle and pistol marksman. The trailers have gunsmiths on staff to work on the handguns for the competitors, and there are several shooters waiting on the gunsmiths to do their magic.

The U.S. Army Marksmanship Unit utilizes their trailer to support the team when traveling to and at the matches. The trailer has a staff of gunsmiths that are ready to work on any of the team's firearms if needed.

The All-Guard team has its trailer at the ready. For those young competitors who are thinking about a part-time military career and still want to shoot, it's a great way to go.

This is the Headquarters Building to Camp Perry

The Quonset huts are a Camp Perry staple, and were used to house German POWs during WWII. These have been rebuilt since I stayed in them in the mid-80s. They are still spartan, but not as bad as they were back in the day. The huts really add to the ambiance and history that is Camp Perry. I highly recommend that if you ever get the chance to shoot at Camp Perry, stay at least one night in the huts.

Commercial Row at Camp Perry is a great place to check out what's new in parts, ammo and accessories, and gives shooters the opportunity to talk with shooters from all over the country who love bullseye shooting.

The Camp Perry historical marker is a reminder of the long history of competitive shooting there.

The morning of the first day of the National Matches is a quiet time before the pomp and circumstance of opening ceremonies.

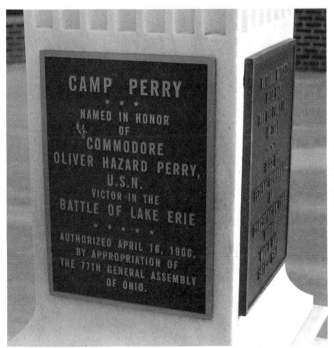

This plaque states how Camp Perry came about. There are a lot of reminders like this around the base, reinforcing the history of Camp Perry.

This WWII Sherman tank will be the main battle tank in the skirmish against a squad of German Wehrmacht soldiers in the re-enactment battle prior to firing the opening shot to start the National Matches at Camp Perry.

Opening ceremony at Camp Perry.

The skirmish between the WWII U.S. Forces and the Germans for the Battle of Camp Perry's opening ceremony commences!

The Sherman tank takes out the Germans in the battle.

The B-17 and other warplanes performed a flyover and was one of the high points of the opening ceremony at Camp Perry.

The pistolsmiths in the Civilian Marksmanship Program (CMP) repair van perform trigger pull checks on competitors' firearms to make sure the trigger pull weight is legal for the gun and match they are competing in. Always consult the rulebooks to see what is legal for the gun and match.

Note the yellow tape around the trigger guard, signifying the trigger pull has been checked and the gun is legal to compete. The tape must stay on when the competitor moves to the firing line.

The .22 pistols are also checked for correct trigger weight of pull and tagged with yellow tape around the trigger guard to show they have been inspected by the CMP pistolsmiths.

The Sherman tank poses for pictures after defeating the squad of German attackers. I believe this is an M4A3 Sherman tank with the bigger main gun that was produced later in the war.

The entrance to Camp Perry hasn't changed in decades.

The vanquished re-enactment German army poses with smiles along with a couple of the American troops for a post-battle photo.

The NRA referees stand watch over the match proceedings, and are indispensable to running the National Matches.

The "Wailing Wall" is where the day's scores are posted. Competitors will spend quite a bit of time here once the matches start.

Congressman Bob Latta (R-OH) fires the ceremonial first shot to officially start the matches

EQUIPMENT

Up until about 30 years ago the revolver was shot almost exclusively for all three events, and shooters used the .22 rimfire revolver, a .38-caliber revolver and a .45 ACP revolver. In fact, back in the early 1980s when I was shooting bullseye, a couple of shooters at Camp Perry still competed with all revolvers just for the nostalgia factor. They weren't so much concerned about their score, although they were competitive and wanted to do well, they were more concerned about being competitive *with the revolvers*. They were still firing scores in the high 2500s, which is excellent shooting with any gun, but is even more amazing when performed with a revolver.

For the .22 event, an accurate pistol is a must, and while alibis are allowed, the pistol has to be reliable. An alibi is where the shooter gets a refire due to a malfunction of the pistol. The classic bullseye target pistol has been the S&W M41 since it burst on the

scene in 1957. The upside to this gun is that it's ready to go right out of the box if you want to compete with iron sights. Mounting options for the gun are many. The pistol is available with either a 5-inch heavy barrel, or the 7-1/2-inch version. The shorter barrel is very good for the timed and rapid fire events, since the added weight of the heavy barrel makes recoil recovery much quicker. With the longer 7-1/2-inch barrel, the longer barrel gives a longer sight radius for shooters using it with iron sights. A longer sight radius makes it easier for the shooter to pick up small deviations in sight misalignment, so the longer barrel is inherently more accurate for the shooter, all things being equal.

[N-sa}My preference is the longer barrel with its longer sight radius for slow fire event, but I like the shorter, heavy barrel for the timed and rapid fire stages. My all-time favorite barrel for the M41 was a custom job made up by one of the MTU pistolsmiths, who installed a front sight blade on an

This competitor uses the 7-1/2-inch barreled S&W M41 with iron sights. This is the gold standard handgun for .22 LR pistols in bullseye competition. It combines an excellent trigger, outstanding ergonomics and match grade accuracy right out of the box.

This competitor is using a .22 LR conversion, with an optical sight, for the .22 match. The competitor to her left is using the popular S&W M41 with ergonomic grips. Both guns are equally competitive.

This shooter has experienced a malfunction and the Safety Officers will verify that it's a legitimate and allowed malfunction, and will be given a reshoot, otherwise known as an alibi.

Some gunboxes are homemade from wood, and work perfectly, and some are converted guitar cases.

extension and machined that into the front of the heavy barrel so I had the best of both worlds: a longer sight radius for slow fire and a heavy barrel for the timed and rapid fire events.

[N-sa}The M41 is a great pistol, but the retail price is around $1200, so it's a little daunting for a new shooter to justify the price for top level pistol like that. A great alternative is the Ruger MkII or the newer MkIII. The gun is very accurate out of the box, and there is a plethora of aftermarket parts and accessories to enhance the pistol.

The gun and your scores will be enhanced with a trigger job from a good pistolsmith, Also, match quality barrels are available, and the pistol can be mounted with electronic sights. Older Hi-Standard

These competitors are getting ready to fire either timed or rapid fire from the 25-yard line. They are setting their stance and position, which will give them a natural point of aim. The next step will be to get the pistol out of the box and get the grip situated.

This shot shows how the American Ruger .22 LR pistols can compete with the high end European Walther target pistols side-by-side. The economical Ruger has the accuracy to shoot highly competitive scores.

The Ruger MkII and MkIII with iron sights are very popular, accurate and economical pistols at Camp Perry, and very effective.

This shooter keeps previous targets in the box as positive reinforcement. The shooter can remember what the thought process was when they shot this target or that target, and it will help replicate that performance.

guns are still plenty accurate for bullseye competition, and parts are still available. The Hi-Standards are excellent bullseye guns.

The M52 was later chambered in 9mm, and the last M52 was manufactured in 1992. I talked to several shooters from the Army team while I was shooting there, and there were two reasons the gun never caught on in a big way. First, it was more difficult to learn to shoot three guns in a bullseye match, rather than just learning and becoming proficient with just two, so it took more work to fire the same overall scores. The second reason was the ammunition required better follow-through, especially in the slow fire matches. This was because the very slow velocity of the HBWC .38 Spl ammunition meant that the bullet was moving out of the barrel very, very slowly, and any movement between when the primer was struck and the bullet was out of the barrel was detrimental to accuracy. The shooter could exert enormous influence on the point of impact. So, most shooters these days simply use their .45 ACP wadcutter gun for both centerfire and for the .45 event, which is perfectly legal.

The NRA Referee is always available. This ref is using a scoring plug in order to determine the value of the shot. The glass of the plug magnifies the plug, which is inserted into the bullet hole, and if the plug breaks the line on the scoring ring, the competitor is given the higher point value.

It's also an advantage in that the shooter only needs two types of ammunition and only needs to learn one centerfire gun. If you are trying to earn your Distinguished Pistol Shot Badge, your President's Hundred Tab, you will also want to shoot the hardball gun. If you don't aspire to that yet, and want to earn your NRA 2600 pin, then forego the hardball gun and just shoot .45 wadcutter for both the centerfire and .45 matches. Then, once the 2600 Pin is achieved, add in a hardball gun to the .45 match, and use the wadcutter in centerfire. Shooting a steady diet of hardball will get you ready to compete in the EIC and President's match.

A secondary effect of shooting all that hardball is that it will make you a better bullseye shooter overall when you go back to shooting all wadcutter, since the hardball gun is more difficult gun to shoot. The recoil generated by the hardball gun is what makes it a more difficult gun to shoot. Recoil recovery is more difficult, the trigger is heavier, sight radius is relatively short, and it's just a more difficult gun to shoot well. After a steady diet of hardball, switching over to wadcutter will make the wadcutter scores skyrocket.

So, for firearms, you will need a good, accurate .22 semi-auto, and a good .45 ACP 1911, which is set up for either wadcutter or hardball. The competitor can actually have one gun that can handle both loads, but you will need to switch out recoil springs. The

This competitor shows how to control the recoil of the 1911A1 hardball gun when firing one hand.

This shooter gets a proper grip by placing the gun into the firing hand with the non-firing hand, and then making adjustments. Most shooters take from several seconds to over a minute in order to get the "feel" of a good grip prior to firing the string.

wadcutter gun gets the lighter spring, usually about a 12-14-lb spring, and the hardball gun gets either a factory 17-lb spring, or possibly a heavier 18-lb. The hardball gun can only be fitted with iron sights only, no

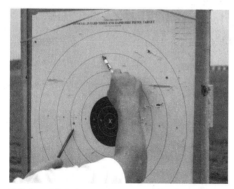

This target is being scored by the scorer, while the competitor is looking on. Note the bullet has struck the right side of the target frame, and the bullet fragments have splashed across the target. This shot will be scored as a miss. This is a common occurrence when the targets are turning either toward the shooter or turning away during the timed and rapid fire stages.

optics are allowed.

The 1911 will need to be able to fire at least 3-inch groups at 50 yards, with the type and brand of ammunition used in competition. The shots going into 1-1/2 inches at 50 yards is ideal. Colt pistols are popular as a starting point, as are various models of Springfield Armory. The extreme accuracy required of the game necessitates using the most accurate guns and ammo possible, so this usually means a custom gun, or at least a production gun that has been customized by a bullseye pistolsmith who understands and knows how to build a 1911 that can deliver the accuracy required of the game.

Once you have the gun in hand, test it with as wide a sample of ammunition you will shoot. Factory ammunition is expensive, and reloaded ammunition is what most shooters use. However, it's difficult to load ammunition that will deliver the accuracy needed, so many shooters use factory match ammunition for the slow fire matches, and

Not all guns boxes are the same, and you don't need fancy equipment in order to get started. Note how one competitor uses a traditional gun box, and the other brought his gear to the firing line with a hard shell case.

Some shooters don't even need a gunbox. Just a simple bag, gun and magazines, and some way to spot the bullet holes on the target.

Note that these gunboxes are all similar, but at the same time different. Also, note the fishing net to catch the brass. The empty cartridge cases are the most expensive part of the cartridge, so reloaders are always trying to scoop up the brass any way they can. It also helps keep brass out of the face of your shooting neighbor.

The referee is using an overlay on the target to determine if there is more than a single bullet that has gone through a hole. The overlay has a ring that is of bullet diameter, and when placed over a hole that is suspected of having two bullets passing through a single hole, the overlay will show this because if two bullets go through one hole, the hole will be slightly oblong, and the ring on the overlay will show this elongation very clearly.

reloads for the timed and rapid fire stages fired at 25 yards. Other necessary equipment is a good gun box.

Many new shooters may not need a gun box at first. USAMU Blue team member and later National Champion Tom Woods carried his guns and equipment to the firing line in two small suitcases. Good glasses and ear protection are a must.

I usually wore two types of hearing protection – ear plugs and ear muffs. If there are 50 shooters on the firing line, there will be quite a bit of noise during timed and rapid fire.

Another piece of essential equipment is a good spotting scope. It's impossible to see the bullet holes at 50 yards, and really difficult to see them at 25 unless the sun is right. A good stopwatch or timer will help manage time during the slow fire match, and I always kept some rosin in my gun box for hot summer days when the humidity was high. Rosin on the shooting hand will really help the grip, especially with the hardball gun.

One piece of equipment that many shooters don't think of is a good scorebook. Champions Choice has good bullseye scorebooks. It's great to sit back after the match and analyze the good and the bad, but don't dwell on the bad, just figure out what went wrong and that will help correct it next time.

Don't fall into the trap of thinking about your score *while* you are shooting. Too many shooters try to "shoot and compute" and it can really negatively affect your scores. It's very easy to shoot a ten-shot string, say a 97 on the timed fire stage, and think, "Ok, I'm only down three points, I need to shoot a 99 on the next one in order to break 2600." That's shooting and computing, and is one of the worst things you can do when trying to compete.

These two competitors are firing in the Excellence-in Competition match. The competitor on the left uses blinders to keep his concentration focused.

Civilian and military shooter compete side-by-side at Camp Perry. Here a civilian fires in the EIC match with a member of the All-Guard team. The four main service teams are the All-Army, All-Guard, All-Reserve, and the Marine Corps Team.

These competitors firing in the M9 EIC Match, uses the fishing net to catch the flying brass.

This competitor has a disc over the left eye. This blocks out the vision of the non-dominant eye, and is a better method than closing the eye. This lets the shooter keep both eyes open bringing in more light to the both eyes and producing clearer vision.

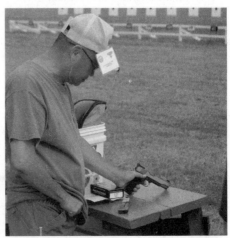

This shooter uses his registration badge as a blinder, which is legal. He is also gathering his thoughts in the EIC match, prior to the targets turning and commencing fire.

Blinders are also good to keep on the shooting glasses, as they help with focus and concentration. These work just like blinders on a race horse. If you've ever watched a horse race, the blinders are put on the horses so they don't get distracted by the horses on the side, and blinders on a bullseye shooter work the same way.

It can be a little distracting, with 50 shooters on the firing line all getting ready to shoot a string of fire. So blinders are a good way to help block out any distractions. Those are the basics.

As you get into the game, you will accumulate other gadgets that will help you shoot more comfortably. These things may not help your score, but they make it more comfortable to shoot well, like a towel hanging off the gun box strap. If heat causes sweating you can wipe the sweat off your hands and reapply rosin. This is a great way to keep a good grip on the guns, especially when shooting the heavier recoiling hardball guns.

This shooter is setting his stance and position to the target prior to shooting a string at the short line, either a timed or rapid fire string. Obtaining a natural point of aim is important so that the sights are centered in the black when the targets turn.

This competitor is getting ready for the 25-yard timed and rapid fire targets to turn and commence firing. Bringing the pistol up, then down to the target while taking several deep breaths, and then getting mentally ready to fire the string is a common technique in bullseye.

A good bullseye stance: feet apart, knees relaxed and head pointed toward the target.

The screens help keep flying brass from breaking the shooter's concentration. Also note the towels and spotting scopes. These shooters get a ten-minute prep time prior to firing the slow fire stage.

When firing either a timed or rapid fire string, and experiencing a malfunction, do not try to clear the malfunction, simply raise the hand and a referee will come over to verify and you will get a reshoot. The lowest ten shots will become your score.

Other things to keep handy are rain gear and hand warmers. Bullseye is an outdoor game, and some ranges like Camp Perry do not have overhead cover, so rain gear is important. Shooting in the off season, some matches will be shot in cold weather, especially in northern states. Some kind of a barrier, or screen clamped to the gun box, is also a handy item to have.

It can really ruin a string when the hot brass from the .45 of the shooter next to you is bouncing off your arm or flying past your field of view.

Awards in this game include the NRA 2600 Club Pin. This is where the competitor fires a score above 2600 at a sanctioned match out of a possible 2700 point course of fire. The NRA 2600 Club pin is very prestigious. In fact, in the 1940s and early 50s, it was thought that firing a score above 2600 was physically impossible, something akin to running a four minute mile, or breaking the sound barrier, none of which had been accomplished, and many thought that none of those events ever would be accomplished. Now scores above 2600 are routine at any decent sized match, and the four minute mile and the sound barrier have been broken for decades.

The other award is the Distinguished Pistol Shot Badge. The competitor fires a special hardball gun only in the Dinstinguished Match, and is awarded points toward the badge based on the score. Thirty points are needed to earn the badge.

The last award is the President's Hundred

Tab. This is given out to the top 100 rifle and top 100 pistol shooters only at the National Championships at Camp Perry every year. What makes this award especially tough is that since it's only given out to the top 100 shooters, if the top 99 shooters have already have the award, this means that only one new shooter will get the award that year. And all shooters always shoot that match since they are trying to be the overall winner, regardless if they already have the tab or not, so there are very few opportunities for new shooters to get the tab. The match is a National Match Course, with an additional slow fire match added. I received the NRA 2600 Club pin and my Distinguished Badge in 1983, and the President's Hundred tab in 1984. It's the Triple Crown of bullseye pistol shooting.

GUN MODIFICATIONS

My old bullseye gun was upgraded with a upswept beavertail grip safety and a lightweight hammer, but still keeps its BoMar rib with the adjustable rear sight.

This Bomar rib was customized at my request with an extended front sight blade by John Videki, inventor of the Videki aluminum 3-hole trigger. Note the barrel muzzle. I recrowned the muzzle with an 11-degree target crown.

The Ruger MkII and MkIII target are good starter guns for bullseye competition. Image courtesy Ruger, Inc.

This is a bullseye gun that I built and competed with many years ago, upgraded with a lightweight trigger, beavertail safety, 30 LPI checkering on the frontstrap, a new match barrel and a lightweight hammer. I recently removed the Bomar rib and installed the Ultradot electronic sight on the Clark solid rib on the slide.

The Ultradot Matchdot II is a popular electronic dot sight used by many Bullseye competitors. The sight has a dot that is adjustable for size and intensity. The sight also has different styles of reticles.

The Springfield Armory 1911 wadcutter gun is a solid pistol for centerfire and .45 courses of fire. Image courtesy Springfield Armory, Inc.

The Aimpoint 9000SC is another popular electronic sight for the bullseye game.

CHAPTER TWO

USPSA/IPSC COMPETITION

USPSA/IPSC is the granddaddy of practical shooting competitions in the United States today. Just to clarify, IPSC, the International Practical Shooting Confederation, first grew out of an informal group of shooters and handgun self-defense experimenters. These early groups of men challenged the status quo of self-defense handguns and handgun training. Informal competitions evolved with these disparate groups in the early 1950s with the "Leatherslap" competitions around the Big Bear Lake area of Northern California. Gradually, the matches became more sophisticated and formalized, and IPSC was officially formed in 1976 in Columbia, MO. USPSA, the United States Practical Shooting Association, is the U.S. region of IPSC and was incorporated in 1984, so membership in USPSA automatically gives the competitor membership in IPSC. Today, over 400 affiliated clubs around the world offer competitive matches almost every week.

The USPSA is a great training ground for practical shooting. The organization has been around for over twenty years and the

This shooter has received the start signal, has drawn the pistol from the holster and is bringing both hands to the gun in the center of the chest. Next the gun will get thrust out toward the target, then he will engage the target. These are excellent practical shooting fundamentals in action.

Here is the next shot in the firing sequence, where the pistol is out and the arms are fully extended, just prior to the first shot being fired. Note the concentration and focus on the sights.

This is how you move safely from one position to another. Notice how the shooter is looking at the spot he wants to get to, while keeping the pistol pointed downrange with the finger off the trigger.

This shooter shows how to move from left to right, while keeping the gun pointed in a safe direction with finger off the trigger.

This is an Unlimited Class shooter, engaging the target. Note the relaxed posture and concentration.

matches have been developed over time, competing in a USPSA match is an outstanding test of shooting skills and gunhandling.

I first became aware of IPSC in the mid 1970s. I was 19 years old and living in Santa Monica at the time. I heard about some people who were shooting some fun obstacle course-type pistol matches out in the desert.

I used to visit at some of the gun shops in West Los Angeles. One of them was a big shop by the name of London Guns that was one of my favorite shops. The store had Old World wood paneling on the walls and smelled of Hoppe's #9. They had everything there, even old English double rifles and Parker shotguns that went for 60k each, and this was in 1970s dollars.

They had a flyer in the store advertising the match and I decided to drive out there and check it out. The first time I went I didn't take a gun, I just wanted to see what it was all about. The match director was a person by the name of Mike Dalton, later to become a huge figure in the development of practical shooting in the 70s and 80s. Another director there was a person by the name of Mickey Fowler, one of the top competitors at that time and the winner of the USPSA World Championships in 1979. The course design at the time was very much like an obstacle course, and I specifically remember a 6-foot retaining wall that had to be scaled. They also had Cooper Tunnels, where the shooter had to crawl through a tunnel of 2x4s that were laid across posts in the ground. These posts were about two feet off the ground and the 2x4s were just laid on top. If the competitor knocked one off, it was a time penalty for each 2x4 that was knocked off. The 6-foot wall was particularly difficult for the younger and older shooters.

The next time I came to the match I brought an older Colt Trooper 6-inch 357

This competitor starts with both hands on the barricade, then draws and engages the Poppers in sequence.

This shooter ran from one side of the red box to the other, staying in the box and engaging targets along the way, and upon reaching the final shooting position fired on the last set of targets. Note the son recording the string with the cell phone, a very common occurrence at competitive matches today.

This shooter is getting the required firing sequence in his mind before getting the start signal from the RO. Being mentally prepared to shoot is almost more important than being physically ready, whether it's a USPSA match, or any form of competitive shooting.

Magnum with +P loads. I was told not to bring light target loads, and I wasn't reloading at the time, so +P loads it was. That, combined with the heavy double action trigger pull and the fact that it was my first match, led to some pretty dismal scores.

That was also the first time I had experienced "match nerves" and it was something I've dealt with ever since. I shot a few more matches with that revolver, and then went to a Colt Commander for a few more matches. Shortly after that, I enlisted in the Army and volunteered for the 82nd Airborne Division, and found that there were IPSC, USPSA and other formal and informal "practical" pistol matches pretty much everywhere across the country. I've shot matches in Denver, North Carolina, Northern and Southern California,

New Jersey, Kentucky and other places, and have found that the matches are always professionally run, fun, and attract a great group of people.

While I've competed in USPSA matches for decades, it's always been an on and off relationship, and I've never shot enough classifiers to actually get a classification card. Therefore, every time I enter a match I'm unclassified, but when I was competing fairly regularly I was shooting low B scores. Back in the day, a competitor needed to shoot a certain number of classifiers per year, but now, USPSA has a more sophisticated classification system in place, so if an unclassified shooter like myself enters a match, they can get classified very quickly, weeding out the sandbaggers.

This shooter engages the targets out in the open, while the target is partially obscured. This is more typical for a USPSA match rather than an IDPA match, where the competitor would be firing from behind cover.

Here the shooter runs from start position to the table, where the loaded pistol will be picked up and the targets engaged.

This shooter has just engaged the three targets to his right, and is now reloading on the move and moving to his left in order to engage another set of targets. Note the safety factor is always in play.

Junior Class shooters get into USPSA is a big way. Here is a Junior Class competitor showing the folks how it's done with a stock Glock.

The stages don't always start from the holster. Here the shooter draws the pistol from a slot, simulating a drawer. Mixing things up always keep the stages interesting and fun.

Here is another shooter firing the string with a 1911, probably the most competitive pistol in practical shooting. Note the GoPro on the hat.

USPSA competitors are broken down into a classification system based on a formula of scores and time. The classifications are as follows:

- Grand Master – 95-100%
- Master – 85-94.9%
- A Class – 75-84.9%
- B Class – 60- 74.9%
- C Class – 40- 59.9%
- D Class – Below 40%

The classification system represents the score at it relates to the highest scores on file for a particular course of fire. So your score is compared to the high scores, and is a percentage of that high score. It's a great way to see how you compare to other shooters across the country.

Here the shooter has finished firing at this position, has dumped the magazine, and is reaching for a fresh magazine while moving to the next firing position – and doing all of that safely.

Women shooters compete right along side with the men and do just as well. There is a Women's classification, but the scores are comparable to the men. Here this shooter controls the recoil of the .45 ACP to great effect.

It was out of these early matches, grounded in defensive handgunning, that IPSC and USPSA grew. Over time, as techniques became more sophisticated, the guns themselves became more and more specialized.

Additionally, there are various categories that a person can compete in, these include Junior, Lady, Senior, Super Senior, Military and Law Enforcement.

The basic tenets of practical shooting center around three core values that are grounded in defensive pistolcraft: accuracy, power and speed. In fact, the early motto of IPSC was *Dilgentia-Vis-Celeritas*, which is Latin for: accuracy, power and speed. I still have a patch from those early days as a member of the club with this motto on it. These three fundamentals of defensive pistol shooting were developed by the father of defensive pistol shooting, Col. Jeff Cooper. He realized that in order to have a positive outcome with a handgun used in self-defense, the shooter must have all three. Accuracy is of no use if you cannot deploy the pistol fast enough in a gunfight, and power is no good if you cannot hit your target. And, using a handgun quickly in a gunfight is useless if you cannot hit your target or do so with a gun lacking stopping power, so in order to

win, you must have all three. You must shoot accurately, with a pistol that has sufficient power to stop a fight, and you have to engage the target quickly or you lose.

Courses of fire today stick to those basic principles of defensive pistol shooting, but these days have a more competitive spin. The course of fire can really run the gamut of the course designers' imagination and really test the shooters skills.

The courses laid out are as follows:

Short Course – The Short Course is designed to be a test with few rounds fired, not so much as the distances involved. The Short Course is designed to be shot with no more than 12 rounds in order to complete it and no more than two shooting stations. This is a "quick and dirty" stage that can be shot quickly.

Medium Course – This is a more involved stage, where it must take no more than 20 shots to complete, and no more than three shooting positions. Distances also tend to be fairly short, and the shooter must be forced to shoot from multiple firing positions. They cannot shoot from just one position. This theme of shooting and movement is replicated throughout most practical shooting, not just USPSA, but other forms as well.

This stage has the shooter start with the hands on the board, but the competitor is looking to where he needs to be to begin firing. Always thinking one step ahead is a big part of wining in this game. The mental challenge of competitive shooting is what makes it fun.

The shooter has just moved to the spot at a dead run, but still keeps the pistol out in front of him, to shorten the time to push the pistol out and begin firing again. These are the little techniques that shave time off the run.

Here is the third shot in the sequence; note how the shooter is still moving forward, but firing through the window at the same time. This is called economy of motion.

Long Course – This course is set up to require the competitor to fire the stage with no more than 32 shots, so these tend to be petty elaborate courses of fire, with multiple firing points and sophisticated props and design. Here the course designers can really show off their imagination.

Standard Course – There are specialty courses of fire as well. These courses are found and many club level matches and most, if not all of the larger matches. The Standard Course is used to help competitors establish a base level of skill.

Classifier – Classifiers are used in order to allow the competitor to obtain a classification rating as a way to gauge their level of skill as measured against other competitors. This way, competitors of equal skill are competing in a class, based on their skill level, and you avoid having shooters with unequal skill competing against each other. So for example, you won't have Grand Masters competing in the same class as a D-level shooter. Classifiers are generally set up as a straightforward stage, and are not usually very complicated, but still allow the USPSA to properly set the skill level for comparison purposes.

Speed Shoot – Speed shoots are just that – speed shooting. They are shot with no more than 16 rounds from a single firing position, at multiple targets, as fast as possible. They may be shot with a least one mandatory reload, and could be shot either strong or weak hand after the reload, depending on the course designer.

TARGETS

The targets used in USPSA competition are the usual targets used for other types of practical shooting, the IPSC paper target, and steel targets are used. There are two types of paper targets and several types of steel targets, including Pepper Poppers, and square and disc steel targets that may be used as well. The classic IPSC paper target has scoring zones that relate to the quality of hit the competitor places on the targets, the closer to the center, the higher the hit value. There are two "A" zone areas, corresponding to the center of the target, and the center of the upper scoring area, hit values then decrease, as the shot placement gets away from these "A" zones, going to "B," "C" and "D." Shots outside the "D" zone are scored as a miss.

Pepper Poppers are steel targets that are meant to be knocked down with a center hit using a handgun of sufficient power. Remember, this game is about accuracy, power and speed. Poppers are calibrated to fall using a cartridge of sufficient power that would reasonably be expected to be effective in a self-defense situation. That means they won't fall with a .38 Special target load. Normally, Poppers will fall with standard load from a 9mm handgun shot at close range. Poppers are calibrated prior to the match.

This target array has it all, the brown targets are the targets to engage, the black portion is hard cover, simulating a hard wall or other barrier, and the white is a no-shoot target. Speed counts, but accuracy counts too!

Reloading under match conditions is challenging for the revolver class, but no less fun. Note the shooting glove on the weak hand side of this competitor.

This shooter is firing on the Pepper Poppers hiding around the plastic barrels. Note the foot position of the shooter, on the line but not going over the line, which would be a foot fault penalty. This competitor uses a Glock to good effect. No fancy gear needed to be competitive.

The loads the competitor uses must also fall in a minimum power category, and there is a formula for this. (I promise this will be the only math throughout the book.)

There are two categories that a competitor's ammunition can fall under: Major and Minor. The formula is bullet weight x velocity/1000. If you compete with a gun/load combo that meets Minor, that will be scored differently than a competitor shooting a gun/load falling under Major power factor. The minimum score for a Minor load is 125, and for Major it's 165. So, using our formula, if I'm shooting a .45 ACP handgun with a 200 grain SWC at 900 fps, the equation

would be 200x900=180,000/1000=180. Well above the threshold for a 165 power factor and I would be shooting Major caliber. If, on the other hand I was shooting that same 200 grain SWC .45 ACP load at 700fps, the resulting Power factor would be 140, and I would be in the Minor category. If I keep all of my hits in the "A" zone throughout the entire match, this is not a problem since hit in the "A" zone are scored equally, but I get a lower score for hits out of the "A" zone if using Minor power loads. Since firing all "A" hits every time is not practical, even Grand Masters don't get all "A" hits all day long, it's in my best interest to shoot Major, or be very, very accurate with my Minor power loads.

Remember, it's all about a balance of accuracy, power and speed. Most .45 ACP loads, except the light target loads will fall into Major caliber, as conversely, most 9mm loads will fall into the Minor category. Can you reload the 9mm to make Major? Yes, and some do. There are advantages in using a 9mm handgun for the Open category that have to do with recoil management and magazine capacity.

Shooting a course of fire for a USPSA match involves similar procedures to other forms of practical shooting competitions. The holster, magazine pouches and the gun will all be put on in the safe area designated specifically for this purpose at every range. Once your equipment is on your person, you may not touch or unholster your firearm for any reason. These rules apply to all practical pistol type matches, not just USPSA events. Once you are assigned to a squad and the match has begun, your squad will start at a particular stage. There is usually a stage description set up for each stage, and the RO will also give you a walkthrough.

You are allowed to walk through the

Shooting through a window of a wall is common in USPSA matches, the key is to keep the concentration on the sights.

Here the shooters get a walkthrough prior to the string. This lets them see how the targets will be presented upon reaching that shooting position. It's not good to have surprises.

Doing a walkthrough, noting the angle to the target and what the sight picture looks like prior to shooting the stage, is an important part of success in a USPSA Match.

Junior shooters make up a growing part of USPSA matches. Here is a Junior shooter getting ready to receive the start signal from the RO. Note the pistol and the magazine on the table. Starting positions can vary widely from stage to stage, making the entire match more interesting.

course of fire to plan your method of solving the particular shooting problem that has been presented.

The competitor will come to the firing line with the unloaded gun already in the holster, with the loaded magazines in their pouches and eye and ear protection on. The range officer will come up and give you the command to make ready.

This is your signal to draw your pistol and insert a magazine. At this point, many competitors will have a magazine in their back pocket to load what's known as a "Barney round." This is a reference to Barney Fife, from the 50s TV Show Andy of Mayberry, where actor Don Knotts played the character Barney Fife, who was allowed to carry a gun, but was also only allowed to carry a single live round in his shirt pocket. The "Barney round" will load the chamber with the round from the magazine, which is then removed and replaced with a fully charged magazine. This procedure ensures that the gun is fully charged with a round in the chamber and a full magazine. The firearm is then holstered.

The next command the range officer asks will be, "Is the shooter ready?" At this point, the shooter will either nod yes or no, or verbally communicate whether or not he/she is ready. Then, the RO will give the command, "Stand By." The next sound will be the start signal from the shot timer, and at that point the shooter will draw and engage the targets. Once the shooter has stopped firing, the RO will give the command, "Unload and show clear," or they can also say, "If you are finished, unload and show clear." At this point, the competitor will remove and secure the magazine from the gun, clear the live round from the chamber and show the RO that the chamber is clear, all while keeping the trigger finger out of the trigger guard and the pistol pointed downrange. The RO will then give the command to the shooter, "Slide down, hammer down and holster." This is where the shooter lowers the slide on the now empty chamber, presses the trigger to lower the hammer, or if a DA semiauto, presses the decocking lever to lower the hammer, and holsters the now unloaded and safe firearm. The RO will then declare the range is safe, and the RO, the competitor, people repairing the targets and scorer can all go downrange.

One note here, range etiquette dictates that it's always appreciated when people help out on the range, either by keeping score, or if you are not comfortable doing that,

repairing the targets. The faster the targets get repaired, the more smoothly the match will progress. The only time you shouldn't go downrange to help is when you are the next shooter up on the firing line to fire. You should be getting mentally ready to shoot the stage, and not be distracted by repairing targets.

All of the loading and unloading procedures MUST be performed with the trigger finger outside of the trigger guard and away from the trigger.

Always get into the habit of making sure the trigger finger is WELL outside the trigger guard area, it makes the job of the RO much easier when you are running between firing points and they can easily see that you are doing it in a safe manner. If they feel that your trigger finger is getting too close to the trigger when reloading or moving, you

This shooter has already engaged the targets displayed through the open door, and now moves to the next position while reloading on the move. Note the magazine falling away from the gun.

This competitor has dropped one magazine and replaced it, while moving to the position from right to left. Note the footwork, keeping in balance and the pistol out in front while on the move.

Pro Shooter Mike Foley shows how it's done, by reloading safely while moving quickly from position to position.

The shooter "looks" the magazine into the gun, while still moving to the next firing position. Keeping the eyes on the reload while still moving to the next position is a good practical shooting fundamental.

will be given a verbal warning. If you get a command to STOP, you must freeze in place, and stop doing whatever it is that you were doing. The RO has seen something that is unsafe and has to immediately stop all action of the competitor.

If everything goes right, you will have a good total time, and well-placed hits on target. But let's talk about what happens when things go wrong.

There are specific procedures that need to be followed in every stage. Let's say the stage is set up that you have to engage certain targets in a certain order and you fail to do that. You would be incurred a procedural penalty, usually something like a five second penalty, for example.

Foot faults are another area where procedural penalties are common. If your foot goes over a line while you are engaging a target, that's a foot fault, and again, it's usually time added to your total time for that stage. Procedural penalties are aggravating, but not uncommon. It's always best to avoid them if possible, but sometimes in the heat

of competition the shooter is so focused on the sights or the target that they are oblivious to foot position or other small details. This is where procedural penalties can hurt.

If you compete in handgun matches for long enough, you may, but hopefully not, incur a DQ at some point. A DQ is a disqualification, and it is where you violated a safety procedure. A shooter can be disqualified for many reasons, so I'll cover some of them here. For a complete list, always consult the USPSA rule book.

One of the basic rules of firearms safety states that you must always keep your finger off the trigger until you have identified the target, have the pistol lined up on the target and are ready to shoot. Trigger finger violations, especially when reloading the pistol or while moving between firing points, are the most common grounds for a DQ. I have seen a competitor fire a round while inserting a magazine during a reload. The pistol was pointed up in the air at about a 45-degree angle when it went off, so the person actually violated two rules. I have also seen people drop loaded pistols when drawing from a holster, and get DQ'd.

Match disqualifications fall under four general areas:

1. Accidental discharge (AD), where the gun went off unintentionally, and other than when directly pointed at a regulation target.
2. Unsafe gun handling.
3. Unsportsmanlike conduct.
4. Prohibited substances.

As an example for #1, the person I witnessed that pressed the trigger when reloading was immediately DQ'd. I have seen people accidentally fire the pistol when transferring the pistol from strong hand only to weak hand only, and got their fingers crossed up and fired the gun. Even though the shot went into the berm, it was still an accidental discharge, and the person was DQ'd. The only exception to this rule is where the competitor has what's known as a "squib" load. A squib load is where the reloader either didn't get any powder into the cartridge case, or insufficient powder to get the bullet out of the barrel when the gun goes off. Sometimes the primer is enough to get the bullet out of the barrel but not

usually. If there is a little powder in the case, and the bullet strikes the ground within ten feet on the competitor, that shooter will not be DQ'd.

Unsafe gun handling can happen in many ways, but one of the most common violations is where the shooter "sweeps" the range.

There is a 180-degree rule that states that the firing line extends for 180 degrees in both directions from the shooter. Both to his or her left and right, if the shooter turns his or her body and points the gun behind them or breaks this 180 degree plane, that would be an example of unsafe gunhandling and a DQ would result. Another common reason for a DQ is sweeping the body during the draw, most commonly sweeping the weak hand. Another situation with the potential for unsafe gun handling is where the shooter starts the stage facing uprange, or with their back to the target.

At the start signal, the shooter is facing away from the targets, and has to turn to face the targets, draw and engage. Sometimes the competitor will draw before fully turning to face the targets and will sweep the competitor behind the firing line. I've seen that happen on more than one occasion.

I have never seen a person DQ'd because of #3 or #4, although I have heard stories. Sometimes, competitors can get heated up

The shooter navigates his way through the course while the RO keeps a careful watch, and a second shooter tapes the entire stage with a GoPro on a stick for later viewing and evaluation.

The shooter is reaching for the door, while at the same time reaching for the handgun. The shooter then goes through the door to engage the targets behind the door. Running through these types of stages safely and quickly is the fun part of USPSA matches.

This Junior shooter moves through the stage while dropping the magazine and reaching for fresh magazine at the same time.

about certain stages and tempers can flare. The best thing to do if you think you have been given a wrong score or a procedural penalty for the wrong reason, or whatever it is that is upsetting you, is to remember that it's only a game and there will always be another match.

USPSA competition is a fun and exciting sport if you are interested in practical shooting. The organization has been around for over twenty years, and some of the equipment and techniques that have been developed are used by some of the finest law enforcement and military personnel around the world. It's a fun game but also has practical real world applications.

The entry requirements to the sport are low, it really just takes a serviceable firearm, either in semi auto or a revolver, in 9mm or .38 Special or above, a few good magazines and a quality holster and magazine pouch, good eye and ear protection, and you are on

the way. The people are great competitors and are always friendly and willing to help out new shooters and get them going on the right track with good advice and helpful suggestions.

USPSA matches have a new shooter orientation that usually lasts about 30-45 minutes prior to every match, where the RO will go over the rules, what is required and how to stay safe. I always suggest to people that want to try the sport, or any of the other shooting sports, to go to a match and look it over.

Try to go with a shooting buddy who is somewhat familiar with the sport to help explain things, or get with one of the shooters after the match and help break down the stages, or come out early and help set up. Any help either setting up or breaking down is always welcomed and it's a great opportunity to ask questions about the guns and gear needed to get going as well as get a general feel for the sport.

This shooter moves quickly to the door and opens the door with one hand while keeping the gun pointed safely above the door handle and the finger off the trigger.

Service-type firearms are always competitive in USPSA matches. Here, the shooter engages the target that has a no-shoot target in front of the regular target.

This competitor uses the stock Glock MOS series to good effect. This is a popular gun for not only USPSA, but IDPA and 3-gun steel matches as well. This MOS has a Leupold Delta Point installed.

EQUIPMENT

In order to decide what load and/or caliber to choose if you are thinking of entering a USPSA match, it's prudent to understand the various categories of firearms and calibers that make up competitive USPSA shooting today. I'll also cover holsters for the various categories.

Open division

In Open division, pretty much anything that is safe is allowed. This division is usually for the most advanced competitors, since the firearms are highly modified and mostly the top competitors are in this category.

This is where you will see all sorts of high capacity magazines, optical sights and

The Open class gun from STI comes with all the bells and whistles needed for the most challenging form of USPSA shooting. Image courtesy STI, Inc.

This shooter uses the C-More RTS small tactical reflex sight on his Unlimited class pistol to good effect.

The Safariland 014 is a good example of a minimal holster for Unlimited class guns. Image courtesy Safariland.

Unlimited class guns are a fun way to compete in USPSA. They are softer shooting than the Limited class because of their compensators and also the extra weight of their optical sights.

The Springfield Armory TRP would be a good choice for a Limited class USPSA pistol, as well as a good gun for IDPA and 3-gun matches. Image courtesy Springfield Armory.

The Limited class gun from STI is a good example of a custom pistol when the shooter decides to take their game to the next level. Image courtesy STI, Inc.

compensators mounted on the barrels in order to reduce recoil. Also common are highly specialized holsters and magazine pouches. The gun caliber is a minimum of .38 caliber, and there are three calibers that are most popular: 9mm, .38 Super and .38 Super Comp.

There are no restrictions on size, weight or trigger pull, no restrictions on modifications to the pistol and no restrictions to the holster. There is a minimum bullet weight of 112 grains. These guns are nicknamed "race guns" because of the highly modified nature of the gun.

Limited class

In the Limited division, the custom pistol still reigns supreme, but with some restrictions. The gun cannot have optical sights, so iron sights are the rule. The gun has to be .40 caliber or larger in order to make Major, which is the only way to be competitive in this division. So most competitors have their pistols built in .40 S&W. There is no restriction on magazine capacity, so the high capacity guns are the norm. These are very similar to the Open class gun, but

cannot have compensators or optical sights installed. There is a Limited 10 division, where the gun cannot be loaded with more than 10 rounds in the magazine at the start signal.

Production class

This is where the factory guns come into play. In this division, there is no Major power factor, the gun and load must only meet the minimum for Minor or 125. The minimum caliber is 9mm, and the magazine capacity cannot be more than 10 rounds. There are also restrictions on the holster. There is a maximum size that the gun with the magazine inserted must not exceed. This is known as the "box rule," where the gun with the magazine inserted must fit into a box of a specific dimension. This is to eliminate factory guns that may have high capacity magazine. There are many guns that are competitive in this category, one of which you may already have in your firearms collection. Guns such as Glocks, S&W M&P and various Springfield XD series guns are all popular in this category.

The Glock G35 with the new Leupold Delta Pro makes a great gun for many types of practical competition, including USPSA. Image courtesy Leupold, Inc.

Single stack

This category is where the 1911 handgun really shines. The 1911 is the pistol that really popularized practical pistol shooting in the 70s, 80s and early 90s, and is still used by law enforcement and military tactical teams and firearms professionals around the world for good reason. So it was in the sport's best interest to keep the gun in the game. The 1911 has a very strong and loyal following, and many people use the 1911 for several matches, not just USPSA. They build one 1911 handgun and can use it for IDPA, 3-gun, USPSA, and even Steel matches.

The Single Stack category favors the

Another good example of an appropriate gun for Single Stack USPSA competition. Image courtesy Kimber, Inc.

single stack magazine of the 1911, but there are other guns that can also be used. The gun can only be fitted with iron sights, and the magazine capacity can only be eight rounds if making Major power factor. If using a single stack gun in 9mm for example, that would be a Minor power factor and you could have 10 rounds in the gun.

Revolver

In all the talk about practical shooting, revolvers generally get the short end of the stick, but there are some hard-core aficionados of revolvers that keep them in the game. Also keep in mind that revolvers are very much competitive in Steel type matches, since the firing strings are only five rounds, so it's convenient and fun to use one revolver for several types of competition.

Like other guns, there are restrictions are far as caliber. It must be .38 caliber or larger, and you cannot have optical sights, barrel porting or compensators.

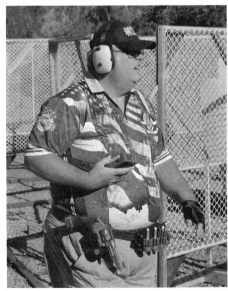

Revolvers are not excluded from USPSA competition by any means. This competitor uses the popular S&W revolver with a Match grade aftermarket barrel, fiber optic front sight and speedloaders.

Revolvers are fun to shoot in USPSA matches. They compete in their own category, and provide a unique shooting experience. Here, the shooter is attempting to reach for the speedloader on the belt, while keeping the gun safely pointed downrange.

Revolvers compete in their own category against each other and can really add a fun dimension to the sport.

CHAPTER THREE

STEEL SHOOTING COMPETITION

S teel competition is one of the most fun and challenging forms of handgun competition, in my opinion. There are several reasons for this. It's relatively easy to get started. The equipment needed to get into the game can be as simple as an inexpensive, used .22 LR caliber pistol and five magazines, proper eye and ear protection, a couple of hundred rounds of ammunition, a range bag to carry everything and the desire to learn and have fun.

The sport is really one of the best avenues for the new shooter, or maybe a shooter that is transitioning over from another shooting discipline to the action shooting sports. The reason is that the targets are large, there is no or very little movement required, the game is simple to learn, and it allows the new shooter who might not have had the opportunity to compete in an action shooting type sport to get their feet wet.

Additionally, the rules at the club level are normally very simple: when the buzzer goes off, shoot the targets in a particular order as fast as you can.

For example, at my club, we have a monthly match called the Steel Showdown. Many shooters from several of the pistol shooting disciplines come to the match. We get the USPSA shooters, the IDPA shooters, some of which are just weekend plinkers,

A shooter's-eye-view of a typical steel target array. Targets are placed up close and personal, making hits easy, with speed being the deciding factor.

and some older bullseye competitors. Being a recovering bullseye competitor myself, I see how the steel matches can really help pistol shooters from any discipline, or people who just want to try a fun new game.

Bullseye is a very static game, so a bullseye shooter wanting to get into an action sport would do well to get started in steel.

This shooter has received the start signal, and is drawing the gun to engage the target array, while the RO, scorer and other shooters in the squad look on. The shooter is wearing a glove on the non-shooting hand.

This shooter uses the Ruger MkIII to get a sight picture with the gun held at the low ready to start the stage, no holster needed.

Junior shooters can get into the game in a big way as well. This junior female shooter uses the Ruger MkIII .22 LR pistol with iron sights to ring the steel plates.

The revolvers get into the steel matches with a category all their own. Here, the competitor uses the ubiquitous S&W 686 stainless steel revolver to good effect.

This shooter uses a USPSA holster rig to hold the pistol and to draw from. This will give him more repetitions with his regular competition gear; more muscle memory equals greater skill and proficiency.

Additionally, at our club match, we have several junior shooters who are trying to hone their speed skills before entering some of the action sports like 3-gun or USPSA. Steel is a great training ground for that because the game is all about speed, so the shooter needs to focus on sight picture and not sight alignment.

The only downside for a bullseye or silhouette shooter getting into one of the action sports is that steel, or any action sport, can be detrimental to a precision game like bullseye or silhouette.

Steel is about speed and acquiring a fast sight picture. Precision sports like bullseye and silhouette require very fine trigger control and a high degree of sight alignment, or if using electronic sight, the shooter needs to maintain a very fine aiming point. Action sports like steel, IPSC and others may ingrain bad habits that are difficult to break if going from one discipline to another.

So, for shooters who would like to transition more or less permanently to an action shooting sports, steel is a great way to go. Just remember, if you still want to compete in the precision sports like bullseye and silhouette, then the action sports like steel,

Controlling recoil is key to getting through the stage quickly. This is where stance position, grip and other marksmanship fundamentals come into play.

This shooter uses the Ruger MkIII .22 LR to gain additional practice on sight alignment and trigger control by shooting steel matches. Plus, they're fun matches to shoot!

While one shooter in the shooting box readies her magazines, the shooter on deck takes a sight picture in order to get mentally ready to shoot next.

Using good form, this shooter uses a glove on the shooting hand for additional control.

The popular MkIII in action. There are several models available to accommodate any shooting style.

The S&W M41 isn't just for bullseye competition. This shooter uses the iconic pistol to good effect on the steel targets. Accurate and reliable, the M41 is probably the Cadillac of steel competition .22 LR pistols.

This shooter uses the MkIII with the C-More sight to engage the steel.

Since speedy reloading isn't a factor, the shooter can take a little time to get ready between strings. Each stage consists of five strings of five shots each and a match usually has five to six stages, so there is a lot of shooting to be had.

Pro shooter Mike Foley gets ready to shoot the string. Mike uses steel matches as a tune-up between his regular schedule of USPSA and IDPA matches.

IPSC, IDPA and others may develop bad habits that are tough to break.

Examples of these bad habits are using a sight picture instead of sight alignment, yanking the trigger when getting a good sight picture or sight alignment, and speeding up the shot when getting good sight picture. These things are all detrimental to a precision game like bullseye or silhouette.

RANGE ETIQUETTE

So, now that you've made the decision to get started, what is the game and how do we play it?

First, before explaining the courses of fire, there are some range etiquette rules that steel competitions and most all ranges adhere to. Almost all competitive pistol ranges operate under the assumption of a "cold range" what this means is that the range does not allow loaded firearms anywhere except on the firing line under direct supervision of the range officer. Only the military, some law enforcement tactical team ranges and certain civilian training ranges operate under "hot range" conditions, where every firearm is loaded and assumed to be loaded.

At a cold range, all firearms are kept in the range bag, and only in the safety areas are the shooters allowed to handle any firearms. The safety area at the range is where shooters go to put on holsters, belts, magazine pouches, etc. The shooters can take their firearms out of the range bag, dry fire them and generally get prepared to go to the firing line or the match registration desk. Under NO circumstances is live ammunition allowed near the safety area for obvious reasons. In steel matches, the shooter is not required to have the pistol in a holster to start the stage, unlike other types of practical pistol sports, so the shooter need not put on a holster. The pistol can be kept in the range bag, and the bag is carried to the firing line in order to start the stage. This is the only form of competition in the action shooting sports where this is allowed. After register-

Mike's short-barreled MkIII uses the C-More sight to simulate his Open class USPSA gun.

This shooter uses the 1911 style pistol with the C-More sight mounted sideways to get it lower to the axis of the bore, helping the shooter to better control recoil.

Shooting a firearm with minimal recoil, Mike is seen here using the steel match as a regular practice regimen.

With a competition holster and a speed-shooting pistol, the gun/holster combo can also be used for USPSA competition, serving double duty.

ing for the match, the shooters are normally put into squads, where they will move as a group between the various stages set up for the day's competition.

SHOOTING THE MATCH

Usually, there are four to six stages set up for the day's match. Sometimes, the match can be fired twice, if time allows, so the shooter can compete and fire the match with a rimfire pistol, for example, and then shoot the match again with a centerfire gun. The caveat to this is that if you start the match with a rimfire gun, or any gun, you have to complete the match with the same gun.

So you can't change guns in the middle of a match unless your gun has a complete mechanical malfunction and you can't finish the match. Some matches will allow you to complete the match with a similar pistol, but you cannot switch guns in the middle of a match, and you cannot go from CF to RF during the same match; once you start a match with a certain gun, you must complete the match with the same firearm.

When the shooter's turn to fire the stage is called, they will carry the range bag, gun and ammunition to the firing line. The command "Load and make ready" will be given, and the shooter will remove the gun and five magazines and place them on a small table provided for that purpose.

The competitor will then load the gun with a one of the magazines and holster the pistol. Then the next series of commands from the range officer will be, "Is the shooter ready?" The competitor should nod if ready, if the shooter is not ready, now is the time to let the range officer know. The start position is usually with the hands at the sides with the gun in the holster. If the shooter does not have a holster (remember, in steel matches there is no requirement to start from a holster, and .22 LR competitors do not usually have one), then the start posi-

tion is "low ready" with the pistol pointed toward the ground at a 45-degree angle with both hands holding the pistol.

Once the competitor nods in acknowledgement that he/she is ready, the next command from the range officer will be "Stand by," then immediately the buzzer from the shot timer will go off, signaling to the shooter to begin firing the string. Each competitor will fire at five targets per stage, and will fire each stage five times, or five strings, with the worst time for each string thrown out.

The four run times, or the time for each of the four strings, are then averaged together for a total average time for the stage. Winner is the shooter with the lowest overall total time for the match after all of the times for the stages are added up. The winner gets bragging rights, although I've been to some steel matches at other shooting complexes where small trophies were awarded. Remember that you as a shooter can compete in more than one category, lady

Shooting teams get together and compete on a regular basis. Here, a junior shooter gets through the targets quickly.

Holding the pistol at the low ready position, the shooter gets ready to receive the signal from the RO.

This shooter uses a variation of the Ruger pistol to engage the steel.

This shooter uses the MkIII with iron sights. Note the red fiber optic insert in the front sight. This is one of the more popular options on competition handguns with iron sights.

and junior, or lady and military, for example, which increases your chances of coming out a match winner.

The really great thing about shooting steel matches is that the shooter gets instant feedback. It's not like shooting paper targets where you don't know if you have good hits on the target or complete misses until you have completed shooting the stage and then go down to patch the targets and can see your hits and/or misses. When you shoot a steel target, it will ring loudly, even with a .22 LR.

The five targets for each stage need to be shot in a certain order, and the order of engagement will be explained for each stage. The buzzer of the shot timer that the range officer uses to start the stage will start the time, and the last target engaged is the

Note the puffs of smoke coming out of the eight compensator ports at the end of the barrel. This is what controls the recoil in this rimfire pistol, as well as the centerfire guns in matches that allow the use of compensators.

Junior shooters don't just use rimfire pistols in steel matches. Here is a shooter using a CZ pistol in centerfire caliber to go through the stage.

Here the heavily fluted-barrel MkIII with a C-More sight and a compensator make for a great experience. The fluting, or grooves on the barrel, save weight, making the gun easier to swing from target to target.

It's not always about scope sighted .22 LR pistols. Just about any gun can be used in a steel match. Here a shooter uses the S&W M&P in centerfire caliber to get through the course.

This junior shooter looks like he has his hands full, but actually controlled the recoil of the full size pistol really well.

Here the shooter uses the S&W M&P is .22 LR to get through the stage. These guns, which are .22 LR versions of their centerfire cousins, are an effective way to get familiar with the service gun by shooting a .22 LR version of the same gun.

stop plate. When the bullet hits this plate, it's recorded, along with the other shots into the timer, so the start and stop times are recorded. The stop time is the total time for the string.

After all five strings have been fired, the range officer will give the command to "Unload and show clear." This is when the shooter removes the magazine from the gun, cycles the slide to remove the round in the chamber, and holds the slide back and show the range officer the empty chamber. The range officer will then give the command, "Slide down, hammer down and holster." At this point, the pistol is placed back in the range bag. The range officer will declare the range safe, the shooter can remove the bag from the firing line, and the other shooters not on deck to fire next can go down and paint the targets.

PENALTIES

At any match there are rules, and steel is no exception. Although the rules are fewer than at many other matches, they are no less important. Penalties usually fall into two categories: procedural penalties and disqualification penalties. Shooters should refer to the appropriate rule book for a complete list of penalties, but procedural penalties are usually in the form of foot faults and shooting the targets out of order. Foot faults are where the shooter has to engage the targets from a shooting box, and the shooter moves the foot either partially or completely outside the box. These penalties are in the form of added time to your overall time. For example, a procedural penalty like a foot fault will get three seconds added to your time. Remember, this game is all about who can shoot the fastest, so a three second penalty may not sound like much, but sometimes it can be the difference between winning and losing.

A disqualification penalty is an entirely different ball game. This is where the shoot-er has performed a dangerous act that puts the safety of him/her and other shooters at risk. There can be several types of disqualification penalties. Again, refer to the appropriate rulebooks for a complete list, but some of the most egregious would be: dropping a firearm (loaded or not); pointing a firearm at yourself or another person; breaking the 180 Rule (see Glossary); being under the influence of drugs and/or alcohol; and having an accidental discharge.

One area that many shooters violate that will get them disqualified, usually without the shooter even noticing they are doing this act, is NOT keeping the trigger finger outside of the trigger guard when moving from one shooting point to another or executing a reload. This is considered unsafe gun handling. At some club level matches, if the violation is marginal, that is, the range officer *thinks* they saw the trigger finger *close to* but not actually touching the trigger, the shooter may get one verbal warning, and if the offense happens again at the same match, it will result in immediate disqualification.

Some shooters try to get a competitive advantage by trying to keep the trigger finger close to the trigger when moving or reloading. You will sometimes see this at local matches, but at higher level matches with pro and semi-professional shooters, you have shooters who have good safe gun handling fundamentals so ingrained that you will always see them with the trigger finger well outside the trigger guard so the range officer can clearly see that the finger is well away when they are reloading or moving. Remember, some of these matches the action is fast and furious and the range officer is trying to watch many things at once. The best place to practice this is at home, always start with an unloaded gun, and work on reloading with dummy cartridges and moving while keeping the trigger finger outside and alongside the gun.

SCORING

Scoring in steel shooting is easy: your time is your score.

Many different combinations of optics, guns and calibers are suitable for steel matches.

If the shooter utilizes a holster, then the start position is hands in the surrender position.

This shooter uses a box-stock revolver to have some fun at a steel match.

Most stages in a steel match are stand and shoot-type matches, but sometimes the shooter may have to move from one box to another. Here, the shooter is stepping into the box, and getting ready to engage the target.

Most steel matches are stand-and-shoot matches, but sometimes the shooter may have to move from one shooting box a few feet to another box. Here the shooter moves from one position to another while keeping the gun pointed in a safe direction with the finger off the trigger of his Ruger MkIII pistol.

This shooter, using a stock Glock, suitable for IDPA, USPSA or even 3-gun competition, takes a sight picture prior to getting the start signal from the RO.

Shooter's-eye view of another target array in a typical steel match.

Repairing the targets is fast and easy in a Steel match, no need for pasters, just paint and go.

Controlling recoil with the centerfire pistol is essential in steel competition. This shooter controls the gun well.

This shooter shows good footwork when moving from shooting box to shooting box.

MALFUNCTIONS

If a malfunction occurs during your string, the timer is running, so you need to do whatever it takes to clear the gun and get back into the game. Remember, if the malfunction is not too bad, sometimes the time can be made up by shooting well on the next few strings. The point is to not give up by thinking just because you have one malfunction the game is over. Remember, there are other shooters who may be experiencing a bad string or have malfunctions on their own. The late Yogi Berra said it best: "It ain't over till it's over," and that is very true in the shooting sports, regardless of the shooting game. This goes back to one of the fundamentals of shooting, and that is the mental game, which is so important to competitive shooting.

Giving up because of one bad string, one bad shot or one bad series of shots is the surest way to not win. I've shot countless matches where I had a bad shot, a bad string or bad stage, and forgot about the bad, and focused on the next shot, or next string, and ended up winning, or at least doing as well

as I would have if I had not had the bad shot or string. The point is to be mentally tough, and focus on the next shot, or next string, because you certainly cannot do anything about the shot or string you just fired. Those bullets are downrange and you can't get them back. Focus on what you have to do next to be successful.

The only point to remember is that there is a time limit to each string. If the shooter goes over 30 seconds, they have exceeded the time limit for the string and any shots over those 30 seconds are counted as misses.

COMPETITION DIVISION

In steel competitions, there are three divisions that the competitor can shoot under.

The first, the **.22 division,** is further broken down into open sights and iron sights. The open division is pretty much where anything goes. As long as the pistol is firing .22 LR ammunition, optical sights, compensators, trigger work and other modification are allowed. The other equipment division in .22 rimfire is the iron sights division. These guns

This shooter uses a factory pocket pistol and moves between shooting positions with good footwork. Steel shooting is pretty much "shoot what you bring," and there is a classification for it.

No fancy equipment here. This shooter uses a factory Glock to ring the steel.

are kept in more stock configuration, as no compensators or optical sights are allowed, although fiber optic sights are specifically allowed.

Centerfire division is any centerfire handgun of 9mm or .38 Special calibers. Centerfire division is further broken down into six classifications. The first is the open class, and this class is where the race guns come out! Optics, compensators and pretty much any other modifications are allowed.

Also, any safe holster and holster position is also allowed. The next is limited class – this is classification is for iron sights only, no optical sights, no barrel ports or compensators are allowed. Production class is for production handguns, either double action or safe action pistol is allowed. This class follows USPSA Production Class rules. No race holsters are allowed.

IPSC production class is pretty much the same as production class, but race holsters are allowed.

Single stack class is governed by the USPSA single stack class. In USPSA, this class is only for 1911 handguns and no race holsters are allowed.

The last classification is **Revolver**. This is actually a game where the revolvers do

really well, since the stages are set up to be revolver neutral, meaning that it takes no more than five rounds to shoot each stage. In this classification, the revolver cannot be ported or have a compensator or optical sights, although the gun can be fitted with the popular fiber optic iron sights, and there are no restrictions on barrel length, maximum number of rounds, and also no restrictions on holsters.

Check out a steel match if you can. They're a lot of fun, easy and inexpensive to get into, and probably one of the best ways to get into the practical shooting game. Get

This S&W stainless revolver with a speed hammer, heavy match grade barrel and reflex dot sight makes for a fun steel gun to shoot.

an inexpensive used .22 LR pistol, a half a dozen magazines, and some inexpensive .22 LR ammunition, and get started. If you don't have a steel match in your local area, go to your range and start one. The targets are inexpensive, and once you have them they last for a long time. I know several semi-pro level shooters who take their .22 LR pistol to steel matches from time to time just to use for a "tune up" for other matches, because of the speed element of the match. Once you can get started in steel shooting, it's easy to move over into one of the other practical shooting sports.

EQUIPMENT

Steel is probably one of the easiest shooting games to get into since the equipment needs are pretty basic. Eye and ear protection and a good range bag are essential. Holsters are not even required, since the shooter starts from the low ready position and doesn't have to draw from the holster.

Specialized speed holsters are useful, but not necessary when using the match revolvers in steel competition.

Notice how the hammer has been cut down from a stock hammer, decreasing its mass and making it lighter. This makes the hammer fall faster, decreasing lock time, as well as making the hammer easier to pull rearward when firing double action.

Since the shooter fires five strings in a row, the shooter needs to have five reliable magazines that are loaded and ready to go when the called to the firing line to shoot. If firing a revolver, the shooter should have five speedloaders loaded up and ready to go. Short-barreled Ruger MkII and MkIII pistols are very popular, and beyond that, the game is pretty much open to any safe, serviceable firearm.

Many models of Kimber handguns make excellent pistols for double duty in steel and practical pistol matches. Image courtesy Kimber.

The S&W 625 JM is a Signature Jerry Miculek Edition. Chambered in .45 ACP, this would make an excellent revolver for the diehard revolver shooter wanting one gun for steel, IDPA and other types of practical shooting competitions. Image courtesy S&W.

The S&W 686 is a popular base gun to start with. It lends itself to serious customizing, or it can be competitive right out of the box. Image courtesy S&W.

The Ruger 22/45 Lite, with a blue anodized alloy upper receiver, threaded barrel and rail for mounting various types of optics, is a popular pistol for steel matches. Image courtesy Ruger.

The S&W Thunder Ranch Model in .45 ACP makes a great home defense, practical shooting and steel match pistol. Image courtesy S&W.

The Glock MOS in .40 S&W is an excellent pistol found at many steel matches, as well as other types of practical pistol matches. Image courtesy Glock.

The STI Steel Master pistol is an example of a full-blown custom racegun specifically designed for steel competition. Image courtesy STI.

This Ruger MkIII semi auto is probably the easiest and most cost effective method to get started in competitive shooting, especially if the shooter wants to get into practical shooting sports. Starting with iron sights, the pistol has an accessory rail for mounting optical sights as the competitor gains skill. Image courtesy Ruger.

The Springfield CD Tactical model in .45 ACP is a versatile pistol that can perform in a wide variety of competitive shooting sports, from steel shooting, to IDPA, USPSA and 3-gun. Image courtesy Springfield Armory.

CHAPTER FOUR

SILHOUETTE COMPETITION

The IHMSA World Championships target array shows the bank of targets. The shooter will fire at a single lane of targets at the four distances for smallbore and field pistol: 25, 50, 75 and 100 meters. For big bore competition, the distances are 50, 100, 150 and 200 meters.

Silhouette competition is one of the oldest forms of competitive shooting. The roots of this exciting and challenging sport began in Mexico in the early 1900s. *Siluetas Metalicas*, metallic silhouette in Spanish, began, as the story goes, with Mexican banditos that would, in between raiding ranches and towns, challenge each other as to who was the better shot. Live farm animals, at first live steers, were tied to the trees at a distance, and any shot to the animal that drew blood was counted as a hit. The idea caught on, and soon, other animals such as pigs and chickens were also used as targets.

This practice continued, usually at large *fiestas*, until after World War II, when the practice of using live animals was replaced with steel cutouts. Still, the practice of using live animals continued in the outlying areas of Mexico until the 1950s.

The matches began to take the form of organized competition in Mexico starting with the first match in Mexico City in 1948.

It was somewhat formalized in 1952 close to its current form with the targets being *gallinas* (chickens) at 200m, *gualotes* (turkeys) at 385m and *borregos* (sheep) at 500m. It would take several more years before the *javelina* (pig) target came into use.

Rifle shooters were the first to embrace the sport and handgunners came later, although there was some anecdotal evidence that the first bandits that originated the sport

This competitor uses the popular T/C Contender pistol with a rifle scope, in the standing position, to engage the bank of targets.

The shooter is in the Creedmore firing position, using the Freedom Arms .22 LR pistol. The popular revolver uses a hooded target-type front sight to good effect.

This shot shows how the shooter controls the recoil of the pistol, and tries to keep the scope reticle on the target during recoil. Follow-through is a very critical aspect of silhouette competition, more so than other types of shooting, with the exception of bullseye.

used both rifles and handguns. Modern Mexican competitors brought the sport to the Arizona border towns around 1972, and the next year the NRA brought the first NRA sanctioned event into the U.S. and held the first match in November that year.

The matches themselves are not complicated. There are various classifications and divisions, and various firearms that can be used, but by and large the game is simple, but very, very challenging. Set up four banks of five targets each at four different distances, and knock them down in order. Simple, yes? In theory it is, but it's a very challenging and addictive sport.

There are two governing bodies for competitive silhouette shooting, and the rules vary by which sanctioning body you are competing under. The International Handgun Metallic Silhouette Shooters Association, or IHMSA, and the NRA both offer sanctioned events. IHMSA, of course, only covers handguns, while the NRA events also cover rifle silhouette shooting.

The format of handgun competition, which is the focus of this book, is by and large, the same for both sanctioning bodies, so this book will cover the rules, format, courses of fire, and equipment in general terms. For specific rules, consult the appropriate rulebook for the sanctioning body your club is organized under.

IHMSA has four categories: big bore, small bore, field pistol and air pistol, and

This competitor gets ready to fire the next string by placing the gun into the firing hand. The pistol's loading gate is open and will be closed prior to getting into position to shoot.

This is a classic Creedmore firing position in silhouette competition.

This is another shot of the competitor firing the T/C in .22 LR in the standing position. Note the face is kept close to the scope. These are full size rifle scopes, not long eye relief pistol scopes. They have superior optical qualities, higher magnification, and finer windage and elevation adjustments. Also note the shooting gloves, and the use of a wood stock on the firing hand, and the synthetic material on the forend.

This angle shows the grip and arm position of the standing event. Along with the use of custom stocks on the firing hand, note the scope has parallax adjustment capability on the front objective bell of the scope – another reason for using rifle scopes, as opposed to handgun-type scopes, for silhouette competition.

Here the shooter can shoot off the bench as long as no part of the gun touches the bench. Note how the ammo is neatly organized and the shooter keeps track of the time with the stopwatch.

they are further divided into subcategories. These categories are: production, revolver, standing, unlimited, unlimited standing and unlimited any sight.

The NRA also has four categories: hunter pistol, long range pistol, smallbore and air pistol, and these are also further subdivided.

When competing under either sanctioning body, there are opportunities to compete at a very high level, or simply get started with basic equipment that can be purchased off the shelf and used without any customization, so it's very easy to get started in the sport.

A homemade shooting box, using a couple of plastic parts bins, keeps everything organized and at hand. This is a common theme throughout all forms of competitive handgun shooting, whether it's bullseye, IDPA, or silhouette; keeping the gear at the ready gives the shooter less to worry about, and the shooter can focus on developing a plan to shoot the match.

The long barrel and hooded front sight of the Freedom Arms revolver makes it a popular choice in the silhouette game.

This shooter shows great form in the standing event.

A good spotting scope and a knowledgeable spotter are keys to knocking down the targets and being successful at this game.

Here are two shooters firing simultaneously in the standing event, using a similar stance toward the target and similar grip on the pistol.

This competitor shows great form in the Creedmore position, while engaging the targets with the Freedom Arms .22 LR revolver. This pistol is the Cadillac in the small bore class.

Here, a spotter can actually spot the bullet impact for two shooters at the same time.

This competitor uses the Aimpoint electronic red dot sight on the popular T/C Contender pistol in .22 LR.

This shooter uses the T/C pistol in the Creedmore shooting position with a leather blast shield on his leg.

The courses of fire are basically the same for NRA and IHMSA. Four banks of five steel cutout targets are set at various distances. The competitor is required to fire one shot at each of the five targets, and has to do this under a certain time limit. The competitor fires at one bank, and then when time runs out, moves to the next bank of targets, the time resets, and so forth, until all four banks of five targets have been engaged, each target with a single shot.

The shooters get a prep time where they can dry fire, and there is also a period where they can engage spotters in order to establish a zero for that particular gun load, and to "warm up" prior to the match.

The firing line and targets for IHMSA competition go as follows:

	BIG BORE	FIELD PISTOL/ SMALL BORE	AIR PISTOL
CHICKEN	50 M / Yd	25 M / Yd	10 Yd
PIGS	100 M / Yd	50 M / Yd	12.5 Yd
TURKEYS	150 M / Yd	75 M / Yd	15 Yd
RAMS	200 M / Yd	100 M / Yd	18 Yd

Each bank of targets needs to be engaged with 10 shots minimum, therefore, a course of fire is 40 shots. A usual match would consist of 40, 60, 80, or 120 shots.

Targets must be engaged from left to right, and all targets must be knocked down or off the table to count. Additionally, for firing ranges that lack the requisite real estate to hold matches out to 200 yards, there are 1/5th scale targets that allow shooters to still hold sanctioned matches, with smaller targets at shorter ranges.

Tiebreakers are determined by "reverse animal count," where the number of animals knocked down, starting with the ram at the longer distance, determines the winner.

So, for a tie, the shooter with the most rams knocked down would be the winner, if multiple shooters have the same number of rams, then the next animal or turkeys, are counted, then pigs, then chickens. If there are multiple shooters still with the same score, then a shootoff is held to determine the match winner. Shootoffs are used with any five targets, determined by the match director, and set out at the ram distance. So you may have the smallest target (chickens) at the longest distance, for a 5-shot shootoff.

The name of the game in silhouette is precision. You, as a competitor, are engaging relatively small targets, at relatively

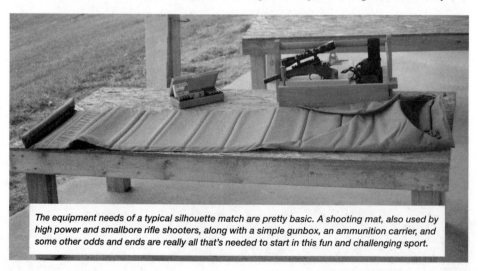

The equipment needs of a typical silhouette match are pretty basic. A shooting mat, also used by high power and smallbore rifle shooters, along with a simple gunbox, an ammunition carrier, and some other odds and ends are really all that's needed to start in this fun and challenging sport.

Making small sight adjustments is easy and repeatable, critical when firing at long distances.

A custom stock, Match grade custom stainless barrel and a rifle scope make a very effective setup for silhouette competition.

With the shooter firing off the bench, as long as the pistol does not make contact with the bench, it's a legal firing position.

long range, firing from an unsupported position at times, with a handgun. If you are coming from a bullseye background, and if you were a solid slow fire shooter, then you will be very comfortable and a very tough competitor in this sport. If, however, you are more of a run-and-gun type shooter, then this sport will be more difficult for you. This sport demands a high level of concentration and precision, with very fine trigger control, and the ability to fire single, well-aimed shots. Time limits are generous, but they are still there, so you cannot take an excessive amount of time to complete your string.

When I shot with the Army team in the mid 80s, one of the members of the Army Blue Team, comprised of the top shooters on the Army team, was a Master Sergeant by the name of Max Barrington. Max was an excellent slow fire shooter and always posted high scores in the slow fire stages of the National Match Course and the slow fire matches. After he retired from the military, I believe he stopped competing in bullseye altogether, switched over to pistol silhouette and became a champion silhouette shooter in the Pacific Northwest.

Remember, in bullseye slow fire, you are trying to keep all of your shots into a target that is about three inches in diameter at 50 yards, holding a .45 ACP pistol in one hand, and you have to do that ten times in a row. Silhouette shooting is much like that, so translating those precise bullseye skills over to silhouette is fairly easy. At least, it's easier than someone who has never shot small targets at a distance with a handgun under time limits. This is another reason bullseye competition is a great training ground for virtually all other forms of competitive pistol shooting.

The long barrel and corresponding long sight radius of the Freedom Arms is an advantage in silhouette. This shooter gets into the Creedmore position while the spotter waits patiently.

It's not all about custom guns and specialized equipment; this shooter is very competitive with a stock T/C and iron sights.

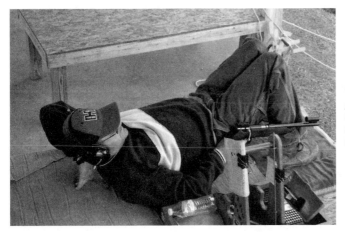

The bolt action Anschutz pistol in .22 LR makes a very effective and accurate handgun for the silhouette game.

It doesn't have to be pretty to work. This shooter has a homemade forend on the gun, but uses the pistol to great effect on the steel targets, while shooting in the prone position.

These shooters demonstrate the two main firing positions: standing and Creedmore, with the spotter helping both shooters in the Creedmore position with their hits on target.

Note the fold-out eye blinder on this shooter. This allows him to keep both eyes open, but only use the dominate eye to actually aim. Bullseye and silhouette shooters use this technique to great effect. Elbow pads also make shooting from prone more comfortable.

In order to be competitive, the shooter needs to be able to assume two basic firing positions, standing and freestyle. For standing, it is pretty easy to get into position, but most difficult to shoot from because it's the most unstable position.

In the freestyle position, the shooter lies on his or her back, feet flat on the ground, with the knees bent and rests the gun on the side of the calf, with the non-firing hand supporting the back of the head. This is known as the Creedmore position. It's actually a pretty comfortable way to hold and fire the handgun for long periods of time. Also, many shooters firing revolvers use some type of blast shield for the side of the pants, otherwise, blast and powder burns will quickly ruin a pair of jeans. For people with disabilities or physical conditions that preclude them from getting into some of these shooting positions, there are rules in effect that accommodate virtually any

shooter's inability to get into position and still allow them to be competitive.

CARTRIDGES

The types of cartridges used in silhouette competition are pretty standard, until you get into the unlimited category. Then, pretty much anything goes, although even then there are some standard and non-standard rounds that have become very popular with shooters over the years. For the big bore category, any straight-walled, or bottleneck cartridge is acceptable. For smallbore, only .22 LR is allowed. For field pistol, straight-wall, center fire pistol cartridges of standard manufacture with a maximum case length of 1.29 inches, as specified for that cartridge. 22 Hornet, or some of its variations are very popular. For air pistol, pellets must be .22 caliber or smaller, made from lead or similar soft metal. BBs or other round balls are not allowed.

Air pistol silhouette is a popular match, and is a good and fairly inexpensive way to stay sharp. Image courtesy IHMSA.

Close up of a Benjamin air pistol, when mated with a Leupold scope makes an effective combination. Image courtesy IHMSA.

The Wichita Arms bolt action pistol is a very popular pistol for the unlimited class.

Safety is always paramount at any match. Here the shooter is getting ready to shoot, but the finger is off the trigger until the sights are on the target. Image courtesy IHMSA.

It's not all custom single shot or bolt action pistols at a silhouette match. Here a shooter tries his hand at knocking down the steel beasts with a S&W revolver and iron sights. Image courtesy IHMSA.

Many people may scoff at the idea of shooting air pistol silhouette, thinking it's akin to shooting BB guns as a kid. But next to dry firing, it's probably the one of the best forms of training you can do for competing with other pistols.

Just like in bullseye, where we would fire air pistols in the winter when it got too cold in Maryland to fire outside, air pistol is a great training modality for slow fire or other types of shooting where time doesn't really matter, but extreme precision does. Plus, other than the cost of the air pistol itself, ammunition is very inexpensive, and it's something that can be set up in a garage or basement. From 10 ft away, and with a small backstop, is very safe to shoot indoors.

EQUIPMENT

Necessary equipment for silhouette competition is a good shooting box, a timer and a good quality spotting scope.

The Thompson Center Contender domi-nates the production class, and the Freedom Arms revolver dominates the revolver class, although the Ruger and Dan Wesson revolver is also represented in match results. It comes in a variety of calibers suitable for competition. The accuracy in the gun is from the solid engineering, the three locking lugs up front, and the match barrel. In the unlimited class, the discontinued Remington single shot XP-100 has dominated the class for many years. Used XP-100s are still available, but are getting scarce.

Quality optics is also a necessity, Leupold long eye relief handgun scopes and some models of rifle scopes are popular depending on the position and category the shooter assumes. For example, shooting standing position, the shooter can use a rifle scope with the .22 LR and get it close to the face. If shooting in the Creedmore position, the long eye relief handgun scope is needed.

A good shooting mat is allowed and makes it more comfortable to shoot. Shoot-

The T/C Hunter pistol is a good base model to start with. The interchangeable barrels can be switched out with a single hinge pin and provide a multitude of calibers suitable for the sport. With a little trigger work and a good scope, it's probably the most popular pistol in metallic silhouette competition today. Image courtesy Thompson/Center Arms.

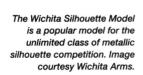

The Wichita Silhouette Model is a popular model for the unlimited class of metallic silhouette competition. Image courtesy Wichita Arms.

The Leopold MkIV Spotting scope can do it all – hunting, competition and virtually anything else. It's one of the most popular scopes for military and law enforcement, and also works well for IHMSA.

ing gloves are also allowed, as long as they do not offer artificial support. Also, when shooting in the Creedmore position and using a revolver, a blast shield will protect the pants from powder residue and blast gasses coming sideways out of the revolver's chamber/cylinder gap.

There are also custom barrels that can be purchased for the T/C. Match grade barrels from Bullberry Barrel Works have been a popular addition for the T/C for decades, and can really make a difference in the accuracy of an already accurate pistol. Remember, going to a match grade barrel will usually put the shooter into a different class, so always consult the rulebook before shelling out the money for an upgrade.

Spotting scopes are a necessity for silhouette competition, and there are many on the market. Scopes for handgun competition are needed for spotting hits on the steel, or in the dirt, as the case may be. Since the range is relatively short, any decent optic with generally do, but if the competitor is like many shooters and has a variety of guns, then a lower quality spotting scope may not be enough to do all of the jobs asked of it. One excellent spotting scope that can do it all is the Leupold MkIV 20x60 tactical spotting scope. The optics are among the best in the business, and it's the one scope that can do it all, from competition to hunting. It's what the military uses, so you know it's good.

CHAPTER FIVE

IDPA

One of the most fun types of competitive pistol shooting is known as IDPA. IDPA stands for International Defensive Pistol Association, and is the governing body for the sport. Started in 1996 as a way to compete in action-pistol type handgun marches but in a more practical environment than other types of practical shooting type matches, IDPA grew out of a desire to get away from the "equipment races" that had plagued other sports for years.

Other practical shooting-type matches were no doubt fun, but increasingly you needed more and more expensive equipment to keep up, and while the shooting scenarios were challenging to competitive handgunners, they were not practical, which was how many of the action-pistol events started. Some shooters felt that the action-type matches had drifted from being practical to just being gun games. Some shooters wanted to return to the original roots of practical

shooting, and IDPA was formed.

In 1996, IDPA was formed and organized to advance the idea of using competition to sharpen self-defense handgun skills.

The equipment used in the matches is primarily what you would find on the hip of just about any CCW (concealed carry weapon) holder, and in fact, these types of firearms and holsters are perfectly suited for the matches.

It does not take a lot of money to get started in IDPA: a serviceable firearm in a suitable caliber, usually 9mm and above, a few magazines, a quality holster and a double magazine pouch, eye and ear protection, a couple of hundred rounds and the desire to have a blast at the range is really about all you need to get started. Indeed, for most of the competitors, including the top shooters, this is all the equipment you will ever need, since the sport is intentionally designed so that stock, or nearly stock firearms are

This shooter engages the target while sitting inside the front seat of a car. You never know what to expect at an IDPA match, which is part of the fun. Image courtesy IDPA.

The new shooter orientation takes place for any shooter who has not fired in any form of practical shooting event. This is to make sure the competitor can safely load, draw, fire, move and shoot, and unload under a controlled and safe manner. The shooter is also given instruction on targets and scoring, and how the courses of fire are shot. These are the rules of the host range, not of IDPA.

This is the new shooter orientation practical portion, where the competitor has to show that he/she can safely engage the target while moving, among other skills, before being allowed to fire in a match.

This shooter is drawing from behind an automobile, simulating having to engage targets while filling up the gas tank. Note the firing hand sweeps the clothing out of the way, while with the same motion, draws the pistol, keeping the trigger finger well away from the trigger, and the weak hand moves to the center of the chest, ready to assume a two hand hold. Image courtesy IDPA.

The RO gives detailed instruction to the new shooters on how the targets are scored and how to engage the targets.

This shooter, firing a revolver, still has to manipulate the gun, and get through the course in the most effective manner. Note the "tablet" has been dropped, and the hand goes to the pistol, while the trigger finger is well away from the trigger guard.

This competitor moves off the bed to the pistol on the nightstand, simulating real world circumstances. Image courtesy IDPA.

all that need to be used. You will not see "equipment races" at an IDPA match. The goal is to use service-type handguns and holsters, with full power ammunition in real world scenarios.

This is really a test of the shooting skills and gun handling ability of the competitor, leveling the playing field and lowering the entry barriers for people to engage in the sport. Currently there are around 25,000 competitors including shooters in 50 countries.

Now that I have your interest, let's look at the format. IDPA is actually made up of two different types of exercises contained in every match. There is the self-defense exercise and the standard exercise.

The self-defense exercise is exactly that, simulating a real world self-defense scenario or problem, exclusively solved with a handgun. As such, typical distances of target engagement run from a yard or two, to generally about 20-25 yards. Many times, the shooter has to start from typical shooting positions that would be required in a self-defense environment: lying in bed, sitting on the porch, changing an automobile tire, etc.

These matches typically require that the shooter move from one position or another, but not generally very far. So as the shooter you may start the stage sitting in a chair, but you then get up and engage one or more targets, then continue on with the scenario. Also, you will be presented with scenarios that force you to engage targets in different shooting positions other than just straight up shooting. There are almost always barricades

This competitor moves to open the door and engages the targets behind it. Note the orange and black stripe on the door, this is a fault line and the pistol's muzzle cannot dip below this line, this is a safety measure to make sure the muzzle of the pistol does not sweep the hand when reaching for the doorknob. Image courtesy IDPA.

This shooter engages the targets through the open door, still using cover. This is made more difficult since she is a right-handed shooter firing around the right side of an open door, making for an awkward stance, but still maintaining cover, a critical aspect of IDPA competition. Image courtesy IDPA.

This competitor fires from behind a jewelry case, simulating a shopkeeper being robbed, while still using good form and recoil control. Image courtesy IDPA.

This competitor sweeps the jacket away while at the same time reaches for the pistol and moves toward the target. Footwork is key in all practical pistol competitions. Image courtesy IDPA.

never see the exact same stage twice, no matter how long you've been competing or how many matches you've been to. There may be some that are similar, but the match director can always come up with creative ways to make each stage, fun, different, challenging and interesting. It's really up to his or her imagination.

Keep in mind that the stages are set up to test the shooters' skill and gunhandling expertise. You may find yourself at an ATM machine being robbed, or a victim of a carjacking, or you are picking up groceries at the convenience store that is being robbed. Sometimes you will start the stage with the gun in a box or by the bedside and not even in a holster.

All of these matches are designed with one thing in mind, they are set up to test actual or possible "real world" situations, so you will be challenged and

and/or walls to shoot around, windows to shoot through, doors to open or close, moving targets and more at an IDPA match. One of the fun aspects of the matches is that there are usually around 5-8 stages, and you will will, more likely than not, need to move around while shooting each individual stage. The sport does not require great physical ability, but you will need to be able to be somewhat mobile.

This competitor from Team Smith and Wesson fires a controlled pair at an IDPA match. Note the two pieces of brass in the air in close proximity, a sign of a quick double tap. Image courtesy IDPA.

This competitor was standing at a simulated ATM machine when attacked. Creative, realistic scenarios are a staple of IDPA competitions. Note the two pieces of brass in the air, denoting a double tap, another staple of practical shooting. Image courtesy IDPA.

The shooter starts the stage from the seated position, reading their (simulated) tablet, and will then move to the wall to begin firing.

This competitor has moved from the seated position and started the string, shooting through the window of the wall. Note the camera attached to the bill of his baseball cap. More and more shooters are videotaping their strings for review later. Video feedback is a great way to identify areas that the shooter can improve at the game.

No "race guns" here, just an everyday service-type revolver being used in a practical competition. These types of guns and the shooters who use them are the basis for IDPA shooting.

These shooters are getting the mover set up prior to starting the match. On this stage, when the pepper popper is struck by the shooter and falls, it releases the mover, which slides down the rails, and must be engaged while moving.

This shooter gets ready to shoot a standard stage.

Shooters always need to engage targets while behind cover.

The target array makes for a fast and furious match, with a lot of targets and a lot of shooting. The hands on the targets are no-shoot targets.

Here the RO gives the walk-through to the shooters at each stage prior to starting the match. The RO will explain what the scenario is at each stage before the match starts, and the stage description will be posted at each stage as well.

This shooter has to engage the targets while holding onto a briefcase. Realistic scenarios keep the match interesting and fun. Note he keeps the left foot on the blue piece of wood. Moving the foot off the wood and engaging the targets will result in a penalty. Procedural penalties like this can add up fast.

This shooter engages the targets and moves while shooting. This is a critical skill to develop for all types of practical shooting.

IDPA stages start with the pistol under cover of clothing. Here the shooter sweeps the jacket out of the way in order to draw and engage the targets.

The shooter has already opened the door, is sweeping the jacket out of the way and moving through the open door at the same time.

Reloading skills are also emphasized, and reloading is always performed while utilizing cover. Note the shooter is looking at the gun while pushing the magazine into the pistol.

Here the shooter engages the target firing with the weak hand, while making sure not to shoot the no-shoot target.

The second type of match you will see at an IDPA match is the standard exercise. Standard exercises are designed as purely a test of shooting skill, and not running and jumping ability.

Classifiers are used to be able to assign the shooters into various skill level classifications. There are several classifications for shooters based on skill level: Novice, Marksman, Sharpshooter, Expert, Master and Distinguished Master. These tests are a great way to measure your progress in your marksmanship and gunhandling techniques, such as firing with the strong hand or weak hand only (meaning firing one handed with the right or left hand only, respectively, assuming you are a right handed shooter) and testing your accuracy, using good sight alignment and trigger control at short to longer ranges.

This shooter uses a set of shooting gloves to good effect. Some shooters like them and some don't. Anything that's legal by the rulebook is allowed, and if it helps, then by all means use it.

Notice how this competitor shoots around the corner and doesn't step out away from the door opening. Shooting under cover is critical and is part of the rules of the game.

A tight target array utilizing a mix of shoot, no-shoot and pepper poppers makes shooting this stage quite a bit of fun.

Firing through the window while still maintaining cover is mandatory in IDPA. Exposing oneself and engaging the target will incur a procedural penalty.

This competitor uses a one-hand hold to engage the targets with a double action semi-automatic. These DA service-type guns are very popular in IDPA matches.

This moving target is activated when the pepper popper is struck and falls down completely.

Moving through the obstacle while keeping the gun pointed in a safe direction with the finger off the trigger is very important in any type of practical pistol match.

The 1911 pistol is a popular one for IDPA. Here the shooter fires from the seated position.

This competitor fires from behind a wall, which is required in IDPA matches. If the shooter were to fire from an exposed position, he/she would incur a procedural penalty.

One of the main points of competing in an IDPA match is that the equipment, meaning the gun and holster, has to be concealable. The focus of the sport is the CCW holder, or at least people who are interested in obtaining their concealed carry card. Although you do not need a CCW card in order to attend or compete in the matches, the equipment must be concealable, in the "spirit of the game." Therefor, a holster or gun that is meant strictly for competition is not allowed. In fact, the gun and holster must meet certain rules of concealability in order to be allowed to compete. Also, the stage will be started with the competitors' firearm in a concealed position. In other words, even if you don't have a CCW, you will still be required to start each stage with the gun covered up by a shirt, jacket or other piece of clothing and fully concealed, unless all competitors have to start the stage with the pistol in a box or on a table, for example. If that is the case, this information will be posted. Each scenario is posted at each stage, so as you walk up to the stage with your squad, you will be given the opportunity to review the scenario and will also be given a walk-though by the match director or safety officer.

Two concepts that you will need to be familiar with if you decide to get started in IDPA competition are tactical priority and tactical sequence.

Since this sport is designed to simulate real-world situations, you need to engage the targets in the most effective tactical man-

Drawing the firearm from a seated position is a common skill in many practical shooting type matches, and IDPA is no exception.

This shooter leans way out in order to get to all of the targets. The less the shooter has to move his/her position in order to engage all of the targets presented, the better.

The RO, second from left, scores the targets while the scorer records the score, the two shooters on the both ends are pasting targets. The shooter on the far left is waiting until the RO scores the target before the target can be repaired.

Firing weak hand only is an important skill in IDPA and one that is used in many of the stages.

Note the shooter still stays behind cover, in this case the corner of the wall, while firing.

Footwork is important, and this shooter keeps the focus on the sights while moving to his right.

A service-type pistol, a good holster, a few good magazines and a desire to have some fun are all that is needed to compete at an IDPA match.

Note that the shooter does not make contact with the wall while firing, yet still stays behind the wall and using it for cover while engaging the target.

Getting the range set up takes a little time, and help is always appreciated. New shooters to the sport of IDPA can learn quite a bit by coming a little early and staying a little late, helping to set up and break down the course. Talking about the match with experienced shooters, both before and after, will greatly help new shooters learn about the sport and improve their skills.

Moving and shooting in either direction is a common aspect of an IDPA match, this shooter keeps the focus on the sights, while executing good footwork.

This shooter is negotiating the course at a dead run, while at the same time keeping the handgun under control, keeping the finger out of the trigger guard, and getting into a good firing position to engage the next set of targets.

ner that you can. This means that you have to engage the target that poses the greatest threat to you, and then keep engaging them in lower priority.

Tactical priority would go something like this: You are faced with three targets at three different distances, a near target at 5 yards, a middle target at 12 yards, and a far target at 22 yards away. Tactical priority means that the closest target is the greater threat, and you would fire two rounds on that target first, then two rounds on the target the next furthest out, and finally, two rounds on the target the furthest away from you. That's tactical priority. You are prioritizing the targets based on the actual greatest threat to you, and working your way from near to far.

Tactical sequence, on the other hand,

means that you have targets at equal distance, and are all an equal threat, so you have to engage them equally. Take our same three targets we used before, but now they are at equal distance from you. How do you engage three targets at practically the same time, since they are all an equal threat to you? By engaging them with one round first, and then going back to reengage. So, for example, you are in an alley and three armed men confront you and tell you they going to take your wallet and then kill you. You would engage them by firing one round on each target, and then going back with another round since all targets must be engaged with at least two rounds in all IDPA matches. So, going from left to right or right to left, your firing sequence would be 1,1,

This shooter shows how to lean around a set of barrels, keeping under cover while engaging all of the targets presented.

It's one thing to be able to run fast, but a shooter needs to stop as well. This shooter is careful not to go past the edge of the wall, which would expose the shooter, who would have to then back up before engaging the target; otherwise, the shooter would incur a procedural penalty. Notice the trigger finger is almost into the trigger guard, so that when the shooter comes to a stop, he will be ready to engage the target.

2, 1, 1. Or one round on the first target, one round on the second target, two rounds on the third target, then back to the middle target with another round and the last (or first) target with another round.

Most new shooters forget tactical sequence and instead engage the targets with 2, 2 and 2. This sequence is wrong and will get you penalized as a procedural penalty. It's always good to collect your thoughts before you nod your head when you are on the firing line about to start the string and the RO asks you if you are ready!

The targets shot at an IDPA match are paper and steel. Paper targets are similar to the USPSA targets, but have different scoring rings and different scoring areas.

Steel targets are also used and come in four different types: pepper poppers, which have an 8-inch round section in the center of the 24-inch tall target, and a popper, which has the 8-inch round section at the top of the target. There are also 8-inch round steel targets, and 6-inch square targets. These usually have a small flat plate attached to the

This shooter is on a dead run, keeping the trigger finger out of the trigger guard, the pistol pointed downrange in a safe direction, and looking ahead to the next firing position, where he needs to stop and engage the set of targets.

Here the shooter has swept way the jacket, drawn the pistol, and at the same time, the weak hand is coming up meet the pistol at the center of the chest, to get the two handed hold and start the firing sequence. Notice the trigger finger is blurred in the photo, meaning it is moving into the trigger guard. All of this should be performed in one smooth motion, like this shooter is doing. These motions can be practiced at home, with an unloaded pistol, of course.

Getting into a kneeling firing position, keeping behind cover, while keeping the pistol pointed in a safe direction and thinking about how to engage the targets, makes the IDPA matches fun to shoot.

This shooter is reloading the pistol while still keeping behind the cover of the wall, which is critical in an actual armed confrontation, all hallmarks of the guidelines and "spirit of the game" of an IDPA match.

bottom so the targets can stand on their own.

Shooting and IDPA is exciting and challenging. Give it a try, you don't need a whole lot of expensive equipment, and it's a blast.

EQUIPMENT

Equipment needed for IDPA competition is actually pretty basic, which is what makes the game so popular.

There are several divisions in IDPA covering the guns that are legal to use. They are:

Stock Service Pistol – These are normally semiautomatic handguns in 9mm or above, double action, or striker fired handguns. There are modifications that can be performed and some that are outlawed. Always consult the rulebook to see what classification your handgun falls into.

Enhanced Service Pistol – These guns are similar to the Stock Service Pistol, but can be modified with more custom touches, including sights, barrels and trigger work.

Custom Defensive Pistol – These guns are can be more enhanced than the Enhanced Service Pistol Division. They must be chambered for the .45 ACP cartridge, and are designed to allow the popular tactical 1911 handguns that have been a mainstay of competitive handguns for decades. The modifications allowed include checkering, and heavy coned style barrels, and many more. Again, always consult the rulebook when considering entering the match. Just remember, pretty much any centerfire handgun in 9mm and above will fit into one category or another.

Compact Carry Pistol – This division is similar to the Enhanced Division, except that the barrel length must not exceed 4.10 inches.

Revolver Division – Revolvers are categorized as stock or enhanced. The caliber for stock revolver is .38 Special or larger, and enhanced revolver is .357 Magnum or larger.

BUG Division – This is the Back Up Gun division, and is a specialty division that may or may not be included in a local match. Sometimes BUG Matches are a completely separate match or can be included into a regular IDPA match. BUG Matches may be set up as semi-auto matches or revolver, and will be designated as BUG-S, for semiauto, and BUG-R for revolver matches.

NFC – This is the Not For Competition Division. This Division is for guns that do

The Springfield Armory Range Officer would make a good gun for both IDPA and CCW holders wanting a good 1911 pistol. Image courtesy Springfield Armory, Inc.

The S&W M&P, in either 9mm or .40 S&W or .45 ACP, makes an excellent pistol for IDPA matches for a shooter wanting a striker-fired pistol, rather than an exposed hammer-type pistol like a 1911.

The Fobus GL26 is paddle-type holster popular for CCW holders and IDPA. Image courtesy Fobus, Inc.

not fit into the other six categories. These include guns that are smaller than 9mm, or include active lasers or tactical lights. In fact, many local club matches offer night competitions using tactical lights and lasers. These are popular at indoor ranges, where they can lower the lighting.

Holster requirements are pretty stringent, since this game is geared toward concealed carry. The holsters must conform to the type that would be worn if carrying concealed. In fact, the start position of every shooter must be with the gun covered by clothing, whether the competitor actually has a CCW or not.

The first line in the rulebook on holsters states, "Must be suitable for concealed carry and all day continuous wear." This line pretty much tells you what you need to know about holster and magazine pouches. Again, when in doubt, consult the rulebook.

Once you know you have the proper gun for whatever division you are interested in competing in, make sure you have several

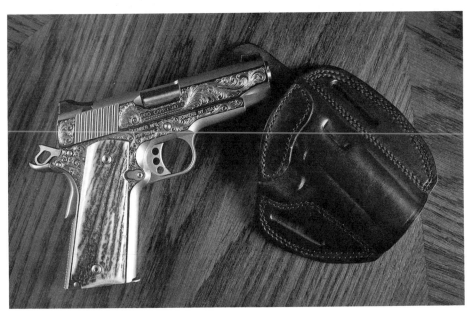

For shooters wanting an excellent leather holster, the Kirkpatrick compact undercover paired with a 1911 pistol makes a good combination. Image courtesy Kirkpatrick Leather, Inc.

reliable magazines, a couple of hundred rounds of ammunition or more, a range bag and eye and ear protection.

Always wear comfortable clothes and shoes that will let you move around the range without slipping. Hiking shoes are always a good choice.

The Alien Gear Kydex holster is made for a variety of firearms, like this Springfield Armory XD. Image courtesy AlienGear Holsters.

The BladeTech Total Eclipse is a popular holster for IDPA matches. Made of Kydex, the synthetic holster is durable and keeps the pistol solidly secured while moving and maneuvering through the various IDPA stages during a match. Image courtesy Blade-Tech, Inc.

The Alien Gear Outside the waistband holster is made from Kydex and is concealable and durable. Image courtesy AlienGear Holsters.

CHAPTER SIX

GLOCK SHOOTING SPORTS FOUNDATION

Since the introduction of the popular polymer pistol, the Glock has been adopted by a majority of law enforcement departments across the country. The civilian market has also embraced the Glock, and it is a popular firearm for the 100,000 CCW holders in the U.S. today. Simple to operate, customizable, possessing the fewest parts of just about any handgun on the market, and reliable as they come, the Glock is a natural choice for many of the shooting games that handgunners engage in across the country.

IPSC, IDPA, 3-gun and even steel matches always see a good representation of Glock products, so it was natural for Glock themselves to design and develop a match specifically for the popular, polymer framed pistol. In 1991, the Glock Shooting Sports Foundation (GSSF) was formed. The Foundation now boasts over 100,000 members and hosts hundreds of matches across the country every year.

Each competitor needs to join the GSSF in order to compete, and of course the only firearms allowed are Glocks. Memberships are inexpensive, only $35.00. As with other forms of handgun competitions, there are several divisions, categories and classifications, so a review of the rulebook should be the first step for any new shooter coming to a GSSF match.

The Glock stage is a challenging one, but a lot of fun. The check-in tent is in the center and one of the two outer tents is where the competitor goes to actually shoot the stage. Image courtesy GSSF.

The registration table is where the shooters first come to, and the prize table at the GSSF matches is always full.

The prize table at a Glock match includes Glock pistols given away to the top shooters. Image courtesy GSSF.

Morning range officer orientation makes sure all of the ROs are fully briefed before the match starts. Safety is paramount, and the ROs do an exceptional job making sure the match is safe and fun for all. Image courtesy GSSF.

This competitor is using really good form to engage the target: arms out, and shoulders rolled forward, with a high grip on the gun for recoil control. Image courtesy GSSF.

The range is fairly short for all of the stages, which makes the action fast and furious.

With very little equipment needed, the ranges short yet challenging, Glock matches are fun for everyone. Note this competitor does not use a holster or magazine pouches, just a range bag and a reliable gun and magazines.

The category a shooter falls into largely depends on what firearm they want to compete with. One of the great things about shooting in GSSF match is they are not complicated or intimidating courses of fire, but are challenging enough for even seasoned professional competitors, and the equipment needed is inexpensive, and readily available. You really don't even need a holster, since at each stage there are tables set up at the firing line, so the shooters can bring the firearm and ammunition to the line in the range bag.

Three points about the GSSF matches that really make it unique are that there is a Certified Glock Armorer at every match to work on pistols that may be needed repairs, and there are firearms given away at even smaller matches. The third point about GSSF matches is the breadth of people coming to compete in the matches. Come to any GSSF Match and there will be families competing, not just Dad, or Dad and son like at many matches. You will see wives, girlfriends, and daughters at the matches. Glock matches are very family-friendly. The match consists of three stages: Glock the Plates, 5 to Glock, and Glock'M.

In the Glock the Plates stage, the competitor stands facing a bank of steel plates that are placed 11 yards downrange. The plates are standard 8-inch steel, and the bank consists of six of the steel plates.

Steel plates at 11 yards represents a great stage in that the plates are small enough to be challenging to top shooters because they are trying to go as fast as they can, always competing against themselves, and the plates are also close enough to present a hittable target to the first time shooter. So the challenge is speed.

The shooter needs to start the stage from the low ready position, which is both hands on the pistol, with the finger out of the trigger guard and the pistol pointed toward the ground.

At the start signal, the shooter engages the plates in any order, and the pistol cannot be loaded with more than 11 rounds, 7 if the shooter is competing in Major Sub category. All plates have to fall, not just hit, and any

The Glock the Plates is always fun. Plates give instant feedback when hit, or not.

plate left standing after firing the string is counted as a miss, and is accrued a 10 second penalty.

The shooter fires four strings of six shots each, for a total of 24 shots for the stage. The four strings are fired separately, so they are four individual strings of fire, reloading the pistol and starting each string from the ready position.

I've always found steel plates to be great fun to shoot, because the shooter can always improve their time, it's always a challenge, and it's very uncomplicated, the shooter does not have to "think" about how to shoot the

This range officer gives the command to the shooter, who is collecting his thoughts before giving the nod to start the stage.

Law enforcement shooters are always tough competitors. Note the RO keeps the timer close to the shooter to properly register each shot.

Regardless of what type of competitive shooting event it is, just prior to the start of the string, all shooters will collect their thoughts and get mentally prepared to fire. All shooters at GSSF matches start from the low ready position.

The RO calls out the score, based on the bullet hole location on the scoring rings, while the scorer records the score and the competitor looks on.

This shooter uses more of a Weaver stance with one of the smaller pocket Glock pistols, and does a good job of controlling the smaller pistol's recoil.

stage, or where or when to reload, or how to move through the course of fire. The shooter simply needs to stand and shoot.

The Glock to Plates can also be shot as a paper option if the range facility does not have a plate rack available. The targets are the NRA D-1 or Tombstone target, and any hit inside the "C" ring is counted as a hit. The "C" ring is eight inches in diameter, so it matches the diameter of the steel plates.

The difference between the Steel Glock the Plates match and using paper targets for this stage is that the paper targets are place at 7 yards instead of 11 yards with steel.

The next stage at a GSSF Match is the 5 to Glock. Again, as with other GSSF stages, the key here is simple and fun. The stage is basically 5 NRA D-1 Tombstone targets, placed at 5, 10, 15, 20 and 25 yards, alternating from side to side in a straight line. These distances and heights can vary from match to match, at the discretion of the range master due to range, and other conditions. For example, at a recent match where I took these photos, the targets are placed next to each other, rather than being staggered, but the concept is still the same: five targets engaged with two shots each in any order.

As with other GSSF stages, this stage is shot starting from the low ready position.

The stage is shot with three separate strings of two shots per target. At the start signal, the shooter engages each target with two shots each, in any order.

This competitor uses one of full size Glock pistols with the interchangeable backstraps, which gives the shooter a higher grip on the gun and more recoil control.

This competitor engages the plates with a full-sized Glock. Note the heavier recoil.

Proper application of the shooting fundamentals will allow the competitor to shoot groups like this all day.

The Glock matches are easy to get involved with. Just bring whatever Glock you have; there is a category for you to compete in.

Three separate strings are fired and the best six hits per target are scored. Again, as with the other two stages of the GSSF matches, stages are simple and fun, and scoring is easy to understand. One twist of this stage that is different from the Glock the Plates stage is that the D-1 target has scoring rings. There are A, B and C rings, and the competitor incurs a time penalty. For example, if the shooter scores a hit in the A/B zone or ring in the center of the target, the shooter incurs no time penalty. If there is a hit in the "C" ring, the shooter incurs a one-second penalty per hit which is added to the total time. If there is a hit in the "D" area of the target outside of the scoring rings, he/she incurs a 3-second penalty per hit in the "D" area. Misses get 10 seconds added to the shooter's time. So, as with other action type events, the shooter needs to go fast but not too fast and a lack of accuracy has negative consequences.

The last stage at a GSSF match is the Glock'M stage. In this exercise, there are 4 D-1 targets and three steel pepper poppers. This stage is the most complex, but still very straightforward to shoot and score. There are two D-1 target set at seven yards, three poppers set on a horizontal line parallel to the firing line at 11 yards, and two more D-1 targets set at 15 yards. At the signal, the shooter engages each paper target with two shots each, and one popper. The targets are engaged at the shooter's discretion, and the stage is three strings, hence the three poppers. Scoring paper targets is the same, and misses get a 10 second penalty. The popper needs to fall in order to be scored a hit.

This competitor has good recoil control with one of the smaller Glock pistols. Note the two pieces of brass in the air at the same time. Image courtesy GSSF.

First and second place prizes money given out. Here R. Lee Ermy, (center) of Full Metal Jacket movie fame, showed his support at the GSSF match. Image courtesy GSSF.

One of the great features about the GSSF matches is the fact that at the matches, not only is prize money available, but Glock firearms are also given away. In fact, prizes at a typical outdoor GSSF match consist of a round $5,600 and over 25 firearms, in addition to bragging rights!

In addition to the cash and prizes, when you become a member of the GSSF, you also have access to the Glock Armorer's Course, which will show you have to assemble and disassemble, clean and maintain your Glock firearm, as well as being allowed to participate in the Glock Pistol Purchase Program.

EQUIPMENT

As mentioned, the GSSF matches need to shot strictly with Glock pistols, but one of the great things about Glock is that there are many different makes and models to choose

from. So which ones are the most competitive? GSSF encourages the stock category to promote the ease in which a large number of people can compete without getting into an "equipment race" where gadgets and modifications are used to gain a competitive edge. Stock division is just that: stock, meaning no modifications or parts can be used unless those parts were manufactured by Glock themselves.

Any use of aftermarket parts normally puts the shooter into the Unlimited division.

I have two Glocks, a G17 and a G35 MOS, so using my guns as an example, the G17 is a full size pistol chambered in 9mm, the magazines hold 17 rounds, but that's no advantage since the stages cannot be fired with more than 11 rounds anyway, 10 in the magazine and one in the chamber.

My G17 has Tritium sights, and also has

This competitor uses a Glock with a compensator installed to help control recoil, it also makes for a softer shooting gun because the extra weight on the end of the barrel helps slow the unlocking of the pistol when it's fired, it also has a Leupold Delta Point electronic sight. Image courtesy GSSF.

This competitor takes down the plates using good form. Image courtesy GSSF.

This young shooter uses a laser marksmanship trainer to warm up before a GSSF indoor match. Image courtesy GSSF.

The competitor, after using the laser trainer, put the skills to use during the GSSF Indoor match. Image courtesy GSSF.

a Bar-Sto Match barrel that I installed many years ago, so because the pistol is no longer stock due to the installation of the match barrel, I would fall into the unlimited division, where many modifications are legal.

I would generally prefer to re-install the original factory barrel in the gun since the yardages are so close, there really isn't much advantage to having a match barrel on the gun, and the stock category is where the most people shoot, so I feel stock category would be more competitive.

My other pistol, the G35, is chambered in 40 S&W and is completely stock, although my G35 is the MOS version which is the Modular Optic System.

Competing with this pistol would, again, put me in the unlimited category, since the sight is not Glock equipment, although if I shot the gun with iron sights, I could shoot in the stock division. About the only modifications allowed in the stock division are fiber optic iron sights and grips, such as the "skateboard tape" type grips that wraparound the frame or the Hogue-type grip sleeves.

The stock-centric nature of GSSF competition makes it very talent driven, and very little gamesmanship is apparent. This keeps the fun in the matches and is one reason why the GSSF matches are so wildly popular.

The firearms fall into subcompact, major subcompact, heavy metal, unlimited, competition, and pocket Glock categories. It's best to consult the rulebook or talk to an active competitor to see which fall into which category. Pretty much any stock Glock can fall into one category or another, meaning is you have a Glock in 9mm, .40S&W, 10MM or .45 ACP, it will be allowed in one category or another, and would be very competitive.

For shooters new to handguns, the G17 in 9mm would also be a good choice. If

The Glock G35 MOS in .40 S&W is another good choice for competitive practical pistol shooting and allows for the use of dot sights like the Leupold Delta Point, the C-More and other types of sights. Image courtesy Glock.

The Glock G22 in 40S&W is a popular Glock model and a good choice to get started in the GSSF matches. The gun could also do triple duty as a carry gun for CCW holders and in other forms of practical pistol matches. Image courtesy Glock.

The G23 is the compact version of the G22, and comes in the same caliber. This is also a good choice for a starter gun. Image courtesy Glock.

you have the G42 it would fit into the pocket Glock, category. If you compete in the pocket Glock category, the steel pepper poppers are shot under the "ring and paint" method, meaning that the .380 ACP cartridges have difficulty knocking them down, so they just have to be shot and hit, which will leave a mark on the paint, noting a hit.

A note about ammunition: Shooters only need to bring about 150 rounds of ammunition to shoot the three stages, not including any side matches that may be set up. Ammunition is the single most common reason for a gun malfunction, so if you reload, make sure that your ammunition is well tested in your firearm, and as an alternative, buy ammunition in bulk and save some money. 9mm, for example, can be purchased by the case and will last for several matches. All GSSF matches are "lost brass" matches, meaning that the brass that comes out of your pistol is "lost" when it hits the ground. You are not allowed to retrieve any spent brass on the range at any time.

The inclusive nature of the GSSF matches extends to female shooters. Many of the GSSF matches have a Glock Girls Side Match, which is open to female shooters in either Amateur or Master categories. Competitors can use the stock Glocks used in the other categories, or the long slide versions such as the 17L and others.

For GSSF competition, there are no holster requirements. In other words, if you don't have a holster for your Glock, no problem, you can come to the firing line with the unloaded gun in your range bag, and when the RO gives the command, you simply unbag the gun and bring out the loaded magazines. The RO will then give you instructions on how to proceed. If you do have a holster, there are no specific requirements about what type of holster you need to use, but the gun must be able to go back into the holster with the slide locked to the rear.

This is different from other practical type handgun matches where the unloaded gun is required to be secured in the holster with the slide forward.

If you have a Glock, find a GSSF match in your area and get out there and compete. If you don't have a Glock, now's a great time to get one and get started.

CHAPTER SEVEN

SASS

The action gets up close in SASS (Single Action Shooting Society) competition. This competitor thumbs the revolver with the left hand and fires with the right, which is the preferred technique. Pistol targets are set at 7-10 yards. Image courtesy SASS.

One of the most unique forms of competitive shooting today is known as collectively as "Cowboy Action." Formed from a desire to blend the action of a USPSA/IPSC match, with the firearms and "feel" of the Old West, Cowboy Action Shooting matches under the Single Action Shooting Society (SASS) are unique in not only the types of firearms that are used and the courses of fire, but also the "look and feel" of the Old West. To be sure, the costumes worn and the courses of fire can get quite elaborate, especially if you attend one of the bigger matches. But even at the club level, the costumes are as big or maybe a bigger part of the overall shooting experience.

For example, you cannot show up for a match and try to compete wearing any kind of non-period clothing, so that means no baseball hats, tennis shoes or sports-type clothing.

Everything worn during the match has to be period-correct, and as authentic as pos-

The clothing at a SASS match is as correct for the period as possible, and is part of the unique aspect of SASS competition.

This is a typical stage in a SASS match. The loading bench is on the right, where the handgun and rifle are pre-loaded, the actual stage where the shooter engages the targets is in the center, and the unloading table is at the left. The competitors watch the proceedings and wait their turn. Note that each shooter has a unique cart to carry guns, ammo, cleaning equipment and other supplies needed for the match.

The costumes are required and are an important part of SASS competition. Here is a shooter in Civil War-era dress, next to his cart carrying his long guns and equipment.

sible from head to toe. This period clothing extends to family and friends at the matches, as well as at banquets and award ceremonies. It really adds to the festive nature of the matches.

I was fortunate enough to attend one of the larger regional matches that was held near my area, and not only were all of the competitors wearing full dress costumes of the Old West, the match stages, as well as the simulated Old Western town itself was made up to look like a scene from a John Wayne western. It really felt like you were standing on a Hollywood movie set. It was very cool to see the Jail, the Blacksmith Shop, the old Saloon and a General Store. Another great aspect of the matches is the friendliness and camaraderie of the shooters.

They are very welcoming to new shooters and very helpful in explaining what the game is all about. This camaraderie aspect of the sport is even in their Rulebook. There is a chapter on the "Spirit of the Game", which states that the shooter doesn't look for ways to gain an unfair advantage over other shoot-

Here the RO gives the safety briefing and also goes over the course of fire for the competitors.

Some of the larger matches offer a taste of the Old West. This period town is set up outside the shooting area at a large regional match. This is the SASS equivalent of Commercial Row at Camp Perry, where the vendors set up their accessories for sale.

ers, and that the shooters fully play by the rules of the game, and go above and beyond the term "sportsmanship."

I've been to SASS matches where there was a call that could have given the shooter a higher score, but instead, took a lower score because it wasn't clear if the shooter should have received it or not, and rather than argue the call, which many shooters may be inclined to do, the shooter elected to take a lower score, in the *spirit of the game*.

The Single Action Shooting Society is the governing body of the organization and sets the rules of the game. There are several unique divisions of the competition and will be covered in this chapter. When a shooter decides to get into Cowboy Action, the one of the first things a shooter needs to do after signing up is to pick an alias.

This is a fun, first step toward really getting immersed into the sport. The alias the new shooter select needs to be representative of a character or profession that was around in the Old West. There are, of course, some caveats to selecting an alias. Rule number one is that it needs to be "printable" meaning it needs to be fairly clean. It also needs to be unique, so that you cannot have an alias that is a duplicate or similar to another shooters alias. It means that you cannot have a Wyatt Earp, or a Marshal Wyatt Earp, those are considered too similar.

Beyond those few simple rules, it's a fun way for new shooters to really get creative. The SASS Headquarters gets to be the final arbiter on alias names.

So what are the courses of fire and how is the game played? Basically, this is very similar to a modern 3-gun match, except the match is shot with firearms that were appropriate in the Old West. That means revolvers, rifles, which are mostly lever action, and shotguns, either single or double barreled, or lever action.

The matches are also similar to a modern 3-gun match in that the stage scenarios are such that instead of walking into a convenience store and confronting a group of armed thugs, you walk into a saloon and confront Black Bart, or other similar nefarious outlaw, and engage him and his posse in a gunfight with all three firearms.

This competitor in the Duelist category uses the two handed technique to great effect.

Thumb cocking and aimed firing is the preferred technique in SASS competition.

Being able to shoot through the haze is important for this SASS competitor.

This competitor in Civil War dress uses a blackpowder gun at this stage.

This shooter thumbs the revolver and fires with the same hand. Note the different holsters of the shooter and the RO, the RO has a crossdraw-type holster.

Husband and wife teams really get into the game, here the wife shows her husband how it's done as the RO looks on.

The shooters are placed into separate categories, most being age-based, with "Young Guns" being the 14-16 year olds, and the "Buckaroos" being 13 years old or younger at the day of the match.

The Buckaroos' firearms have to meet all of the requirements of the firearms as far as make and model, sights, etc., but need to be chambered in .22 LR. Shotguns are chambered in .410 calibers, and knockdown targets do not need to be knocked down. "Cowboy" competitors can be of any age, and "Wranglers" are 36 and older. "49ers" are those competitors 49 years old or older, and Seniors are 60 and above. Silver Seniors are competitors 65 years of age or greater, and Elder Statesmen/Grand Dames are competitors 70 years of age or greater. There are also sub-categories, so you can enter the match as a Lady 49er, for example.

Once you've been put into an age category, there are other categories to choose from as well. Remember, these handguns

From head to toe, the clothing, firearms and leather gear for a SASS competitor is period correct for the men and the women.

Note the sign at this stage. SASS shooters definitely have a great sense of humor.

The carrying carts keep everything organized and the easy to move from stage to stage during the match.

Young SASS shooters can compete in the "Buckaroo" category for the under 13 age group, but this youngster has to stick with the wood gun for now since he is a little too young to compete. Youngsters this age may compete at the RO's discretion. Image courtesy SASS.

Junior shooters are an important part of any shooting sport and SASS is no different, here a junior shooter uses the thumb cocking technique to good effect.

are single action, and as such, they need to be cocked and fired for each shot, and there are a couple of ways to do this. One way, and is probably the most popular because it's the fastest and most efficient, is to draw the pistol from the holster at the start signal, then with the weak hand, cock the pistol and fire with the strong hand. This way, the pistol can be cocked and fired very quickly.

One method you won't see anyone doing is fanning the revolver, because this is the most inaccurate way to shoot a single action pistol. So, to fire the shots, the drill is to cock, and fire, then recock and fire, going through all five shots.

The other way to fire the gun actually enables the competitor to sign up for and compete in a different category, and that is the "Duelist".

The Duelist is where the pistols is drawn, cocked and fired with one hand. So, the hand that draws he pistol also cocks the hammer and then fires the pistol. There are also some matches that can also be a Double Duelist, and that means exactly what it says, you draw and fire two pistols, cocking and firing with each hand. There are no rules as to

The thumbcocking technique, with careful aiming, is the hallmark of effectively engaging the targets in a SASS match.

This shooter uses a similar one-handed technique that shooters in modern practical shooting competitions like USPSA and IDPA matches use. This technique keeps the upper body tight and helps counter the effects of recoil.

Once the pistol is drawn, the thumb-cocking and firing technique works well for both the men and the women equally.

This competitor fires in the Double Duelist category, and uses two revolvers at the same time.

Having just completed the rifle portion of the stage, this female shooter is moving to the shotgun/pistol portion of the stage and is drawing the revolver in order to engage the targets. After firing the revolver, the will be holstered and the shotgun used. Note how close the targets are, typical of a SASS match. Image courtesy SASS.

how this must be accomplished, but clearly alternating between revolvers, cocking and firing one in the left hand, and cocking and firing the pistol in the right hand, is the most efficient way to accomplish this.

Another category is the B Western. In this category, the shooter is limited to specific types and calibers of rifles, but the handguns are the normal SASS-legal firearms. The main difference is in the costumes worn. They are to be representative of the types of clothing worn in many of the B-Western movies back in the day. So for example, shirts must be the type worn in the movies with snap buttons and embroidery. Pants, boots and scarves of the type worn in the movies are also a requirement, as are spurs for the men!

The Classic Cowboy and Cowgirl category is a category where the pistols must be shot Duelist, or Double Duelist. The revolver caliber requirement are 40 caliber or larger, and there are also requirements for the rifle and shotgun.

There are clothing requirements for both men and women. The men have to choose between a list of five clothing items, as do the women. The men have the following list to choose from and must pick five

of the items: *"Chaps, Western spurs with spur straps, cuffs, tie or scarf worn loosely around the neck or with scarf slide, vest, pocket watch with full length chain, jacket, sleeve garters, knife (screw knives do NOT qualify), botas, leggings, braces; no straw or palm hats allowed. (From the SASS HAND-BOOK)."*

The women have to choose five from a list of items such as: *"Period watch, split riding skirt, bustle, hoops, corset, Victorian style hat (straw allowed), period jewelry, period hair ornaments (e.g., feathers), snood, reticule (period handbag), period lace up shoes, camisole, bloomers, fishnet stockings, feather boa, cape.(From the SASS HANDBOOK)"* This shows that the level of authenticity of the matches is kept intact. It really makes for a fun and interesting time at the range. In addition to watching the match, I spent as much time just admiring the level of detail and craftsmanship in the costumes and holsters as I did watching the competitors shoot, it was that much fun!

Blackpowder cartridge categories are a hoot! When those guns go off, they can obscure the entire firing line with smoke. At the match I attended, there were several black powder competitors on the firing line and the smoke, even from the handguns was enough to obscure the entire firing line of the stage, in addition, the smoke choked several of the shooters waiting to go next. It

This shooter fires in the Double Duelist category, and is in the process of drawing and firing two pistols at the same time.

This competitor starts from the surrender position, just like in other types of modern competitive shooting, while the RO looks on. The pistol and rifle are loaded prior to starting the stage, but the shotgun is unloaded and is loaded during the string.

After shooting the stage, the firearms are unloaded at the unloading table under the direct supervision of the unloading officer and then handguns are holstered.

Women shooters get into the game in a big way as well. Here the shooter draws the pistol using good techniques with the finger off the trigger.

Here the old mixes with the new as the clothing is period correct for the 1800's, but the tablet technology used to track the shooter's score is decidedly 2015.

was a blast, literally. The Frontiersman category is for shooters that want to compete with blackpowder. The pistols are percussion style and can be shot two handed or one-handed Duelist style. The blackpowder category of handguns is required to produce smoke the equivalent of 15 grains by volume of ffg powder.

Two more categories are the Plainsman, and the Derringer. In the Plainsman category, the competitor has to use a blackpowder pistol 36 caliber or larger. There are requirements for the rifle and shotgun as well.

The Derringer/Pocket Pistol category is just what the name implies; the match is shot with Derringers, and is usually a side match that is shot in addition to the Main Match. Pocket Pistols are small handguns,

of pre-1900 design, with fixed sights, and they must not be .22 LR caliber, and the Derringers are external hammers and having one to four barrels. These pistols were commonly called "Pepperboxes" these guns are normally used in "side matches" which are apart from the main match and may be added to a regular match.

As a side note, one aspect of SASS that I wanted to mention, even though this is a book about handgun competition, is that SASS sponsors long range rifle matches using period rifles. If you've seen the movie with Tom Selleck titled "Quigley Down Under," you've seen these types of long range Buffalo rifles, usually Sharps rifles, and some of the incredible long shots they were/are capable of. There are five catego-

After completing the string, the shooter goes to the unloading table to clear all three guns under close supervision of the unloading officer. Shotguns start the stage unloaded, but rifles and pistols are loaded prior to starting the stage.

The loading table is where the revolver(s) and the rifle are pre-loaded under supervision just prior to the shooter stepping up to the firing line.

ries of long range rifles, and the buffalo rifle from the movie is one category. I think these would be a lot of fun for the long range rifle aficionado.

Ammunition for the pistol matches is governed by a set of rules that set the power factor for the ammunition.

This is to ensure a level playing field for all shooters, and to ensure that the ammunition has the power to knock down steel tar-gets. Interestingly, the power factor formula is the same one used by the modern USPSA in Practical Shooting Competition. That is, Bullet Weight x Velocity / 1000= Power Factor. So a 100 grain bullet at 600 FPS has a power factor of 60 (100x600)/1000=60.00). For large matches like the National and World Championships, ammunition will usually be tested to make sure it conforms to this standard, for club matches at the local

This is a typical target array at a SASS match. Steel targets are easy to engage, and don't need to be repaired like paper targets and make the match go quickly and smoothly. Also, feedback from bullet hits are instantaneous.

Another shot of the loading table where the competitors can load their firearms under direct supervision prior to stepping up to the line.

level, all of the shooters pretty much know each other and are friends with each other, and there is the concept of the "spirit of the game" in play.

People do not try to cheat in order to gain an upper hand in the match. The minimum power factor for handguns is 60, and the maximum velocity is 1000 fps. Any faster and the bullets have a tendency to splash back at the shooter and other competitors, making for potentially dangerous situation. Pocket pistols, Derringers and long range rifles are exempt from the power factor rule.

Ammunition needs to meet minimum power factors so it can knock down steel reactive targets. Sometimes the match director will set up pepper popper targets, the same ones used in modern IPSC and other action pistol type matches. These targets, in a SASS match, are calibrated to fall when engaged squarely with a .38 Special cartridge fired using a standard 158 grain load. The targets used in SASS matches are steel cutouts of bad guys, and there are different target shapes such as buffalo, clovers, and other shapes and styles.

Safety in the game is paramount, and with single action firearms, specific rules apply. Firearms are loaded prior to the shooter approaching the line at the loading table. Once the shooter is called to the line, the shooter placed the shotgun and rifle on the table provided, and gets ready to shoot the stage. The shooter will be asked if ready, and if ready, will be given the start signal and begins shooting. Since the pistols are single action, if the pistol is cocked the gun cannot be decocked without firing the gun. In other words, if the shooter cocks the pistol at the wrong time, the shooter cannot decock the gun to correct the error.

Two very interesting aspects of SASS competition are Mounted Shooting and the Wild Bunch. First, Mounted Shooting. This is exactly what it sounds like. This is an Old West 3-gun cowboy match, shot while on horseback. The horses used are accustomed to the sounds of gunfire, and the types of horses that can be used is wide open, even mules can be used. I would love to go to a SASS match where a person shot the match riding a mule, in fact, I would pay to see that! Before anyone gets concerned, the entire match is shot with certified blanks, loaded with black powder. Absolutely no live ammunition is allowed anywhere near the match. No abuse of animals is allowed. Saddles and tack allowed are in keeping with the same spirit of the game that the shooters follow with their guns, clothing and holsters. Targets used are helium filled balloons and should measure about 6x9 inches when inflated. A standard stage consists of ten balloons, and the competitor engages them with two revolvers loaded with five rounds each. Going along with the Mounted Shooting is the Cart Event. This is where the shooter engages ten targets while being pulled around the course in a horse-drawn cart.

The other types of SASS competition is known as the Wild Bunch. This is a one-to-three gun match used with firearms from just after the turn of the 20th century. This means that the competitor can use a semi-auto 1911, but has to be in military form, this means no modern modifications that are popular with practical shooters today. The rifles and shotguns used are also from this period. So Winchester Model 12 shotguns are popular, as is the Winchester M93/97. Modifications of the pistols are allowed, within a narrow range. The finish must be a blued steel or Parkerized finish, and sights need to be what was installed on the pistol when it was issued to the troops in 1911.

There are two categories for the 1911, Traditional, which keeps the pistol as close to the original as-issued configuration as it was in 1911. This category of shooter needs to make sure the pistol is virtually box-stock

The Old West dress runs the gamut from the period for both men and women. These shooters get ready at the loading table.

This competitor uses a good stance and position when engaging the targets. This is an important marksmanship fundamental no matter what shooting discipline it is.

in standard 1911configuration. Springfield Armory makes a mil-spec model that would be perfect for this class. With the spur hammer, arched mainspring housing, short steel trigger and Parkerized finish, it would meet the specifications very, very closely.

The other category is Modern, and the modifications that are allowed in this category are wide open: frame checkering, ambidextrous safeties, hi-rise beavertail safeties, match barrels, and a host of other modifications are legal. In fact, the competitor could take a gun designed for Single Stack competition in USPSA and be right at home. No optics or compensators are allowed, though.

If you love the Old West, or just enjoy firearms from that period, definitely go

check out a SASS match, they are incredibly fun, and the people are absolutely outstanding, you won't be disappointed.

EQUIPMENT

Handguns used in the sport vary depending on the classification the shooter desires to compete in. Cimarron and Ubertis are popular, as are various Ruger single action models. Handguns can be modified to a certain extent, but outwardly must keep the original configuration. In other words, you cannot put adjustable sights on a Uberti copy of a Colt SAA because the original Colt in the 1880s didn't have adjustable sights. Remember, it's about the spirit of the game.

Holsters and bandoleers are another area where the spirit of the game really comes

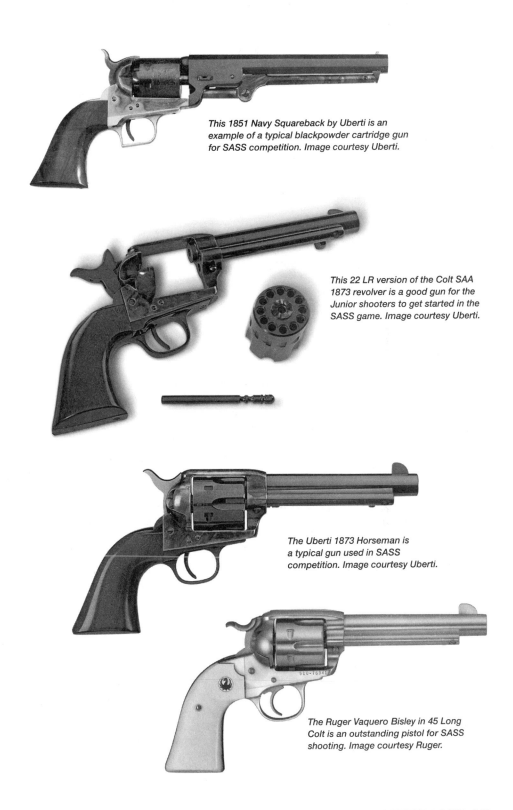

This 1851 Navy Squareback by Uberti is an example of a typical blackpowder cartridge gun for SASS competition. Image courtesy Uberti.

This 22 LR version of the Colt SAA 1873 revolver is a good gun for the Junior shooters to get started in the SASS game. Image courtesy Uberti.

The Uberti 1873 Horseman is a typical gun used in SASS competition. Image courtesy Uberti.

The Ruger Vaquero Bisley in 45 Long Colt is an outstanding pistol for SASS shooting. Image courtesy Ruger.

into play. There are many leather companies that create original hand-tooled leather products specifically for SASS competitors and the authenticity and craftsmanship displayed in these products is amazing. The rulebook emphasizes traditional designs, and safety is paramount.

A cart is really handy to carry the long guns, ammunition, cleaning gear and other items needed for a match; these carts get pretty elaborate and really reflect the personality of the shooter and the spirit of the game.

The Uberti 2nd Model 7 is a reproduction of the top break Model 7 made in the late 1860 by S&W. Designed for the Calvary soldier, the gun could be operated with one hand. Image courtesy Uberti.

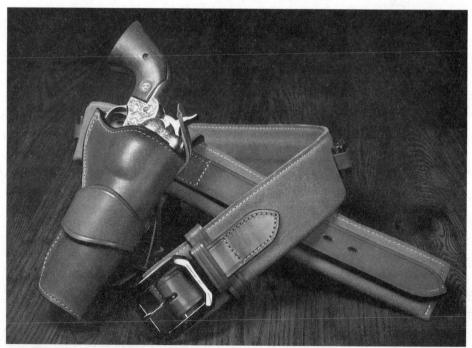

The leather holster for SASS exhibits excellent craftsmanship. Here the Big Jake rig from Kirkpatrick leather is a good example. Image courtesy Kirkpatrick Leather.

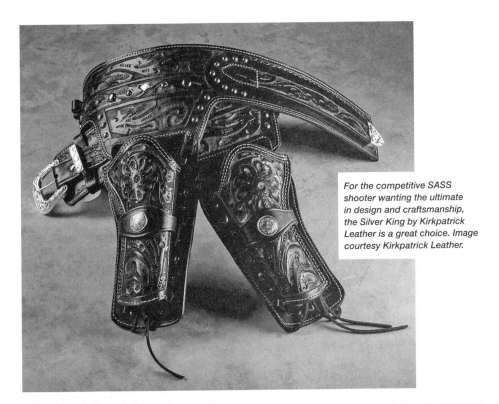

For the competitive SASS shooter wanting the ultimate in design and craftsmanship, the Silver King by Kirkpatrick Leather is a great choice. Image courtesy Kirkpatrick Leather.

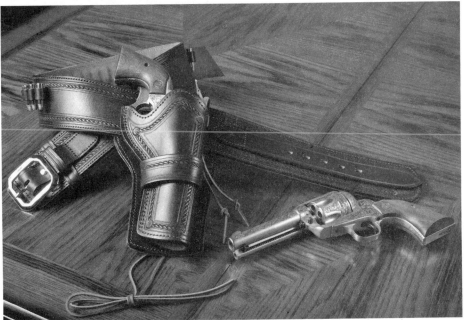

For someone looking for more hand tooled leather product, the Fort Laramie design is popular. Image courtesy Kirkpatrick Leather.

CHAPTER EIGHT

3-GUN COMPETITION

Three-gun competition is one of the most challenging and fun forms of practical shooting events in the U.S. Encompassing the fast and furious of hand-gunning, close quarter rifle, and shotgun all in a close in event, it really challenges the shooter to have all around marksmanship skills to win. Not to say the shooter has to be a Grand Master with all three to win, but definitely good skills with long guns as well as handguns needs to be incorporated to be competitive.

This chapter of the book will cover the handgun portion of the 3-gun competitions.

Three-gun matches are a little different from a typical practical shooting match. The shooter starts with a loaded pistol, but also

The shooter engages targets from the shooting box, with the rifle and shotgun in the barrels.

The range officer will give a walkthrough to the competitors prior to the start of the stage.

Target distances in a 3-gun match, like other practical shooting events, can range from point blank to 50 yards or more. This one is up close, but the trick is to go fast, but not go too fast when the targets are this close.

Some of the target arrangements can get a little complex. The shooter needs to know what to engage and what not to. In this photo, the white target is a no-shoot, and the black space is hard cover, simulating the target is behind an impenetrable wall, and the shot will be ineffective, so the competitor needs to only engage the brown targets.

Complex target arrays are not limited to paper targets, steel targets also get involved.

This shooter is moving into the shooting box, and is getting ready to engage the targets at this firing point.

has a loaded shotgun and loaded semi-auto rifle nearby, usually placed muzzle down in a shooting barrel.

The shooter has to solve the shooting scenario as presented with all three firearms. Shooters familiar with USPSA or IDPA matches will feel right at home in a three gun match, as least for the pistol portion, but also with targets, course design and layouts are all similar, yet different at the same time. Handguns are loaded in the usually manner, at the firing line, when the RO give the command to "make ready."At the beginning of every match, there is a range briefing given to the squadded competitors.

At this point, competitors can ask questions, once that is complete, a "walkthrough" with the competitors is allowed. These stage briefings will be posted at each stage and will list the minimum number of rounds needed to complete the stage, the number and type of targets, time limits, if applicable, the competitors start position, identification of specific targets to be engaged with specific firearms, and any other pertinent information the competitor needs to know in order to safely shoot the stage.

The construction of the courses of fire is also similar to a typical USPSA, or IDPA match.

The courses of fire may or may not have obstacles, walls or barriers, tunnels, or other moving or swinging stage props, as well as doors, and windows that may or may not come into play in during the stage that will serve to challenge the shooter.

Targets used in 3-gun matches are also the same as ones used in USPSA and other practical shooting competitions. The "classic" or turtle target and the metric targets are typically used. There will almost assuredly pepper popper steel targets of different sizes, along a variety of shoot/no shoot targets will almost always be set up.

All firearms have to either make Major or Minor power factor, and the same formula is applied to handguns, and that is bullet weight x bullet velocity divided by 1000. This will give the power factor for the caliber and load, and for Major PF, the minimum score is 165, and for Minor PF, the minimum is 125.

Holster requirement for the handgun stage of 3-gun matches are identical to USPSA and other practical shooting matches: they must be safe and serviceable and retain the firearm when performing rigorous movement. No shoulder holsters are allowed, but tactical style thigh holsters are allowed.

There are multiple divisions within 3-gun matches. They are:

The competitor moves from one firing position to another after first engaging the initial set of targets. Note the shooter keeps the pistol pointed downrange, with the finger off the trigger. Safety is always paramount.

This competitor is left handed and moving from right to left, always using safe gun handling techniques, but thinking ahead at the targets that need to be engaged. Notice the shotgun in the white barrel has not fully dropped to the bottom after being fired, and the shooter is already moving to the next position to engage the targets.

The competitor is moving to his left to engage the set of targets, and keeps the pistol downrange with the finger off the trigger. Good footwork is always important in the practical shooting games.

Open Division. This is almost identical to USPSA Open category, so if you compete in the Open category in USPSA competition, you have the firearm needed for 3-gun matches. The Open category for handguns includes optical sights, compensators, high-capacity magazines, and virtually unlimited modifications to the handguns are allowed. The difference in the Open division of USPSA and 3-gun, are that with handguns, sound suppressors are allowed.

Firearms used in 3-gun are similar to other forms of practical shooting, and the marksmanship fundamentals are also similar. Good recoil control is essential.

Tactical Division – Equivalent to USPSA Limited class. .40 S&W is the minimum caliber to make Major, and there is no barrel porting, barrel compensators, or optical sights allowed.

Targets are often partially obscured to make it more challenging to the shooter. Here, the shooter needs to make accurate shots and not hit the plastic barrels.

Limited Division – Handgun rules are same for Tactical Division, but the rifle rules vary.

3-gun matches often bring out firearms that are used by CCW holders, and also firearms that are suitable for home defense. Note the tactical light this shooter has installed under the Glock.

Heavy Metal Division – Handgun rules use the same Limited 10 handgun rules, which means that the firearm cannot hold more than ten rounds. The caliber is a minimum of .40 S&W, and many people use the venerable single stack .45 ACP. Suppressors and flashlights are not allowed.

Safety areas are provided for the shooter's convenience and safety. This area is for shooters to put on gunbelts, holsters, magazine pouches, as well as to handle and dry fire their pistols, and for the shooter to holster their firearms prior to starting the match. Under NO circumstances is live or dummy ammunition allowed in the safety Area.

Keep in mind that revolvers are competitive in 3-gun matches, and I always see several at just about every match. The start position for competitors is arms at the side, unless otherwise noted, and malfunctions have to be dealt with in a safe manner all while the clock is running.

Other safety rules to keep in mind are similar to USPSA and other practical pistol type matches. Moving from one firing point to another requires that the competitor keep their trigger finger off the trigger and completely out of the trigger guard and the safety should be engaged.

Penalties are allocated for procedural faults, just like with other practical matches, so foot faults, shooting targets out of order, or not using cover, will receive time penalties for procedural errors on the part of the competitor.

Procedural penalties can very quickly add up and really increase the time that is added to the total time. This has an adverse effect to the overall shooter's score.

Therefore, it really is in the best interest

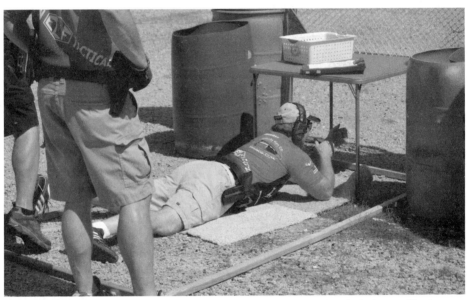

Here the shooter takes a sight picture prior to starting the stage to find out where is the best position to engage the targets

The stages don't always start with the gun in the holster, at this stage, the competitor starts the stage with the pistol in the box.

Baby carts are popular for carrying all of the gear needed for 3-gun competition.

Going prone to engage the target is a fairly common occurrence in the practical shooting games. Here the competitor engages a series of targets from the prone position.

Good shooting techniques are important no matter what the shooting game. Here the shooter uses the weak hand finger wrapped around the trigger guard. This technique is not as popular as it once was, but can still be an effective way to control the pistol under recoil.

of the competitor to do a walkthrough prior to the match, then really listed to the RO when he/she gives the verbal stage instructions, and don't be afraid to ask questions if any procedure of the stage is unclear. Finally when you do your walkthrough really get fixed in your mind exactly how to shoot the stage and formulate a plan, then when your name is called, go to the firing line with confidence and execute your plan. This will help you avoid those costly procedural fault penalties.

SCORING

There are four methods for scoring a 3-gun match, and it follows standard USPSA rules. The four methods of scoring are:

• Comstock – There is an unlimited amount of time to shoot the stage and an unlimited number of rounds can be fired.

• Limited Comstock – This is where there may be a limited amo8nt of time allocated to complete the stage.

• Virginia Count – Where there are a limited number of rounds fired for each stage, but an unlimited time allocated.

• Fixed time – Where there is a limited time, and a limited number of shots allocated.

Three-gun is an exciting way to become a better all-around marksman. If you have a serviceable handgun in at least 9mm, a centerfire semiautomatic rifle in at least .223 caliber and a 20 gauge shotgun, you have what you need to get started. The best way to get involved is to attend a match and watch some of the good shooters go through the various stages. Talk to some of the other competitors and let them know you are interested and would like to know more. There are always experienced shooters at every match that are more than happy to help a potential new shooter get started on the right track.

The Colt Combat Elite is a good alternative for shooters that want an excellent 1911 but don't want to spend the money for a full blown custom pistol. Image courtesy Colt Mfg.

EQUIPMENT

Much of the equipment used in 3-gun competition is similar to the firearms used in USPSA, IDPA and other practical pistol matches.

The Les Baer custom 1911 is an excellent example of a custom 1911 suitable to 3-gun competition. Custom guns are not needed for 3-gun, as many competitors use Glocks, S&W M&P and others, but a custom 1911 is very effective for practical shooting competitions. Image courtesy Les Baer, Inc.

The Blade-Tech Kydex holster is a popular choice for many forms of practical shooting, and is popular for 3-gun. The Kydex holsters are inexpensive, and durable. Image courtesy Blade-Tech, Inc.

The Kimber is another good choice for a semi-custom/semi-factory production gun. Relatively affordable, the gun comes with many of the features that most competitive shooters want. Image courtesy Kimber, Inc

CHAPTER NINE

NRA ACTION PISTOL

The sport of action pistol shooting has been around for decades, and actually since the early 1980s. During that time, the sport began when two of the biggest names in shooting, Ray Chapman, winner of the 1976 IPSC World Championship, and John Bianchi, founder of Bianchi International and a pioneer in handgun holster design, came together and formed the first courses of fire.

This early competition was actually designed to be a law enforcement-only match, but gradually was opened up to civilians when the NRA took over the competition in 1994.

The Bianchi Cup is the NRA Action Pistol Championships, and is one of the most prestigious events on the pro shooting circuit. Because of the high level of accuracy required from the shooters, it's also one of the most challenging events.

Today, perfect scores are routinely shot by the top pro shooters, and X counts separate the winners from everyone else. Doug Koenig was the first competitor to ever shoot a perfect score, firing a blistering 1920, with 157 "X's" occurring in the 1990 Bianchi Cup Match. The Bianchi Cup is considered one of shooting's Triple Crown events, the other two events being the U.S. IPSC Nationals and the Steel Challenge.

There were 12 courses of fire added to the overall match at that point, and the sport is a very challenging mix of PPC, or Police Pistol Combat shooting, which is very revolver-oriented and is mostly focused on standing, kneeling, prone and barricade type shooting, and IPSC, which is geared more toward and run and gun type of match, where a lot of shooting is from a certain position, then moving to another position with a reload usually at some point. With PPC,

As with most practical shooting type matches, these competitors are starting from the surrender position.

Professional and non-professional shooters alike compete at the NRA Bianchi Cup. Different divisions allow shooters to compete with regular production handguns.

Here, Pro shooter Rob Leatham, competing for Team Springfield Armory, fires weak-hand only with a Production class gun at the NRA Bianchi Cup Match.

This shooter, competing for Team Hornady, fires a semi-auto pistol, with optical sight and compensator. Note the wings installed on the gun to facilitate the Barricade Event.

Female shooters get into the NRA Action Pistol game in a big way with the same ability, guns, equipment and techniques as the men.

The Barricade Event is a challenging stage in which the competitor fires from behind the Barricade. This stage goes back to the old PPC matches in the 70s, in which the police officer had to engage the target with his or her service revolver from behind a barricade, later used with Match Grade PPC revolvers.

This female competitor from Team S&W engages the target with a stock S&W 686 revolver, while the shooter to her right uses a stock semi-auto. This is what makes the game so much fun; revolvers and semi-autos, and men and women can all compete on an equal footing.

Shooting prone is a common firing position in practical shooting events, whether is NRA Action Pistol, 3-gun, or USPSA.

This shooter is engaging the Mover with a production gun and iron sights. This is a very challenging event with iron sights. The electronic dot sights can be used to lead the moving target, which is more difficult with iron sights.

the competitor normally has a stage where they are shooting from cover and engaging from a more static position, although also usually with a reload or two thrown in. Many people consider action pistol competition to be a sort of crossover event.

Where people that are primarily bullseye shooters who are looking for something a little more exciting, can get into a form of completion that isn't so repetitive, and shooters who compete in practical events like USPSA, IPSC, IDPA, GSSF, 3-gun and similar events, can compete in a form of competition that is a little more static, a little more predictable, where they know with a fair amount of certainty, what the courses of fire will be. It's a great form of competition to get shooters from disparate forms of competition together.

There is a certain comfort going into a match where you know what the course of fire is going to be. I know when I shot bullseye, it was nice knowing I didn't have to think as much about what the course of fire was going to be: we were either going to be shooting a 900 point course, an 1800 point course, a full 2700 point course, or a 2700, with an additional team match and possibly a leg match which goes toward the Distinguished Pistol Shot Badge. Action pistol is like that. There is also the fact that if the

competitor has a local club that hosts action pistol, or better yet, a range at home, they can set up some of the stages and be able to practice them in order to become more proficient. With the practical shooting event, you don't know what to expect until you show up and get the stage briefing from the RO. Some people like that type of spontaneity and some don't. There are 17 courses of fire, or matches in total, but not all 17 would typically be set up at a normal match, in fact at the NRA Bianchi Cup, the match consists of only four matches. So there is repetition in the courses of fire at the club level, but enough of a mix and enough spontaneity that you wouldn't know what stages you are shooting until you got there. The courses that make up the NRA Bianchi Cup are:

Practical Event – This is actually four stages which are shot at 10, 15, 25 and 50 yards. Shooters are allowed to engage targets from any position and usually shoot prone, although the ten-yard stage must be shot standing. The total number of rounds fired for this event is 48.

The match is broken down this way:

(a) 10 yards - one shot each target within three seconds, two shots each target within four seconds, and three shots each target eight seconds.

(b) 15 yards - one shot each target within

four seconds, two shots each within five seconds, and three shots each target within six seconds.

(c) 25 yards - one shot each target five seconds, two shots each target six seconds, and three shots each target seven seconds.

(d) 50 yards - one shot each target seven seconds, two shots each target ten seconds, and three shots each target fifteen seconds.

The Barricade Event – This event is shot all from the standing position, utilizing the barricade. This is actually four stages, and the barricade can be used, but the pistol cannot touch the barricade. The distances are 10, 15, 25, and 35 yards. Each distance is engaged with two strings of six shots per string, for a total of 48 shots for this event. Each stage is shot this way:

(a) 10 yards - 6 shots in 5 seconds, 2 strings.

(b) 15 yards - 6 shots in 6 seconds, 2 strings.

(c) 25 yards - 6 shots in 7 seconds, 2 strings.

(d) 35 yards - 6 shots in 8 seconds, 2 strings

Moving Target – This Match is exactly what it says it is. A moving target that travels 60 feet in six seconds. The Match consists of four stages, and is shot all from the standing position from 10, 15, 20 and 25 yards. The Match is broken down this way:

(a) 10 yards - 6 shots in 6 seconds, 2 strings.

(b) 15 yards - 6 shots in 6 seconds, 2 strings.

(c) 20 yards - 3 shots in 6 seconds, 4 strings.

(d) 25 yards - 3 shots in 6 seconds, 4 strings.

Think about (d) for a moment and imagine yourself on the firing line at the Bianchi Cup, with the pressure of a major championship where a single shot out of the ten ring means you are out of the running to win the match. I'm sure many of the shooters reading this book can relate to an IPSC or IDPA target at 25 yards.

Now, image that the target is moving across and parallel to the range at 10 feet per second for only six seconds. You are fining from a unsupported standing position and have to fire four strings of 3 shots per string at 6 seconds per string, or two seconds per shot. Close your eyes and mentally go through that firing sequence in your head. Look at some YouTube videos of the Moving Target Event to get a sense of how incredibly difficult this match is.

Falling Plate Event – This event, like other events in Action Pistol, has the competitor fire the 10 yard stage from the standing position, but can switch to prone for the 15, 20 and 25 yard stages if so desired.

This competitor shows how it's done, firing from the Barricade Event. Note how the "wings" on the pistol are used to help brace the pistol against the wall while firing. The index finger wraps around the shroud, or "wings" while the rest of the hand grabs onto the barricade. The recoil is minimal since the guns are usually 9mm using lower powered target loads.

There are four stages, each stage is shot with two strings of fire with six shots per string for a total of 48 shots. The target is a rack of steel plates, eight inches in diameter. The nice thing about this stage is that many local clubs have a plate rack available that can be used for practice. I know my local club, the Bluegrass Sportsman's League, actually has two plate racks that could be used for practicing this match. The match breaks down this way:

(a) 10 yards - 6 shots in 6 seconds, 2 strings.

(b) 15 yards - 6 shots in 7 seconds, 2 strings.

(c) 20 yards - 6 shots in 8 seconds, 2 strings.

(d) 25 yards - 6 shots in 9 seconds, 2 strings.

These are the courses of fire that make up the Bianchi Cup, but NRA Action Pistol actually has other matches within the sport. One fun match is the Flying M, which is a mano-a-mano or "man against man" shoot-off, where two competitors are on the firing line at the same time, and at the start, they both begin firing at two sets of identical targets placed side by side, which form a large M. The last man to hit the last target is the loser. The targets are placed at 7, 10 and 15 yards. So, shooter A, has a target at 10, and 15 yards, on his or her side, and shooter B has another set of targets at 10 and 15 yards on his or her side, there is only one target at 7 yards and the winner is the shooter that is the fastest at hitting their first two targets and ringing the last target at 7 yards.

No time limit on this match as the first one to hit the 7-yard target wins. It's really an exciting and fun aspect of action shooting that you really don't see anywhere else. Technically bullseye could be called man against man, since all competitors are on the firing line at the same time, but you are not really competing against one man, you're competing against your best score.

The target used for action pistol shooting is different from other practical shooting events, it's called a tombstone target and one look will tell you why.

The targets have scoring rings laid out this way:

- X Ring: 4-inch diam. = Tie breaker
- X Ring: 1.12-inch diam. = Tie breaker – (Reduced target)
- A Ring: 8-inch diam. = 10 Points
- A Ring: 2.24-inch diam. = 10 Points – (Reduced target)
- B Ring: 12-inch diam. = 8 Points
- B Ring: 3.36-inch diam. = 8 Points – (Reduced target)
- C Ring: Remainder = 5 Points
- C Ring: Remainder = 5 Points
- (Reduced targets are used for indoor matches at 50 ft.)

Range rules mimic those of other types of matches and DQs are given for similar actions to those at other practical matches; violations of the finger off the trigger rule,

This shooter is making a final adjustment to his pistol prior to raising his firing hand and giving the nod to the RO to begin the stage on The Mover.

The Falling Plates is one of the four stages that comprise the Bianchi Cup. This shooter is engaging the plate rack. Note the use of the Weaver stance the shooter is using, as opposed to the Isosceles stance used by most shooters today.

pointing a firearm up range, sweeping the body and other violations are automatic DQs.

An increasingly popular form of action pistol is the Rimfire Division. This is a game where the same targets are used, except for the falling plates, and provides a very easy and cost-effective way for novice shooters, or shooters that are new to action pistol competition an easy entry into the sport.

CLASSIFICATION OF COMPETITORS

Shooters are classified as either Classified, or Unclassified. New shooters are automatically put into Unclassified status. Classified shooters go from High Master, Master, Expert, Sharpshooter and Marksman, and classification is based on a percentage of the scores posted.

FIREARMS NEEDED

There are several classifications of firearms that can accommodate a wide variety of competitors. In fact, the NRA has been very proactive to get new shooters involved in the sport by adding a production class, which uses more of the off the shelf type firearms like the Sig, Glock, S&W M&P, Beretta, and many other types of service-type semi-auto and revolvers that many people would already have in the gun safes, without have to shell out thousands of dollars on a "race gun" in order to be competitive. The NRA has also added a rimfire class

to entice new shooters and junior class to bring inexpensive rimfire pistols in order to lower the bar for entry into the sport.

Firearms need to meet a power factor, just like other types of practical shooting, but the only stipulation is the gun has to meet the power factor of 125, 000. A similar formula for other practical shooting competitions is used; bullet weight x velocity. The most common caliber for action pistol is 9mm in the semi auto class, and .38 Spl. in revolver. Almost all factory-loaded ammunition meets the minimum power factor, and reloaded ammunition is allowed.

The classification of firearms is:

Open Division – This is pretty much what the name says; it's an open category where many, but not all modifications are allowed. Electronic sights, compensators for recoil control, and "wings" which help brace the gun during the Barricade event. There is a minimum trigger pull of two pounds, and holsters used are a special open type of holster, which lets the shooter draw the gun with very little upward motion. Usually, just an inch or less of upward motion, then the shooter draws the pistol forward toward the target, this is a much faster method than drawing pistol up six inches or more, and then out to draw when drawing from a closed holster design.

Metallic Sight Division – The shooter is not allowed to have electronic sights or "wings" and the same two pound trigger pull is enforced. The gun must have "iron sights" only.

Production Division. The newest and fastest growing segment of Action Pistol is probably Production class. This is where the competitor can use pretty much use any stock, off the shelf pistol. The competitor does not need to have to invest in expensive custom pistols in order to compete. In fact, if you have a 1911, a Glock, Sig, CZ, S&W M&P, Springfield Armory XD, or pretty much any other service type centerfire handgun, you can compete in Production class, as long as it has not been modified. Holsters must be standard top draw type of holster, and Blade-Tech, Safariland and many others are legal. If you have a gun/holster combination that you shoot for USPSA, IDPA, 3-gun, steel-type matches, or other practical shooting matches, it's probably legal and competitive for production class in action pistol. Trigger pull cannot be less than 3.5 lbs for production guns.

TAKING YOUR GAME TO THE NEXT LEVEL

One great aspect about some NRA competitions is the NRA Distinguished Program. It's a way for the NRA and the sport itself to demonstrate excellence in competitive shooting and gives the competitor something to shoot for, pun intended. The NRA has Distinguished shooting programs for many forms of competition. High power rifle, to international pistol to bullseye pistol, and yes, action pistol has a Distinguished Pistol Shot program. Like with the bullseye Distinguished program, the action pistol shooter trying to accumulate the points needed for the badge only needs to reach 30 points. Most matches, if the shooter scores high enough, will get 10, 7 or 5 award points. When the competitor has reached 30, they are awarded the Distinguished badge.

Many new shooters, when they learn about the Distinguished program, whether bullseye or action pistol, often think, "If I get 10 points for a single match and it only takes 30, I should be able to get there pretty quickly." Now, I have known one person that got their Distinguished Badge for bullseye in three matches, which means they won three Excellence-in-Competition matches in a row, but that was the only person I have ever heard of achieving that amazing feat, in the hundreds of people that have the badge. SFC Charlie McGowan did that back in the early 80s. It took me about a dozen matches to accumulate the required points to get my Distinguished Pistol Shot badge for bullseye. What makes it so difficult, especially for civilians, is the points are only awarded at four matches per year, State Championships, Regional Championships, and the National Championships. The competitor can only attend these four matches in any one calendar year. So, if I wanted to get my Action Pistol Distinguished Badge, I could only shoot two State Matches, one regional, and the national Championships in any one calendar year. So it's not like I can go to fifteen or twenty matches in a year to accumulate my 30 points. Add in the fact that since you only have four matches in one calendar year that you are allowed to even *attempt* getting the points needed, it puts additional match pressure on the shooter, in addition to the match pressure already on the shooter just being in a large State, Regional or National Championship. Anyone that has the Action Pistol Distinguished Badge, is a very accomplished pistol shooter.

So, action pistol shooting is a great form of competitive shooting, especially if you are already competing in other types of practical shooting events, or even a conventional sport like Bullseye, the skills learned in those events transfer really well.

* Images in this chapter courtesy of NRA unless otherwise noted.

CHAPTER TEN

MARKSMANSHIP FUNDAMENTALS

B efore anyone gets involved in any sport, they need to have a solid understanding of the fundamentals. It really doesn't matter what the sport is, either. When my son was learning how to play baseball, there were many aspects of the game that he had to understand. How to swing the bat, throw the ball and field his position. All of these physical aspects of the game require a deep understanding and a certain level of commitment to master those fundamentals. All sports have a fundamental way of performing that breaks down into basic steps, the physical steps the participant needs to do in order to ensure success.

The shooting sports are no different from any other sport. They have their set of marksmanship fundamentals that, when properly applied, help the shooter ensure

This picture shows Kyle with his eyes pointed straight ahead, his shoulders rolled forward, and the thumbs on top of each other for good recoil control.

success. Each of the shooting sports has its fundamentals, and, while there are similarities, they are very different when looking at them individually.

For example, take the shotgun game skeet. In a nutshell, this game involves trying to break a clay disc, called a pigeon, when it's launched out of a target house, and while it's on the fly, by using a shotgun firing a large amount of small diameter lead birdshot. Sounds simple, and when described like that, it is a simple to understand. However, in execution, is a very complex and difficult game. The way to break the pigeon is to swing the barrel to a point in front of the pigeon as its flying and pull the trigger, while continuing to swing the barrel, called "following through." So, the fundamentals would be swing the barrel, aim the gun at the target, pull the trigger and follow through. As simple as those basic

These three pistols show the different lengths of sight radius. The longer the sight radius, the easier it is for misalignment in the sights to be recognized by the shooter.

Here, Mike watches Kyle shoot the paster drill, trying to keep all of the shots onto a single paster at three yards. This demonstrates good sight alignment and trigger control.

shotgun fundamentals are the game of skeet, if a shooter tried to apply the same fundamentals to one of the pistol games, it would be disastrous. The reason is that while pistol shooting has fundamentals of aim, pulling the trigger, and follow through, they are very, very different in the application from the shotgun and the rifle.

This chapter will discuss the seven fundamentals of marksmanship as it applies to handguns.

So, to get started on marksmanship fundamentals, we really need to break it down into steps. There are seven basic parts or fundamentals to firing a handgun. These fundamentals are applied to one degree or another whether the shooter is competing at an IPSC match, on the silhouette range or simply plinking with a .22 pistol on the weekend.

Make no mistake, mastering shooting fundamentals is critical to success in the shooting sports. That doesn't mean you have to be a Jedi master, but it does mean you should have solid shooting skills. Sure, you can have fun going to the range and banging away at targets and shooting poor scores if your goal is to get out in the fresh air and sunshine, burn some gunpowder and have fun with your shooting buddies. And for some shooters, that's enough. But even

if you are just a little bit competitive, you will want to be able to shoot at your very best. It's not a lot of fun if you are lying prone, and it takes 7-8 shots to hit a 5-inch square steel plate at 15 yards. Accuracy is the key. Once you have learned to shoot with a decent level of accuracy, depending on what game you have chosen to shoot, you can always speed things up and shoot faster. Shooting fast is nothing more than applying the basic fundamentals of marksmanship more and more quickly. Put another way, a solid bullseye shooter can quite easily become a solid IPSC, IDPA, steel challenge, silhouette, or 3-gun shooter because they have learned the fundamentals of marksmanship and they have the ability to shoot accurately. In the action sports, the application of those fundamentals is merely sped up. Same with silhouette, where a bullseye shooter who has learned how to shoot accurately in the slow fire stage can transfer those skills to hitting the small silhouette targets at long range. It doesn't work as easily the other way; an IPSC shooter would have a hard time in bullseye because of the tendency of the IPSC shooter to shoot sight picture, and not pure sight alignment.

Take some time and really learn to shoot. Remember, it's not about how fast you go in these action matches, it's how good your hits are. Accuracy trumps speed every time, and the more you compete in these events, the faster your times will be. Only go as fast as you can while still getting good hits on target.

The seven fundamentals of basic pistol marksmanship are:

1. Stance
2. Position
3. Grip
4. Sight alignment
5. Trigger control
6. Breathing
7. Mental discipline

Step 1 is the **stance**. The stance as it applies to the handgun is nothing more than the position of feet and body relative to the target. It sounds simple, but it's actually one of the most critical and also one of the most often overlooked aspects of pistol shooting. The reason it's so important is that the stance is the foundation upon which all of the other fundamentals are built. If the shooter's stance isn't solid, then the delivery of the shot or shots to the target won't be at their optimum. The stance may not be as critical if the shooter is on the run, obviously, since the feet will be moving, but there are not too many instances where the shooter will actually deliver a shot on the run. I would say that 99 percent of the time the shooter will be stationary at least for a second to two when the shot or shots are actually delivered. The other exception to this is when the shooter is firing from the prone position, and I'll cover that in this section as well.

So, now that we've established the importance of the stance. Let's delve into how to develop it so it helps the shooter during the firing sequence. The stance for a bullseye shooter is going to be much different than that of a person firing in one of the action shooting sports. For the bullseye shooter, assuming a right-handed shooter, the stance will be standing at about a 45-degree angle to the target, with the feet approximately shoulder width apart, and about 60 percent of the weight out on the balls of the feet. Always keep the knees flexed a little, and keep the non-firing hand in the pocket. Why? Because if the non-firing arm is not anchored with the hand in the pocket, or at least with the thumb hooked into the pocket, the arm will swing slightly during firing, and will act as a counter-balance to the firing hand, causing is to sway slightly and making it difficult to stay on target.

For an action shooter, there are two basic types of stances: the Weaver and the Isosceles. The Weaver stance was developed by Los Angeles Sheriff's Deputy Jack Weaver in 1959, while competing in Jeff Cooper's Leatherslap matches in Southern California, the precursor to today's USPSA/IPSC matches.

Pro shooter Mike Foley shows my son, Kyle, how to maneuver through the barrels, safely with good footwork. Image courtesy Hornady Mfg.

The classic Weaver stance, the body is at an angle, the weak side elbow bent, and the strong-side arm is straight. The firing arm should be pushed forward, and the weak side arms should be pulled back, this helps lock in the upper body and is a great way to control recoil.

Another angle of the Weaver stance. While the Weaver stance was revolutionary for the day, later techniques were developed that came out of the burgeoning combat shooting games. The Weaver stance makes it a little difficult to engage multiple targets that are spaced widely apart since the shooter has to move their feet. This is where the Isosceles stance emerged.

The Weaver stance is very good for managing recoil of some of the sharper recoiling handguns. It does this by using isometric tension between the firing and non-firing, or support, hand. Basically the shooter is creating a push-pull arrangement in the arms. The firing arm is pushing slightly forward, and the support hand is pulling back. It's a very effective way of firing a powerful handgun accurately, and is still taught at the Gunsite Academy, Jeff Cooper's iconic shooting school.

The second fundamental is **position**. This is nothing more than taking the stance and introducing a target. With the stance, we are not yet factoring in the target, we are just trying to establish a good foundation. Now, with position, we are attempting to take the stance and make sure that we are positioned naturally toward the target, or, put another way, we are trying to find our natural point of aim.

On the range, a good way to practice this is to get into a comfortable stance, then, take the pistol in a good firing grip with both hands, close the eyes, and raise the pistol toward the target, open the eye and the pistol should be aiming at the center of the target. If it isn't, close your eyes, lower the pistol and pivot on the left foot and move the right foot slightly forward or backward while holding the pistol out at arm's length to move the pistol left or right relative to the target. Raise the pistol and open your eyes,

In the Isosceles stance, the body is facing straight on to the target, with the arms pushed out, shoulders rolled forward, and the upper body leaning forward with 60 percent of the weight on the balls of the feet.

Another shot of the Isosceles stance. This stance is where the shooter faces the target perpendicular to the firing line. Spread the feet a little wider than shoulder width, with about 60 percent of the weight out on the balls of the feet. Keep the knees flexed and bend forward at the waist. The shoulders are rolled forward a little, with both arms pointing forward. This is where the name Isosceles stance came from, if you look at the shooter from the top or from the bottom, the arms and shoulders form a Isosceles triangle. Tension on the arms should be firm, but without inducing tremors. This stance makes it very easy to engage multiple targets, especially ones that are spaced widely apart.

the pistol should be pointing at, or close to the target.

This drill is especially important on the bullseye range, where we want the pistol to return to the center of the target naturally when fired during the timed and rapid fire stages. You don't want to be fighting the pistol when it's coming out of recoil trying to get it back into center mass of the target. Establishing a natural point of aim will really help out in the speed shooting events like steel matches and some IDPA where there isn't much movement of the shooter. Its main benefit is that of getting the pistol pointed naturally at the target with as little amount of thought as possible.

A good example of this application of position is when firing at steel plate on a plate rack. Just like when the skeet shooter gets

ready for the bird to come out of the house, his feet are in the position where the swing will be at the end, and the gun is pointed at the point where the bird comes out, and the shooter "unwinds" as the he/she swings through the target.

When firing at an array of targets, be it a steel plate rack or an array of paper targets, it's a good practice to line up in the center of the array, then engage the first target and continue on the last. To ensure the shooter is in the proper position, get the feet placed comfortable apart, close the eyes, raise the hands as if firing at the center target, then open them. The "gun" should be lined up in the center of the array of targets. If not, shift the feet so the "pistol" is lined up approximately in the center, this will allow the shooter to go from one side to the other with the least amount of stress. Some shooters like to line up their position on the last target, and then fire on the first target first. In other words, I would line up pointing at the far right target, but begin shooting at the far left target, assuming I was going from left to right. The best method is the one you feel most comfortable with. Talk to different shooters and get their opinion, try different techniques and then decide what works best for you.

The next fundamental is **grip**, and this part sounds easy, simply pick the pistol up, and you are gripping it, right? Not so fast. There are several do's and don'ts when establishing the proper firing grip. Two of the main aspects of establishing a proper grip are consistency and tension. For a bullseye shooter, it becomes even more critical since we are only using one hand to shoot.

Also, the firing hand and arm need to absorb the recoil and be an aid to a quick recovery, especially when firing the timed and rapid fire stages. This is even more true with the hardball gun, where the recoil is the most extreme since we are using full power .45 ACP loads and not the lighter recoiling loads of the centerfire or .45 match Wadcutter guns.

As I mentioned, one of the key aspects of the grip is consistency, not only in the application of the grip but also in the tension applied. Too loose of a grip, and the pistol will shift in the hand during firing. Too tight, and two things happen: the hand will tremble, and the trigger finger is partly immobilized. One way I've found to get the proper grip is to pick up the gun with one hand, and squeeze the pistol until the hand starts to shake, then slowly back off the tension until the pistol stops shaking.

This is a good starting point in applying the proper grip, and you may need to adjust this amount of tension up or down based on the gun and caliber of the pistol and the type of shooting you are doing. One aspect not talked about enough is that the grip should allow the recoil of the pistol, any pistol, to travel straight up the arm and not rotate around the wrist. This is especially important with heavy recoiling pistols. When firing with one hand, a la bullseye, the shooter should be able to draw a line from the front sight through the pistol straight up the arm.

My son Kyle shows excellent form in a Isosceles stance with a good high grip on the Glock G35 MOS pistol.

Getting into a good firing position first requires getting a good grip on the pistol. Here the shooter sweeps the jacket back with the hand and then draw the pistol.

Kyle demonstrates a one-handed technique with the Glock G35. The weak hand is brought into the center of the chest in order to keep the upper body more rigid through the shoulders, controlling the recoil and the gun.

Another angle of the one-handed technique, showing how to lean forward and keep the arm straight.

With a two-hand hold in an Isosceles stance this isn't possible, but the recoil still needs to come up the arm as much as possible. Another aspect of the grip, especially with the two-hand hold, is the shooter needs to "choke up" on the pistol. In other words, the shooter needs to get the firing hand as high up on the pistol as possible. This helps direct the recoil to travel up the arms, and also keeps the pistol from rotating around the central point of the wrist. This "torque" makes the pistol twist up and over, making follow up shots much more difficult. This is why handguns with a high grip, like the 1911 with the aftermarket upswept beavertail grip safeties, are so effective. They don't just look cool, it gets the hand high up on the gun to better manage the recoil. The general rule of thumb is the lower the axis of the bore is, relative to the hand and forearm, the more manageable the recoil will be.

Another aspect of the grip that many shooters discuss is placement of the trigger finger. Like many aspects of shooting, there's really no right or wrong way to place the trigger finger on the trigger. The two most common ways are the pad of the finger and the first joint. Both are used by many champion shooters, so decide which one is more comfortable and go with it. One of the best ways to see if the placement of the trigger finger is correct for you is to dry fire. If, during a dry fire session, the pistol's sights move to the left when the hammer or striker falls, then there is too little trigger finger applying pressure and the trigger finger is moving the gun to the left, assuming a right handed shooter. If the sights move to the right, there is too much trigger finger, most likely the shooter is placing the trigger finger on the joint of the finger and it's pulling the sights to the right.

This brings up another point: dry fire. Dry firing is one of the single biggest methods a new shooter can use to improve their skills. It doesn't matter is the new shooter is a bullseye shooter, IPSC, IDPA, silhouette or whatever, dry firing is the single best and fastest way to improve your shooting. If the shooter is an action-type shooter, IPSC, or IDPA for example, incorporating drawing from a holster into the dry firing routine will also pay huge dividends. With dry firing, the shooter can practice almost all of the basic fundamentals of shooting – stance, position, grip, sight alignment, trigger control, breathing, and mental discipline – and can include loading and unloading safely (with dummy rounds) as well as drawing from a holster.

The UltraDot Matchdot II is a popular pistol for bullseye competition. Note the high grip on the gun, letting the shooter control the recoil and recovery during timed and rapid fire.

The grip on a bullseye gun, being a one-handed grip, needs to make sure the recoil goes straight up the arm, helping to control recoil.

The problem with dry firing is that dry firing to a shooter is like practicing scales to a musician. It's not a lot of fun, it's repetitious and it's a little boring. But dry firing is probably the easiest, most cost-effective method there is to improve a shooter's marksmanship.

One aspect about the grip that a new shooter wants to avoid is known as "milking the grip." This is where the shooter begins to grip the pistol, then shifts the position of the hand, the tension of the grip, or both either during or just prior to the act of firing.

The next feature about the grip is that it needs to allow a natural point of aim. This means that when the pistol is brought up to the target, the front and rear sights should be in natural alignment, and there should not be any need to shift the pistol in the hand in order to get proper sight alignment. If you are a bullseye shooter, you can get a good natural grip before the load command is given. If

you are an action-type shooter and are drawing from the holster, the grip you get out of the holster is the grip you will have when the shooting starts. This is why a good shooter will dryfire for hundreds of hours in order to develop that muscle memory. To get that natural grip and natural point of aim, a good drill to employ is similar to the drill outlined in developing a good stance and position. Get a good grip on the pistol, either coming out of the holster or, if a Bullseye shooter, by holding the pistol at a low ready position.

Close the eyes, and raise the pistol. Open the eyes and the sights should be mostly centered on the target, but also the sights should be MOSTLY in alignment. If the front sight is left or right, relative to the rear sight, then the grip should be adjusted until they are lined up. We are striving to place the body into the center of the target with the stance and position that get us in the general area of the center of the target. Then, by establishing the proper grip and natural sight alignment, we can complete a rapid fire string with good recovery and the front and rear sights will return to a natural state of alignment out of recoil. If the grip has shifted or was not good to begin with, when the pistol comes out of recoil the sights will not be in natural

The grip is one of the most important physical aspects of bullseye. Every person's grip is different, and each shooter needs to develop a grip that is comfortable and repeatable.

alignment. At least with a proper grip, the sights will bounce back to the position they were in prior to the shot.

When using a two-handed grip, I mentioned that the shooter should "choke up" on the pistol, or get as high on the gun as possible. The shooter also needs to push slightly with the firing arm, and pull back slightly with the non-firing arm. This will create a good amount of isometric tension that will help overcome the effects of recoil.

Another aspect of the grip is the thumb of the firing hand. Make sure that the thumb does not drag on the slide, as this can strip energy from the recoiling slide and cause failures to feed and eject.

I've talked about aspects of the grip that the shooter wants to do, now here are a couple of don'ts. Don't use what's called a "teacup" grip. You will see this type of grip in the movies from time to time, and is where the non-firing hand acts as a "saucer" to the pistol's "teacup." This type of grip offers little countering to the effects of recoil. The pistol will twist right out of the non-firing hand with this grip, although it does look cool in the movies. Also, don't fail to use the proper amount of tension in the wrist and forearm. This is really important, especially with semi-auto handguns. The

reason for this is that semi-auto pistols need to have a solid platform for the gun to properly feed, chamber extract and eject. There's a condition called "limp wristing," where the shooter fails to provide enough tension in the wrist and arm and, in effect, takes away energy from the recoil spring as the slide is moving rearward, sometimes failing to fully eject the round. The pistol will also not then have enough energy going forward to feed the next round fully. The classic "stovepipe" jam, where the spent round is caught by the slide that's moving forward, and is sticking out of the ejection port, is usually caused by either too weak of the powder charge, or limp wristing the pistol. Many new shooters can't visualize how this phenomenon can happen, and while it's more prevalent with bullseye shooters since they are only using one hand and arm, it happens with action-type shooters as well.

Think of it like this, if I'm firing a semi-auto pistol and if I was able to move the pistol to the rear as fast as the slide was moving at the moment the gun went off, the slide would never unlock of extract or eject the fired case. If I was able to move the pistol to the rear at the moment of firing, half as fast as the slide was moving, the slide would only unlock and move to the rear halfway, and would only have the energy to move forward to feed and chamber the next round. So, in effect, if you don't provide a firm platform for the handgun to cycle, you are taking away energy from the recoil spring and can induce all manner of malfunctions. How much tension is enough? Remember, apply tension to the hands and forward to the point of inducing a tremble, then back off slightly to where the tremors stop, this is about the proper level of tension for your frame. Each individual shooter needs to experiment in order to fine the amount that is comfortable and provides consistent results with the pistol.

The shooter is keeping the eyes forward toward the target while drawing the pistol from the holster.

The five shots on paper were the result of good application of the fundamentals. The high shot was a zero shot, getting the gun sighted in.

Although the shooter doesn't want to fire a string with a grip that's too loose, having a grip that's too tight has its own issues. If the grip is too tight and there's too much tension in the firing hand, it has a tendency to cause the trigger finger to freeze up, and not be as nimble and quick. This can cause all sorts of trouble when trying to fire off a quick string of shots.

You can take your shot timer and prove this. Fire a series of five or six shots with your normal grip, and then fire the same five or six, *with the same accuracy*, with a grip that is twice as firm. I guarantee the split times will be slower. It may not be much, but it will be measureable. The trigger finger just is not as responsive if the tension in the hand is excessive, because the muscles in the back of the hand are too tight. Excessive tension in the hand makes the muscles in the trigger finger more difficult to move independently. It also makes the trigger pull feel much heavier than it actually is.

Another tip for obtaining a proper grip is for the revolver shooters. Revolver shooters need to employ most of the aspects of obtaining the proper grip that the semi auto shooters need, but with the awareness that the exposed hammer of the gun needs to be taken into account. I've taught many new shooters who started out with the revolver and one of the biggest mistakes they make is to wrap the non-firing thumb over the back of the firing hand. Both thumbs need to be on the same side of the gun, just like with the semi-auto shooters. The reason for this is obvious the first time that the hammer comes back and pinches the thumb during a string of rapid fire when the thumb on the non-firing hand is wrapped over the top of the firing hand. This is also a bad idea with semi-auto handgun shooters. If the thumb is wrapped over the top, the slide can scrape and cut the top of the thumb during recoil.

The next fundamental is **sight alignment**. In order to shoot a handgun with any accuracy, the pistol's sights need to be in alignment, but what does that mean? Sight alignment is nothing more than the front sight post centered within the rear sight notch, with equal daylight on both sides of the front sight post, and the top of the front

Here Kyle is going through some two-target drills, with double taps and controlled pairs, with reloads in between.

sight level with the top of the rear sight. The shooter then has to maintain that good sight alignment when the hammer or striker of the handgun falls and the cartridge is fired. The better the sight alignment is when the bullet exits the barrel, the better the results on the target will be. It's important to understand the difference between sight *alignment,* and sight *picture.* Sight alignment is nothing more than the relationship of the front and rear sights to each other. This is what the shooter should be focusing on, and more importantly, the focus should almost always be on the *front* sight specifically. Bullseye shooters, weekend plinkers, or any shooter who is trying to deliver a deliberate, aimed shot or series of well-aimed shots, needs to focus on pure sight alignment, and must have pinpoint focus on the front sight as the shot or shots are delivered. The target should be slightly blurry, and the rear sight should also be blurry. The front sight needs to be in sharp, crystal clear focus during the delivery of the shot for best results.

Some new shooters have asked me how an accurate shot can be delivered when the shooter can't look at or can't focus the target. It's a valid question, and in order to answer it we have to look at other types of activities that involve the type of hand and eye coordination that shooting requires. Many people who participate in sports such as football, baseball and other sports that require the participant to throw an object have been taught to look at the target. My son is a pitcher on his college baseball team, and when he's on the mound, he needs to focus his vision on the catcher's mitt when delivering the pitch; he does not focus on the baseball. Same with football, hockey or other sports, we are always taught to look at the target when delivering the object. When we are driving a car, we are focused on the road ahead, not at the steering wheel. Not so with shooting, here the shooter needs to bring

his/her point of focus back to the front sight and disregard the target downrange. What will keep the shot or shots accurate will be the shooter's peripheral or secondary vision. The primary vision should be focused on the front sight and the shooter's subconscious focus will keep the sight centered on the target, even though the target will be a fuzzy blur. This sounds very Zen-like, but it actually works. Everything else being equal, a proper stance, good position to the target, and a proper grip will keep everything in the center of the target; the shooter must then focus his/her concentration on the front sight and front sight only in order to deliver the shot or shots, and let the peripheral or secondary vision keep the sights in the center of the target.

This technique works well for delivering a deliberate single shot or a series of aimed shots, but what about when time is critical? It will slow the shooter down to have the front sight in pinpoint focus; it takes time to focus the vision on a single point. What if we have a speed shooting event like IPSC where the game favors the faster shooter, or steel or bowling pin matches, which are all about who is the fastest? In these types of competitions, there's simply no time to properly align the sights and focus on the front sight, so we have to use a different technique. This technique is known as *sight picture.* This is nothing more than taking the concept of sight alignment, or the relationship of the front sight to the rear sight, and adding in the target. So, sight picture is the relationship of the front sight, rear sight and target. So, when I tell a shooter that I'm coaching to concentrate on sight picture, the focus is on the front sight first, but also the rear sight and the target, so, when firing a fast string of shots, the shooter needs to focus on the **relationship** of the front sight, rear sight and target *at the same time* in order to determine whether or not to press the trigger and deliver the shot Notice I didn't say the shooter had to actually focus on front sight, rear sight and target, as this is physically impossible. The shooter should instead focus on the *relationship* of the three when firing quickly. This is not easy and takes some time to develop the technique; this is why shooters need to practice. And while dry fire practice can help, the shooter really needs to actually fire ammunition downrange to see whether the technique is working. There's really no substitute for actual range time.

One drill that can help is to use a .22 rimfire pistol that is similar to the center-fire version you are using in competition. Examples of this would be the S&W .22 M&P, the Ruger 22/45, and the Ruger MkII & III. These pistols will allow the shooter to put thousands of rounds downrange in a short amount of time for a lot less money than it would cost for a comparable number of rounds of centerfire ammunition. I equate this technique with cross-training, in that it allows the shooter to develop the muscle memory and other aspects of shooting for less time and money. The shooter cannot rely on rimfire practice alone, but as a supplement, it really can be a great practice regimen.

So how does sight alignment square with the use of red dot sights? Since we don't have a front or rear sight, there is no sight alignment, so we have to focus more on sight picture. In the early 80s, Army Shooting Blue Team members Bonnie Harmon, Roger Willis, Joe Steed and Max Barrington were all using the then-new Aimpoint electronic red dot sights on of their guns. The exception was the hardball gun, otherwise known as the service pistol, because only iron sights are allowed on that gun by NRA rules. Their scores were essentially the same as what they were able to achieve with iron sights in timed and rapid fire, but the scores

in slow fire, which is shot at 50 yards, went up slightly. The main advantage was that their slow fire scores were more consistent.

Remember, by eliminating the relationship between the front and rear sights, we can shift from shooting by using sight alignment, to shooting by using sight picture. With sight alignment, the rear sight, front sight and target are on three very different focal planes, and the focus needs to always be on the front sight. This can be difficult sometimes and occasionally the focus can drift away, usually from the front sight and ends up drifting downrange, many times without the shooter even realizing it. This can cause groups to open up or flyers in the groups to occur. By using a dot sight, the focus is on a single focal plane, the dot. There is not sight alignment. This causes many shooters, especially new shooters, to want to go directly to the dot sight and bypass iron or open sights altogether. This is a mistake because new shooters haven't developed the high degree of trigger control and mental discipline needed to compete with a dot sight.

There's a reason the Army Blue Team didn't allow the second tier of team shooters, the Grey Team or any other shooters, to compete with the new Aimpoint sights. They had not developed their mental game and trigger control to be able to keep from reacting to the sight of the bouncing dot. That's the main reason the new shooters should forgo using dot sights until they have developed their technique to the level that they employ good fundamentals with respect to trigger control and mental discipline.

During the act of firing, the shooter needs to fire with both eyes open. This is something that is not easy or intuitive. Many shooters are taught early by well-meaning but unknowledgeable shooters to close one eye when shooting. Both eyes should be open for several reasons. First, if both eyes are open, it will let in the most amount of light and the vision will be sharper. Also, the shooter will want to use the dominant eye for aiming, but still keep both eyes open. To determine the dominant eye, pick a point downrange about 15-20 yards away, close your eyes and make the "OK" sign with the hand you normally use to fire the pistol with, raise the hand to the approximate spot where the object is and open the eyes, the dominant eye will be looking at the object through the OK sign. Go to any bullseye or silhouette match and you will see shooters wearing an eye patch over their non-dominant eye. Usually this is a flip-up disc that clips to the shooting glasses. This allows only the dominant eye to come into play when aiming, and allows in the maximum amount if light to the dominant eye. You will also see shooters at a bullseye or silhouette match wearing blinders, similar to the blinders you'll see racehorses wear, and shooters wear them for the same reason thoroughbred racehorses wear them: to block out distractions when trying to perform at a high level. These blinders really help maintain concentration and focus when trying to compete, and virtually all shooters wear them on the firing line in bullseye and silhouette matches.

The next fundamental is **trigger control**. The smooth release of the trigger mechanism of any firearm is a critical factor is the delivery of an accurate shot. On the face of it, it's a very simple act. Simply apply steady building pressure with the trigger finger to a small strip of metal or polymer, until the amount of force needed to overcome the friction of the mechanism is achieved and the tension contained in the sear or striker spring is released. But within that simple act, is a very complex series of events that have to take place.

This drill, the shooter is firing into the berm, focusing the concentration on trigger control without a target, getting used to applying a steady rhythm to the application of trigger pressure, without the distraction of a target. This drill can also be performed indoors, with a blank target and dry firing the pistol, and focusing on the sights without a target.

The interesting aspect of trigger control that shooters must understand is contained in the words "steady building pressure." It's the part of trigger control that high-level shooters have mastered, and new shooters struggle with. New shooters do not yet understand that the trigger must be pressed straight to the rear, with steady building pressure. While at the same time trying to maintain as near to perfect sight alignment as possible. The better the sights are aligned when the sear disengages the striker or firing pin hits the primer and the bullet exits the barrel (which by the way, is a lot longer process than most people think), the better the shot will be.

Trigger finger placement is very important no matter what shooting discipline you are engaged in. Here, there is too little trigger finger applying pressure. This finger position will likely cause the pressure on the trigger to be applied to the left side, and not straight to the rear, as it should be.

As mentioned, it's the steady building pressure that most new shooters have trouble with and there are many reasons for this, but they have to be overcome on order shoot with any degree of success.

New shooters apply pressure to the trigger much like the following description: the application of pressure starts and stops, speeds up and slows down. Sometimes this type of trigger pressure is almost imperceptible to the shooter. The shooter is focusing so intently on the sights, they may not be aware that the trigger finger is applying very uneven pressure to the trigger. They may also be "reacting" to the sights and trying to shoot sight picture, trying to apply all or most of the pressure to the trigger as the front sight swings by the target. This is called "ambushing" the target, also known as "setting up the shot" and is the surest way to get poor results when firing a handgun. And while rifle shooters can sometimes get away with using this technique successfully, it has no place when firing a pistol. So the proper way to apply pressure to the trigger is with a steady building pressure, straight to the rear.

A good analogy of this application of trigger pressure is that of falling off a diving board into a pool. Once the person jumps off

the board, or in our world, trigger pressure is applied, the person accelerates until he hits water. He can't back up, he can't stop. It's a steady pressure on the trigger, or steady rate of falling into the water. Now in bullseye shooting during slow fire, many shooters will stop during the application of trigger pressure, since they have time. Maybe the shooter broke concentration, or maybe the trigger finger and shooter is hesitating slightly. It's ok to stop, lower the pistol, gather composure, and start the process of delivering that single accurate shot again. If delivering a single shot in an IPSC match, say, a stop plate at 65 yards, the shooter has to balance the running clock with the need to deliver an accurate, well-aimed shot. The shooter cannot stop or try to recompose themselves, they need to keep the sights aligned and slowly deliver that well aimed and accurate shot. When delivering a series of shots, for example during timed or rapid fire stages in bullseye, or when firing an El Presidente on an IPSC range or shooting any steel-type match where speed is the name of the game, the shooter still delivers the shot the same way, steady building pressure straight to the rear until the pistol fires. The difference is the rate at which the trigger finger moves to the rear. In the speed type

Here, Mike Foley watches Kyle go through some two shot drills, firing double taps and controlled pairs at close range.

events, the clock is running when the signal to start shooting is given. Think of firing a series of well-aimed shots like wheel that's spinning. The wheel represents the steady application of trigger pressure. Now imagine a fixed point on the wheel is where the sear releases and the gun fires, but the gun only fires when the fixed point reaches the top of its revolution. The wheel spins at a steady rate, and can turn slowly or quickly, but when the fixed point reaches the top, the gun fires. So in our analogy, no matter the speed of the wheel, the trigger pressure is applied at a steady rate. This is trigger control; being able to apply steady building pressure to the trigger until the pistol fires without disturbing the alignment of the sights. It's these kinds of analogies that shooters use to visualize different shooting concepts.

Sometimes, especially in bullseye, but it can happen to a weekend shooter as well, the trigger finger just doesn't want to move. Say we are trying to deliver a shot in the slow fire stage, and we put the pistol up, and something breaks our concentration, or the shooter applies uneven pressure, starting and stopping the application of trigger pressure and lowers the pistol. A good way to overcome this is to fire two shots as if they were timed fire. I first saw Tom Woods, who went on to win at Camp Perry a few years after

I left the service, do this many times. He would be shooting in the slow fire match, get frustrated, and would put the pistol up and fire two or three shots like a timed fire match cadence. Invariably, those would be in the ten-ring. Sometimes, if the trigger finger is hesitating, it pays to be a little more aggressive on the trigger to get a smooth release.

While on the subject of trigger control, I want to reiterate how important it is to utilize dry-fire practice in order to gain the muscle memory needed to becoming a proficient handgunner. Another technique that really helps new shooters gain the experience needed to gain proficiency is to buy a rimfire version of the pistol you will be shooting in competition. This is not always possible, depending on the type of competition you are engaged in and the type of pistol you are using. A good example of this type of cross training that a new shooter can do would be a person who is interested in IDPA matches. The smart thing to do, if they like S&W products, for example, would be to by the S&W M&P pistol in 9mm, then buy the same M&P pistol in .22 rimfire. The new shooter can use .22 rimfire for quite a bit of shooting, for a very small cost, and the benefit is the controls and handling of the pistol is almost identical to the centerfire version. So, 500 rounds of .22 rimfire is exponentially cheaper than 500 rounds of even reloaded 9mm ammunition. The new shooter will still need to use the centerfire gun for practice, but a lot of practice can be had with the rimfire version.

The next fundamental is **breathing**. Good breathing techniques are extremely important in all types of shooting, from the slow fire match in bullseye, to speed shooting steel targets, which typically is over in less than two or three seconds.

First, I'll talk about breathing when delivering a single, well-aimed shot. Many people overlook this aspect of shooting since it really doesn't seem to be that important. They focus on the sights or trigger, which is good, but to overlook proper breathing is to handicap your shooting. Breathing can do many things. It oxygenates the blood, which sharpens your vision and enhances the visual acuity. It also helps the shooter relax and that makes it easier to overcome the dreaded "match nerves." Many shooters don't know that there is a small window where the shooter can deliver a shot or a series of shots and where the amount of movement of the arms holding the pistol, and therefore, the pistol itself, is at its least.

All shooters, and especially handgun shooters, will have a small amount of movement while holding a pistol at arm's length. It doesn't matter is the shooter is using one hand, two hands, or even in the laying down in the Creedmore position on the pistol silhouette range. The pistol will be moving around. Rifle shooters call this the "wobble area." Pistol shooters, being the sophisticated, dashing and debonair marksman we are, call it the "arc of movement." The key to delivering an accurate shot (and remember, if we can deliver a single accurate shot, delivering multiple shots just requires speeding up the trigger finger), is reducing the amount of movement to the smallest level possible, and that's where proper breathing

techniques come in. The key is to get the arc of movement, or wobble area at its smallest, at the point where enough trigger pressure is applied to fire the pistol.

A really good way see what's happening when the pistol is raised and moving around is during dry fire. A good drill is to draw a small target, about an inch in diameter onto a white sheet of paper and place it on a blank wall. Step back about five feet from the wall. At this point you can also practice the other fundamentals of stance, position and grip. Take a deep breath and hold it, raise the pistol and align the sights and place them centered to the target. You will see the sights moving around and the amount of movement will steadily decrease. Then after about 4-8 seconds, the movement will be at its lowest point, and this is when the shot should be delivered. This is also the point where the highest amount of concentration and the vision is the sharpest. If the shooter holds their breath for longer than this, the body runs out of oxygen and the movement starts to get much larger. Practice this a few times and you will develop a routine that works best for you in order to deliver a well-aimed shot. This technique also works for delivering a series of shots. When delivering a string of shots, be it on steel or some other type of action shooting, taking a few deep breaths will relax the muscles and remove much of the tension, ease the match nerves and help the shooter compose themselves prior to the sound of the buzzer. Dry fire really helps with this and good dry fire routines will definitely help lower scores.

The last fundamental of marksmanship is **mental discipline**. Shooting is both a physical and a mental game, which is one reason why I enjoy competitive shooting so much. The ratio of physical versus mental depends on the level of expertise of the individual shooter. By that I mean the experience level of the shooter really comes into play as to the level of mental engagement of the shooter. A good example of this is to compare the level of shooter that competes at the Olympic level, and the new weekend shooter learning how to shoot with their first pistol. With the Olympic shooter, especially in a discipline like free pistol, the shooter gets two hours to fire 60 shots at a very small target at 50 meters. This is considered the purest form of pistol marksmanship and has been practiced since the 19th century. The target is so small, and the time limits so generous, that many times it will take a shooter several attempts to get a single shot off. The shooter will raise and lower the pistol, attempting to follow their plan for delivering the shot, then something will enter their mind to break the concentration and they'll start all over again. These shooters have mastered the physical act of firing a shot. They understand and have perfected things like stance, position, grip and all the physical aspects of pistol shooting. For these shooters, the game is 95% mental and only about 5% physical. All of the shooters on the firing line have mastered these fundamentals, so what separates the winners from the other competitors? It's the mastery of the mental game. It's the shooter that has developed a plan, and has the mental discipline to execute that plan successfully.

Sports psychologist are experts at getting athletes and shooters of all stripes into a winning frame of mind and competing at the highest levels. Compare those shooters to the new, weekend shooter with their first firearm. Hopefully, they've been taught at least the basics of marksmanship, so they understand about stance, position, grip, but probably not. So they are just focused on holding the pistol out at arm's length They are focused on aiming the pistol and trying to get a hit somewhere on the target. For these new shooters, and we've all been there at some point in our shooting careers, they are just focused on the physical aspect of shooting, trying to remember to look at the sights, and trying to press the trigger, so the ratio is 90% physical and 10% mental. Another technique that sports psychologists use is the technique of visualization.

This is nothing more than the ability of a person, in this case, our shooter, to visualizing themselves having a successful performance. Many pro athletes utilize this technique, and many armature and pro shooters do as well. For an example of this, go to any USPSA/IPSC match and stand in front of any of the stages. Prior to the first competitor going to the line, they are

Here, Kyle shows good form with a high grip on the gun, shoulders rolled forward, elbows with good tension but not stiff, and his upper body leaning forward to control the recoil of the G35 in .40 S&W.

allowed to walk the stage to see what the scenario is. They will go through their mind and see themselves firing at the targets and moving through the stage, noting where to place their feet and when to reload. Even if shooting a type of match that doesn't involve movement, such as bullseye or a steel match, most successful shooters use some form of visualization technique.

Whether firing a single shot or a string of shots, there are steps you can take to be successful. One of the most important points is to have a routine. Almost all athletes have a pre-game routine and shooters are no different. That routine can be anything you want, from going to bed at a certain time the night before a match to having the same breakfast the morning of a match. The bottom line is that the routine needs to be something simple and consistent to help lessen the effects of match nerves.

One area that will increase a shooter's anxiety is watching the scoreboard. Golfers do the same thing. Some will look at the leaderboard to see what their score is and everyone else's, and some will not go near the scoreboard on a dare. My coaches used to call this "shooting and computing," where the shooter is trying to keep score in their heads *as they are shooting the match.* The

way it works in bullseye is, for instance, the shooter fires a 93 and a 95 for a combined score of 188 in the first slow fire match. Now the shooter knows they are 12 points down for the match. As the match progresses, they are more worried about their score than proper application of the fundamentals, and their scores will actually suffer because they lack concentration. They become more concerned about the points dropping than watching the front sight.

The bottom line is that the fundamental of mental discipline comes down to developing a plan that comprises several steps or a routine, and it starts with **preparation**. This includes all of the details prior to the match such as making sure your range bag or gun box is ready, and that you have enough ammunition to shoot the match, including additional for alibis or malfunctions. Preparation also includes preparing your ammunition at the reloading bench. Most shooters who compete are also avid reloaders, since reloading saves money and has a side benefit of really getting to know your shooting equipment. So, preparation in the assembly of match grade ammunition should be a top priority. This book has an entire chapter dedicated to handloading, it's that important to the competitive shooter.

Mike teaches the finer points of sight alignment to Kyle.

Next step in planning is to **decide** in advance how you are going to shoot the day's match, how you are going to shoot a particular string or even a single shot. Determine when and where the best place to reload is while on the move, how you are going to handle the wind at Camp Perry, or what is the best sequence to engage multiple targets in a steel match. Remember, having a plan is a very good way to reduce match nerves, because you are focusing on how you are going to approach the stage or string, not focusing on fear of failure, which is the primary cause of pre-match nervousness. Also, remember that having a plan and sticking to it also protects against anxiety when something goes wrong. There are times when shooting competitively that someone will forget some piece of equipment back at the hotel and not realize it until their relay is called up to the firing line. Panic sets in and the shooter, at that point, might as well just pack up and go home, since their thought process is now totally out the window.

The next important phase of mental discipline is to **relax and focus.** The shooter needs to approach the shot or series of shots relaxed and ready to shoot. One way to achieve this is to have positive thoughts. Anything negative that creeps into the thought process is detrimental to successfully executing the shot or shot sequence. Positive thinking reinforces success. I had several shooting coaches that told me that having a short phrase to repeat over and over would help block out negative thoughts, and increase the chance for success. Ask some of the top shooters and they will probably tell you that this type of self-talk is key to their success. It might be something as simple as "Watch the front sight" or "Be smooth." Anything that reinforces in the mind the ability to execute a physically demanding task like shooting will be beneficial. Relax and focus also extends to managing emotions. If you are shooting bullseye and you just put a round into the 5 ring at the 50 yard slow fire target, or you had an early or late round on the rapid fire target at 25 yards, many shooter's first reaction is to blow a gasket. Likewise, if you are shooting an action pistol match and your magazine falls out of the gun after the first shot (I saw that happen last week at an IDPA match) many shooters are ready to pack up and go home. How many times have you seen or heard of golfers throwing their club into the lake after a bad shot? How many times have you seen or heard of Major League baseball players breaking a bat over their knee after striking out? These types of reactions to bad performances may make the person temporarily feel better or let off some steam, but actually, it will impact their ability to be successful the next time they are asked to perform. Because they weren't able to control their emotions, the inexperienced shooter will remember a bad performance and will be thinking about it on the firing line, ramping up their anxiety of repeating that bad performance will creep in and hinder their ability to be successful because they weren't able to analyze *why* they performed poorly, and therefore, were not able to make corrections and set themselves up to be successful the next time.

The next part of mental discipline is to **analyze**. I feel this is one of the most critical aspects of shooting. If a shooter cannot analyze a shot or a string of shots, they will never be able to improve and will just keep making the same mistakes over and over. So, how does a shooter analyze the shot or shot string? Before we can answer that the shooter has to be able to perform a function known as "calling the shot." I'm not talking about the time that Babe Ruth allegedly pointed to the center field bleachers during fifth inning of Game 3 of the 1932 World Series. I'm talking about the ability of the shooter to determine where the impact of the bullet will be, based on relationship of the sights, or the dot, at the instant the pistol fired. The ability to call the shot, or to determine where the bullet or bullets' impact will be, based on how the relationship of the front sight to the rear sight, is a critical skill for any pistol shooter.

In 1984, I was on the firing line at Camp Perry getting ready to fire the last leg match of the year. We were issued 30 rounds of Lake City Match Grade .45 ACP ammo from the ammo point and took that ammo to the firing line. My relay was called to the line and the commence fire command was given, for slow fire. I had to make sure I was able to call the location of the shot since I was using different ammo than what my hardball gun was zeroed for, so I knew that the first shot was probably not going to be where the gun was zeroed, and for all I knew, the first round could be a foot away from my original zero.

So if the sights looked good when that first round went off, I needed to be sure of my ability to look at the relationship of the front and rear sight, and trust my ability to adjust my sights to this new ammo based on the new zero. Remember, this is the leg match and I was trying to obtain points toward my Distinguished badge. They don't give you extra ammo to zero, so if I wasn't

able to call the shot and adjust my rear sight based on what I was seeing in the spotting scope, I may have adjusted the sights the wrong way. I've heard many stories from other Army and Marine shooters that this is exactly what happened to them. Fortunately, the Lake City ammo wasn't too far off zero-wise from the Federal Match I had been using, so I only needed to make a slight adjustment, and was awarded a 6-point "leg" and that put me over the top for my Distinguished Pistol Shot Badge that year.

What is needed in order to call the shot? The shooter needs a high level of concentration, and the shooter also needs the ability to follow through on the shot or shots. So, what is follow-through as it pertains to pistol shooting?

Follow-through is nothing more than the shooter's ability to keep the sights aligned as long as possible as the pistol is fired. I'll apply a sports analogy to explain. In the game of baseball or softball, when the batter swings the bat and makes contact with the ball, the bat continues through the contact with the ball and until the batter completes his or her swing. The bat doesn't stop at the moment of contact, the bat continues *through* the ball. Similarly, when throwing a football or rolling a bowling ball, at the moment the ball is released, the arm continues

Something to be avoided is crossing over the feet when moving from position to position.

Here, Kyle shoots his custom Caspian 1911 with full power loads. Notice that the gun is in full recoil and both eyes are open, demonstrating excellent concentration and follow-through.

the throwing motion. This is follow-through, and is the same action for our pistol shooter. Follow-through is nothing more than trying to keep the sights aligned and the vision *focused on the front sight*, as long as possible until the bullet is out of the barrel and on the way. This accomplishes two goals: the main goal is it allows the shooter to maintain concentration on the sights for as long as possible. The second goal is it allows the shooter to be able to call the shot.

Remember, there is actually quite a bit of time between when the sear is disengaged from the hammer or striker, and the bullet is out of the barrel. During that time, the shooter actually has an enormous amount of influence over the sight alignment and direction of the shot. To the majority of shooters, the act of firing a shot happens in an instant, but in reality, there is a window of 10-15 milliseconds where the shooter can exert influence over the direction of the shot. Look at some high-speed video of a firearms going off, there is actually quite a bit of time between the sear disengaging and the bullet leaving the barrel. This is where good follow-through comes in. Because so many people think the pistol fires almost instantaneously, they tend to "give up on the shot," or break their concentration at the moment of firing. Then they can't understand

why the shot went high right or low left, when the last thing they saw was the front sight in good alignment. They first question is always, "How did that shot end up so bad, when the sights looked so good?" The answer is always follow-through, or the lack thereof, and a break in concentration.

So this goes back to our section topic of analyzing the shot or string of shots. If the shooter is looking at the target, they need to analyze what the target is telling them. First, for the bullseye shooter, they need to be absolutely sure that the pistol is zeroed and that the ammunition used to zero the gun is the same that they are using in the match. Most shooters don't know that something as simple as changing primers can have a huge difference with group size at 50 yards. Or

Once the Glock was zeroed, the paster drill is an effective way to measure the shooter's ability to execute sight alignment and good trigger control with any gun.

that changing components can have a difference on zero and group size.

So, to analyze the shot, or shot group, and assuming the pistol is zeroed, the shooter needs to go back and try to remember what the sights looked like when the shot or shots went off. For example, I recently shot an IDPA match that had a single target at 35 yards, which is a long shot by IDPA standards. I was required to put two rounds into it, and I heeled the first two so I put two more just to be sure, I rushed those two and heeled them, so I put another shot into it and heeled that one as well. When I went down to score, I had a nice five-shot group in the upper-right shoulder. I had heeled every shot and saw the front sight jump high right with every shot. But I was ok with that, as I had called every one of those shots. The problem would have been if I had remembered the shots as being good, or in the center, or worse, being left, right or low left or out the bottom. Because I was able to call the shots, I could analyze what I did wrong and make corrections on the next stage. Mentally telling myself to be smoother on the trigger, be aggressive on the trigger but not too aggressive and don't push the shot, but wait for it to break. The next stage was much better. The shooter needs to be able to shoot and analyze what they did wrong or right and make the necessary corrections.

In order to analyze the shot or shots on target, we have to use the pie. Assuming the target is an 8-inch clock face and a shooting right-handed, shots straight out the top at 12 o'clock were either pushed, or the shooter was looking over the top of the sights. Pushing is a form of anticipation, where the shooter feels the need to get the shot out of the gun, usually because the sight alignment looks really good, and applies all of the trigger pressure at once. Heeling is another form of anticipation, where the shooter pushes with the heel of the hand. The shot will always go high and to the right in the 2 o'clock spot. Shots in the 3 o'clock position are usually where the shooter uses too much trigger finger and is not pressing the trigger straight to the rear. The shooter is actually pressing the trigger and the gun to the right. Conversely, a shot to the 9 o'clock position is where the shooter is using too little trigger finger and is moving the gun to the left slightly. Shots in the 6-7-8 o'clock position mean that the shooter executed the classic "jerk" and is another form of anticipation.

The shooter saw good sight alignment in the center of the target, and then tried to apply all of the trigger pressure at once, pro-

Here I shot a decent five-shot group offhand at 20 yards in four seconds. Good shooting fundamentals learned in bullseye are transferrable to any pistol shooting discipline.

Kyle controls the recoil in the Glock G35 with good fundamentals of stance, position and grip.

ducing a shot that goes down and to the left. Shots in the 10-11 o'clock position mean that the shooter lacked good follow-through and/or had a somewhat weak wrist or grip on the gun, allowing the gun to drift up and to the left at the shot. Many times, a new shooter will swear up and down that they are not flinching or anticipating the shot, and will also swear that the gun is not zeroed or that there is something mechanically wrong with the gun.

There are several ways to prove to the new shooter that the fault lies in the application of the fundamentals and there's nothing wrong with either the gun or the ammunition. The first and probably the easiest is for a shooter with known abilities to fire the gun. I do this all the time with my son. He will swear up and down the gun isn't zeroed or the ammunition is bad, or whatever, because he's unable to knock down the steel plates at the plate rack, and then I'll take the

gun and knock them down in order. I always tell him, it's all about the fundamentals. The next way is to mount the pistol in a Ransom Rest. This clever device takes the human factors out of firing a handgun. I'll talk more about the Ransom Rest in another chapter. The third way is by using dummy ammunition, and is a great way to analyze, in a very visual way, what the shooter was doing when the gun goes off. Dummy cartridges can be purchased very inexpensively just about everywhere, but Brownell's Inc., carries a great selection of dummy rounds, snap caps and just about everything else for the shooter.

The drill is to take the magazine from the shooter and have your shooting buddy randomly load a single non-firing dummy round or two somewhere into the magazine, with the live round on top so the shooter does not know where or if there's a dummy round in the magazine. Insert the magazine into the gun without the shooter seeing you

In this drill, Mike coaches Kyle in walking a figure eight pattern around the white and blue barrels, while using good footwork and engaging the target at 10 yards the entire time while moving. This is a critical skill in practical shooting.

do it, then hand the gun back to the shooter, and let them load the first round into the chamber. Let them fire one shot at a time.

The last element involved with the mental game of shooting is **correction.** After you've done all of the previous steps, step back and see if the plan you developed actually worked, if not, what happened and why? This mental aspect of the game can be applied whether you are a IPSC competitor, silhouette shooter, Cowboy Action or simply a weekend plinker. The idea is to formulate a plan prior to firing a shot or series of shots, then look at the results. Look at the target or the shot timer and see if you were successful or not. Usually, if you are not, it's because of a breakdown in the mental part of the game, and as you gain experience and expertise as a competitive pistol shooter, the mental part of the game becomes more and more important.

CHAPTER ELEVEN

BASIC AND ADVANCED TOOLS AND DRILLS

This chapter assumes that you've at least shot in a couple of the various forms of competition, or that maybe you are an experienced competitor in one sport and want to try another. Once you master the basics in a sport, it can get a little boring staying at the same level. Shooters are a competitive bunch by their very nature, and everyone wants to improve their performance. Some people try to buy their way to better scores, and you can up to a point. There are products that will absolutely help you shoot better scores. But mostly, better scores come down to better and more practice, not better gadgets. To that end, this chapter will cover some techniques to help you take your game to the next level.

In the chapter on marksmanship fundamentals, I covered sight alignment, trigger control and the other fundamentals, but putting it into practice is a different story altogether. So, this chapter goes into some practical drills and techniques that will help, presented for each sport.

BULLSEYE

There are several tips to help you achieve better scores. First, look at where you are having the most trouble; is it during slow fire, or do you panic at timed and rapid fire stages? One of the keys to shooting good slow fire scores is to not anticipate the shot. Most shooters have never been taught to

try and achieve a surprise break at the shot, also most shooters tend to hold too long and force the shot. Also, most shooters who have issues with slow fire do so because they have not learned how to work with the movement of the sights. They *react* to the movement and try to force the gun to go off at the instant the sights look good enough to obtain a decent shot, and they'll put all four pounds of pressure on the trigger all at once. This will always result in a poor shot. So the first thing to learn is how to accept the movement of the sights, and that you can never get the sights to stop moving entirely, so you have to use breathing to get the gun's movement down to the lowest amount possible.

One of the best drills to help with slow fire issues is to have a shooting buddy load two five-round magazines with a random dummy cartridge or two, then insert the magazine and try to shoot a ten shot string. This will show when you are anticipating the shot, and will really help cut down on the anticipation. Once you can keep all of the shots in the 7-ring at 50 yards, ideally inside the 8-ring at 50 yards, then you can move on to concentrating on the sights and regular practice.

Another issue many shooters have when shooting at 50 yards is that they hesitate to apply trigger pressure until the sights look great. This happens quite a bit when firing under windy conditions.

One drill to try is to be more aggressive when applying the trigger pressure. This may seem counterintuitive, but what is happening is that the shooter is hesitating, starting and stopping the application of trigger pressure based on what the sights look like. The remedy is to use the tempo you use in timed fire to trigger two shots in succession.

A typical plan I would use when having issues trying to get a shot off in slow fire was to think about what I was going to do, i.e., have a plan. Take a couple of deep breaths, raise the pistol and bring it down to the target, take another deep breath and let it out, settle the sights into the center of the target and begin to apply steady building pressure to the trigger. When the pistol fires, remember what the sights looked like at the shot, recover out of recoil, and realign the sights and begin pressing the trigger again and fire another shot. When you do this, 9 times out of 10, the two shots, and almost always that second shot, will be in the black. This is good enough for now. Don't look in the spotting scope right now. Take a few more deep breaths, and go through the routine again. Once you've shot all ten rounds, look at the target through the scope and you will be surprised at the results. I can almost guarantee that the group will be tighter than usual.

This is also a good technique to use in windy conditions. In a slow fire string, you have ten minutes to get off all ten shots. If weather conditions are not favorable, use the lulls in the wind to get off two or maybe three well-aimed shots.

Another issue with shooting slow Fire is stopping and starting the trigger finger. This was called "chicken finger" back in the day, and also is a result of the shooter hesitating and reacting to what the sight alignment tells him or her. Trigger control should be steady, building pressure until the gun goes off. A good technique for slow fire is to dry fire

with a scale target. I believe most shooters don't dry fire enough, and/or don't think dry firing is all that important. I would say that one of the reasons I was able to have a little bit of success in my shooting career was that I was able to dry fire a lot during the off-season.

The drill is simple: place a white sheet of paper on a blank wall. Draw a solid black dot about ½-inch in diameter, representing the 8-ring of a standard 50-yard slow fire target, and step back until the muzzle is about four feet from the dot. If you want to make the dot larger and step back farther, that's fine, you just want to simulate the size of the 8-ring of a standard NRA 50 yard bullseye target when the sights are superimposed on it. Now you can dry fire and simulate a slow fire stage of the .22, center fire and .45 matches. Watch carefully your front sight. Call every shot you make, and use good fundamentals of stance, position, grip, breathing and mental discipline. Have a plan, and execute that plan. Do this every day and you will start to see good results in no time.

Another good technique a shooter can use is to get a reduced 50-yard NRA bullseye target. This target is made to be shot at 25 yards. Then the shooter can use the .22 rimfire pistol to get in a lot of practice in a very short time. Firing on a reduced target is just as challenging, and in my opinion, more so, than the standard 50-yard target. I always had a hard time with the reduced targets when we shot indoors in the winter months.

For timed and rapid fire strings in bullseye, one of the techniques for good scores is to get the shot off within one second of the target turning and facing the shooter. The target starts at 90 degrees to the shooter, with the target frame edge facing the shooter. When the range officer says, "All ready on the firing line," the targets will turn and face the shooter within three seconds. The objective for the shooter should be to settle in and have the sights already aligned on the center edge of the target frame, so when the target turns, you will be presented with the black 9-ring of the 25 yard target. Pressure should be applied as the target is turning and the shot should be delivered within the stated one second. The reason is this: if you are shooting a rapid fire string, you have ten seconds to fire five shots. If you get the first one off within the first second, you now have a full 8.5 to 9 seconds to get off four, well-aimed shots, which makes this a much easier proposition. If you hesitate, then panic sets in and the shots will be delivered much too quickly, usually resulting in spraying bullets all over the target with disastrous results.

Another useful technique with the timed and rapid fire stages is to have a steady rhythm. If you go to a bullseye match, watch, or actually listen to a shooter firing an alibi round. An alibi round is where the shooter had a malfunction and gets to fire another five-round string. When the targets turn, listen to see how soon he or she gets the first round off, and then listen for a good rhythm on subsequent shots. Listen to see if the shooter holds the last round a little longer to make it more perfect. This is a common error of new shooters. If the shooter is experienced, you will notice that they have excellent rhythm, and this allows an equal amount of time for each shot in the string. Regardless of whether it's a timed or rapid fire stage, having a good rhythm and giving equal time for each shot is crucial. Less experienced shooters will sometimes fire one quick shot, then hesitate, then start to panic and get off a couple more shots, then hesitate, and finally, let the next two go. This stopping and starting of the shot string is devastating to achieving good scores. If you watch either shooter, the experienced shooter or the less experienced shooter, listen to their rhythm and then look at the results on the target. The experienced shooter

will almost always have shot a good score with good rhythm, and the less experienced shooter will have a poorer score, with poor rhythm.

One last tip for achieving good scores in bullseye: get an inexpensive air pistol and some 10-meter targets. You'll need about 33 feet of space, but if you can practice with an air pistol, your slow fire scores will greatly improve. Why? Because the pellet is moving so slowly that you must have excellent follow-through and excellent ability to call the shot.

When I was with the MTU #1 in Ft Meade Maryland in the winter, competitive pistol shooting moves to indoor matches, so in order to stay sharp and help our slow fire scores, we would shoot Feinwerkbau match grade air pistols in the upstairs barracks across from our Headquarters Building where we had an indoor air pistol range set up. These were unused Army barracks that were equipped with open bays, so we had a large open floor to shoot across. These Feinwerkbau's are expensive pistols, they can run $1500 new, but excellent pistols such as the Crossman Competition Pellet pistol are not only used by bullseye shooters, but the silhouette crowd as well. It sells for under $400. The excellent FAS 6004 air pistol is another good choice for under $400, and good used ones can be had for even less. Check these out, and use them to tighten your groups and increase your slow fire scores.

When you start to move up in the ranks of bullseye, or if you are of a certain age like me, at some point you'll want to migrate over from iron sights to some model of red dot sight. In the early to mid-1980s, Aimpoint was being used by the Army's top Blue team. All of them used the Aimpoint electronic sights, not only for practice, but also for competition. Today, many bullseye competitors use some type of electronic sights and they can be a great way to increase your scores, but they require a certain amount of discipline in order to be effective with them. The reason is that new shooters have not developed the trigger control at a high enough level. When using electronic sights, the dot will dance and bounce around, and shooters will react to that movement. The shooter will typically start and stop the rearward movement of the trigger finger in reaction to the movement of the dot, which is the absolute opposite of what is needed to fire an accurate shot or string of shots. Normally, the more the dot dances around, the more the negative reaction will be of the shooter. So it takes a very high level of trigger control in order to use a dot sight effectively in bullseye. The dot on the electronic sights can be adjusted for size and intensity, which makes it nice since the dot can be changed based on shooting conditions, something that iron sights cannot do.

There are two dot sights primarily used in bullseye: the aforementioned Aimpoint, and the Ultradot sight. Both types are popular and which one to use comes down to personal preference. When you are ready for this move, talk to some of the other competitors to see what they like and go from there.

PRACTICAL PISTOL SHOOTING EVENTS

This section will discuss techniques that benefit shooters of all practical-type events, such as IPSC, IDPA, 3-gun, steel shooting, GSSF, etc. For these matches, accuracy is still king, but there are added elements of speed and movement. For many, if not most of these matches, the rule is that the target must be hit twice, although that's not always the case. Still, anybody interested in competing in action-type events must be able to shoot accurately, must also be quick, and must master the art of the double-tap.

To control recoil and be able to execute a proper double tap, the firearm needs to

be held firmly, and the shooter should lean forward with the arms pushed forward and the wrists locked. Remember not to hold the pistol too firmly or it impedes the ability of the trigger finger to press the trigger quickly.

As important as speed is in these events, accuracy is still necessary. There are some drills the shooter can do in order to increase their level of accuracy when delivering a single shot or multiple shots. One of these drills is simple, and doesn't cost a lot. Set up an IPSC or IDPA target at three yards and put a single white paster in the center of it. Draw the pistol and from the low-ready position, fire a single shot. The shot should be inside the paster. You should be able to do this for ten more shots, while still keeping all of the shots inside the paster. Any shots outside the paster will be quickly evident. This little drill is not as easy as it looks, and you will really need to focus on the front sight, as well as use excellent trigger control to keep the shots inside the paster.

A variation of this drill is to start the drill at the low ready position. The low ready position is a popular position to start a shooting string in action-type events like steel shooting if the shooter is not comfortable in drawing from the holster. The low ready position starts with the shooter in a normal firing position with the feet spread shoulder width apart, with both hands on the pistol and arms pushed out, with the pistol pointed at a 45-degree angle to the ground. The shooter can also add a shot timer to the drill, and try to raise the pistol and get a well-aimed shot off in a certain amount of time.

Another good drill to use is to place a paster onto the front and rear sights. Stand back at 10 yards and fire at the center of the target. The shooter should still be able to keep the shots in the center of an IPSC target at that range, just by relying on stance, position and grip.

One drill to show that the sights don't

Here Mike demonstrates to Kyle how to present the pistol by pushing out from the center of the chest, once the hands have come together after drawing the gun.

have to be perfect in order to get a good shot on target is to place an 8-inch steel stop plate, then stand at seven yards, hold the sight on the target and raise the front sight about halfway above the rear sight notch, and fire. You should ring the plate, then lower the sights halfway below the rear sight and fire, then move the rear sight to the left in the rear sight and fire, and then hold the front sight to the right in the notch and fire. You should ring the plate at all four shots. Then move back to the 10 yard line and repeat, then move to the 12 yards line and repeat. You should be able to ring the plate at all of these ranges, showing that the relationship between the front and rear sights does not have to be perfect in order to obtain a center shot on an IPSC, IDPA, or steel target.

One of the critical skills of an action shooter is the ability to have good footwork. Just like with other sports, good footwork is often the difference between first and last place. Fortunately, unlike many sports like baseball, football, basketball, tennis, etc., good footwork in the shooting sports doesn't take great athletic ability; it just takes an understanding of some basic fundamentals and practice good drills. Many shooters that have been shooting action-type events for a while

may have never been taught good footwork skills. A couple of good drills are to set up a target at 10 yards, with two barrels placed in front of each other.

When the shot timer beeps, the shooter moves forward to the right of the first barrel, then moves left between the barrels, then around the front of the first barrel, then back around to the rear barrel. Viewed from above, the shooter would move in a Figure-8 around the barrels, while keeping focused on the target and shooting at the single target while moving, the shooter should deliver a shot about every two to three seconds, reloading as necessary. Another drill is to set up four barrels and the shooter moves in a square around the barrels, shooting as they move. The shooter needs to keep the body center of gravity low, and when moving backward, toe to heel.

Another drill for developing skills when moving is to set up a wall, with targets to the left and right of the wall. The wall should preferably have a window in the center. The drill is at the beep of the start signal, the shooter moves slightly to the left, and engages that target, then moves to the right, and engages the first target exposed in the window, then moves a little more and engages the target to the left of the window as

Here, Kyle walks the figure eight pattern around the four barrels, while engaging the target and reloading as needed. Not crossing the feet, and keeping the gun and body in control is key.

it's exposed. The shooter keeps moving to the right and fires on the target that is exposed off the right side of the wall, then keeps moving and engages the target to the left of that. The drill is to keep moving to the side, while engaging the target, without crossing the feet over, but being able to do it quickly.

Another good drill to practice is called the Bill Drill. The Bill Drill was named after entrepreneur Bill Wilson of Wilson Combat, and is a very simple drill to perform, but instills excellent skills to the shooter. What it teaches is the draw, getting a proper grip quickly, and that the sight picture only needs to be "decent" not "perfect" to get a solid shot on target. The drill is to place a single IPSC target at seven yards. Starting from the surrender position, draw and fire six rounds into the "A" zone. Any shot not in the "A" zone and the run is discarded, so the emphasis is on accuracy, not speed. If you want to change it up a bit, or don't feel comfortable drawing and firing from a holster yet, start from the low ready position, and bring the target in closer, say 10-12 feet or so. A good par time for a beginner should be 4.5 seconds, and for a Master class shooter, around 2.0. Remember, if you are missing the "A"

zone, you are going too fast. I think this is the biggest mistake I see shooters making when competing in action events. Once you can keep all of the shots into the "A" zone, then work on speeding up and moving the target farther away. A shot timer is essential for these types of drills and should be in every shooters range bag. If you don't want to buy a shot timer and own a smart phone, there is an app for that. Surefire makes a free shot timer app for the IPhone that I use pretty regularly.

THE ART OF THE DOUBLE TAP

The double tap, or firing two consecutive rounds at the target, is a staple of competitive action type events and new or even the more experienced shooter should practice these regularly. There are actually three types of double taps: The true double tap, also called a "hammer" where the shooter fires the first shot, then immediately fires the next *without acquiring a second sight picture.* These shots are usually taken when the target is extremely close, ten feet or less, depending on the shooters ability, and a little time can be made up by not taking a second sight picture.

Good fundamentals help control the .40 S&W during recoil.

then come down. Don't worry about where the shot goes. Make sure the trigger finger doesn't come off the trigger and that the gun doesn't shift in the grip. What you are trying to achieve with this drill is to fire two quick shots *with good follow-through.* You should see the front sight flip up and come down. Use a solid stance and position.

The second method of the double tap is the consecutive pairs. This is performed with the shooter standing in front of the berm with no target, just a high berm to catch all of the rounds. If you can, stand as close to the berm as safely possible in order to catch all of the rounds, since the second shot may be quite high. Fire the first shot and try to watch the front sight flip up,

The third method of the double tap is the accelerated pair. This drill is fired using two separate sight pictures for each shot. It's a little slower than either the hammer, or the consecutive pair. What the shooter is doing with this drill is to fire two shots as quickly as possible, but *getting a sight picture with each shot.* It's critical that the shooter focuses on the sight picture at the shot, but when the pistol comes back down out of recoil, to verify the sight picture and quickly reapply trigger pressure. I like to use a paper target turned backward and stapled to a regular IPSC target, this provides a large bright white target to verify sight picture when shooting quickly, without giving a spe-

At the start signal, the pistol is drawn, keeping the finger out of the trigger, while the weak hand is brought to the center of the chest to receive the gun. This move ensures the weak hand is not swept by the muzzle of the gun during the draw. Safety always comes first, before speed. The finger is kept well away from the trigger guard.

The pistol has cleared the holster, and the weak hand comes to meet the pistol at the center of the chest.

cific aiming point that will cause the shooter to shift focus.

This drill is a good one no matter what shooting game you are participating in.

This works for Cowboy Action, steel, 3-gun, and most of the other, except silhouette and bullseye. Set up a target at seven yards. Load the pistol and make the line ready. Once the timer goes off, draw and fire a single round. Reapply the safety, and reholster. Do that for 20-25 shots. If you are shooting a group at the size of a 3x5 card, than step back to ten yards and repeat for another 25 shots. I realize these drills can be a little boring, but I guarantee they will greatly improve your scores.

Once you're accomplished at standing facing the target and feel you're ready to move on, the next step is to add a little body movement to the drills. This time, place a single target at 10 yards. Facing the target, load the pistol, apply the safety and reholster the gun. Turn 180 degrees so that you have your back to the target. At the beep, spin 180 degrees, draw and engage the target. It's really best to have three targets, but it can be done with one. If you use three targets, this drill is known as the *El Presidente*. If you have three targets set up, draw and fire two

rounds on each target from left to right, then reload, and fire two more rounds on each of the three targets from right to left. This drill can be done in either order, but the point is to engage the targets starting with the shooter facing away and engaging the targets with two rounds each from either right to left, or left to right, with a reload. There are a couple of tricks to do this correctly. You can spin in either direction, and I've never seen any difference in either spinning clockwise or counterclockwise. You need to keep balanced and be smooth. I would practice this repeatedly with an empty gun until you are certain that you can spin, draw safely and engage the target(s). Finally, at the beep, your hands can go down to the pistol, but DO NOT draw until you have completed the spin and your feet come to a stop.

Another good drill is to learn how to shoot and move. Set up two targets, one at 12 yards, and one at seven yards. This drill emphasizes keeping the finger out of the trigger guard while on the move and engaging multiple targets. As always, run this drill multiple times with an unloaded pistol until you are certain that you can do it absolutely safely with a loaded gun. The drill is simple; at the beep, draw and fire two rounds at the target at seven yards, then raise the finger out of the trigger guard and move to the second firing point, stop and engage that target with two rounds. If you get confident with this drill, you can mix it up by adding a reload in between the first and second firing point, or making the yardage longer, say 12 and 20 yards. You can reload on the move, or reload either before you move from Point 1, or after you get to Point 2. In some games, you can only move if you are behind cover. Be extremely careful about keeping the trigger finger out of the gun and keep the muzzle pointed in a safe direction. Also, it's a good idea in the beginning to engage the safety while moving between positions.

Sometimes, the action pistol shooting games means that we have to shoot from different positions other than standing on our hind legs and banging away. This means we may have to shoot from either a kneeling, or prone position. A good drill for engaging targets from the kneeling position is this: At the beep, draw the pistol and drop down onto the strong side knee. Keep the pistol pointed straight out and keep both hands on the gun with the safety still on. Once the strong side knee is on the ground, disengage the safety and fire. Always draw the pistol prior to assuming the kneeling position.

Engaging targets from the prone position is probably one of the most difficult positions to fire from. It's not only difficult to get into position, but it has to be done safely, and when the shooting string is completed, the range had to be made safe. The reason this is the most difficult position is because it's so easy to do something unsafe and get disqualified. Just remember, go slow, and go through this drill many, many times with an unloaded pistol before trying it with a loaded gun. In this drill, it's really important to draw the pistol, and keep the finger out of the trigger guard and keep the muzzle pointed downrange. Where shooters get into trouble is when they sweep the weak hand with the muzzle as they are going to the ground. There are a couple of ways to go to the ground with a loaded firearm safely. At the beep, draw the pistol, keeping it pointed toward the target and out in front of the body. Bend the knees, crouch down and place the weak hand on the ground straighten the strong-side leg, putting the knee on the ground, and roll over onto the right side onto the ground while straightening the left leg and going completely to the ground, again, keeping the finger off the trig-

Once Mike has demonstrated the technique, its Kyle's turn to perform the drill while Mike walks him through it.

ger and the pistol straight out in front. There are probably several ways to accomplish this move, and it really depends on your age, and physical abilities. Many times, if the shooter is unable to exactly perform the stage as it's drawn up because of physical impediments; accommodations are normally made on the spot. The important point to always remember is to keep the finger off the trigger, keep the pistol pointed in a safe direction, and don't sweep any part of the body with the muzzle of the firearm.

Once you've completed the string, you will be given the same command from the RO as you were given if you were standing up. The RO will ask I you are finished, and you will be told to "Unload and show clear." At this point, many people will try to get up off the ground, since that's the natural reaction. I usually clear the pistol, let the RO inspect the chamber, let the slide down, hammer down, then get up on my knees, and holster the gun, then stand up. Never try to reholster from the prone position.

The next drill to practice is firing from a barricade. In the action shooting sports, there are always barricades, except maybe is Steel shooting, those are pretty much just a straight-up shootout. But in IPSC, IDPA, 3-gun, there will sometimes be a devious

range designer that has come up with walls, barrels, sometimes tunnels, and barricades, so being able to engage an array of targets from behind a barricade is an important skill to have. One of the first IPSC matches I ever shot had both Cooper Tunnels and a six-foot barricade wall that had to be jumped over. A Cooper tunnel is named after Col. Jeff Cooper, the father of modern practical pistol shooting. The Cooper Tunnel is basically a makeshift tunnel, usually made out of 2x4's, with 2x4's balanced on top, so when the shooter crawls through the tunnel, if they bump the top boards, they fall off and the shooter usually incurs a time penalty. The barricade is an obstacle that the shooter needs to be able to shoot from effectively. Keep in mind that different shooting games will dictate the technique of shooting behind a barricade. In NRA Action Pistol, the barricade is used as a support, but the pistols used for these matches have a shroud around the barrel just for this purpose. In IDPA, or IPSC, the barricade does not come into play, also, the shooter needs to keep in mind that if the cylinder or slide of the firearm touches the barricade in any way, that could easily cause a malfunction. So when performing this drill, if the shooter is allowed to touch the barricade and the target is a long

The hands are almost together, and the finger is moving to the trigger. Every move is performed in a single smooth motion. Start this drill slow and work up to speed as fast as you can go safely. Drawing and dry firing drills can be performed at home, greatly increasing the amount of repetitions needed to ingrain muscle memory of the draw.

distance, say over 25 yards, the barricade can be used as a support, but the back of the hand, or the bottom of the strong hand with the pistol canted slightly can be used to make contact with the barricade while shooting, and at the same time keeping the firearm from making contact with the barricade. In the IDPA game, the barricade is used as cover, and when engaging targets from behind the barricade, cover has to be utilized or a time penalty is incurred. So the shooter should not use the barricade as cover, but needs to imaging that the barricade is not there, and engage the targets in order.

There is a technique in action shooting as well as used by tactical teams from law enforcement and military, which is known as "slicing the pie." The way it works is the shooter needs to engage more than one target from an angle. As the shooter approaches the wall or barricade, the shooter needs to engage the first target that comes into view, then the shooter maneuvers around the barricade or wall, exposing more targets. Each target is engaged as they come into view, and the shooter doesn't move beyond cover until each target is engaged in order. This is why it's called slicing the pie, with each target is a slice of the pie, and the shooter engages each slide as they move around the barricade.

Another vital drill for the aspiring action shooter to be proficient in is strong hand only shooting. In this drill, the shooter needs to draw with the strong hand, then transfer the pistol to the weak hand, and engage the target. The goal of the drill is to be able to safely and effectively engage targets while firing one handed. In this drill, the shooter needs to keep the upper body tense through the shoulders in order to counter the effects of recoil. One way to do this is to keep the body leaning forward at the waist, extending the strong side arm out, and keep the weak side arm tight against the body, with

the hand in the center of the chest. As with drawing with a two-hand hold, a one hand drill with draw, make sure the draw is straight up and out of the holster and punch out toward the target, while at the same time disengaging the thumb safety if the gun is a 1911-style pistol. For other style handguns, do whatever it takes to get the pistol into a firing condition with the thumb and/ or trigger finger once the pistol's muzzle is pointed at, and moving toward the target. It's easy to use a bowling ball or casting type motion discussed elsewhere in the book and we definitely do not want to use this type of motion. Economy of motion is crucial to this technique. Again, this drill needs to be practiced with an empty firearm until it can be performed safely.

The last drill is to draw with the strong hand and transfer to the weak hand and engage the target. This is probably the drill that causes new shooters the most anxiety. This drill and shooting prone are probably the two drills that need to be practiced most with an empty firearm.

There are a couple of ways to approach this drill. One is, at the beep, draw the pistol with the strong hand, the weak hand goes toward the gun as if in a two handed hold. How the shooter disengages the safety will depend on the type of pistol being used. But the main point is that the safety should NOT be disengaged until the pistol has been transferred to the weak hand. The weak hand disengages the safety, not the strong hand. One tip I always give new shooters is to bring the thumb and the palm area off the gun, but keep the three fingers wrapped tightly around the grip of the gun. Bring the weak hand up to the gun with the hand open and place the gun into the hand, wrapping the fingers of the weak hand around the grip, while at the same time, slipping the fingers of the strong hand out from under the fingers of the weak hand. It really sounds more

After walking through the draw in slow motion, it's time to perform the drill at speed under the timer. Here the signal has been given, and Kyle starts the draw.

complicated than it is, and is a fairly easy skill to learn with practice. There is another way to perform this drill. At the beep, grasp the pistol by the butt of the gun, giving some space under the beavertail area of the pistol for the weak hand to fit into, then the safeties of the gun can be disengaged and the targets engaged.

COWBOY ACTION SKILLS AND DRILLS

The Cowboy Action game also has many drills and techniques that can help a new shooter become more proficient in the game. Some of the points of action shooting pertain to the Cowboy Action Shooting (CAS) game as well. First and foremost, never go faster than you can go safely. This is really paramount and I see this in many of the action shooting games. People try to go faster than they are capable of and that's when they get into trouble.

Two main points of CAS are accuracy and speed. Accuracy is something that has to be inherent with the pistol. These guns are shot at fairly close range, but the guns have to be zeroed and shoot point of aim, point of impact, or all of the speed you can muster will be wasted. Make sure the point of impact is right on top of the front sight blade.

Any other point of impact you will need to get the pistol zeroed before competing.

Once the pistol is zeroed properly with the load you intend to use in matches, then a good drill to do is one that also works for the semi-auto crowd. Take a 12x12-inch target and set it on the target frame. Turn the target around so it's a blank page. Step back at about seven yards and draw and fire a six shot group, focusing on the front sight. You should have a very tight group, and having a blank target make sure that the shooter focuses on the front sight and not on sight picture, or even worse, the target. Once you've shot those, step back, say, fifteen yards, and use smaller targets than what you would see at a match. If you are shooting speed drills and are not getting 100 percent accuracy, then you'll need to back off your speed until the hits come back.

Another good technique is a drill similar to the action shooting sports and that's a draw and one shot drill. So, for this one, stand at a blank target with a golf ball sized target on it (many sporting goods stores sell blaze orange sticky targets that work well) or a 3x5 card that has been colored black or blue. Stand with the arms at your side, then draw and fire one round as quickly as possible, then reholster. Do that six times. You should have a nice, tight group on the card. If you don't, then you are probably going too fast. If you have a good group on the target, step back three paces and run the drill again. Getting the first shot off quickly and accurately is really an important key to the action shooting sports, and it doesn't matter what sport it is. Even with bullseye shooting, getting the first shot off accurately is key when shooting a string of shots. When the first shot does not go off quickly and smoothly, the mind starts to panic because the clock is running, and once panic sets in it's difficult to recover. Slow down and focus on being smooth.

When firing one shot or a string of shots, the shooter needs to thumb the hammer. Thumbing the hammer is always accomplished using the thumb of the supporting hand, never thumb the gun with the shooting hand, as it's slow and awkward. Try to keep the sight on the target as much as possible, this will help keep your speed up. You should keep your speed drills separate from accuracy drills. Develop a practice regime that alternates between speed and accuracy. Then, when you have to combine the two in a match it will come more naturally.

SILHOUETTE DRILLS

Silhouette competition is all about precision. There is no movement, no reloading on the run, no barricade. The game is about being able to engage relatively small targets at relatively long range with handguns. Bullseye contains aspects of other types of shooting, like the timed and rapid fire stages. In the case of silhouette, the slow fire stage of bullseye is a great correlation: a small target at long distance. If you are a good slow fire competitor, you will find competing in a silhouette match will be much easier than someone who has difficulty at slow fire. Fortunately, this is a skill that can be learned

with practice.

As with slow fire in bullseye, the key to engaging small targets that long distance is being able to get a surprise break on the shot. What do I mean by this? The shooter should strive to allow the pistol to fire without a conscious effort in *forcing* it to do so. The pistol firing should be a surprise. If not, that means that the shooter is making the gun go off, usually as a result of anticipating what the sights are doing in relation to the target, and reacting to that movement. How to combat this? One way to do this is through dry fire, but if the shooter has already ingrained bad habits, more practice with poor technique is not the answer. This drill requires the use of the buddy system. Use snap caps, or load up some dummy ammunition. While on the firing line, have your shooting buddy load the pistol randomly with either a live round or a non-firing dummy cartridge.

When the pistol goes off, it will be instantly apparent if the shooter is anticipating the shot by the movement of the pistol. Really high anticipation will result in the pistol being yanked in one direction or the other. Whereas, if the shooter is NOT anticipating the shot, there will be very little movement.

I've noticed that the amount of anticipation by the shooter increases when the shooter moves from iron sights to optical or electronic sights. There is a period of adjustment needed when going from iron sights to optic or electronic. One of the keys to shooting with optic or electronic sights is to be able to accept the movement of the reticle or dot, and not to react to the movement. This is hard to do, but is critically important to success with this type of equipment, and using dummy rounds will help. Dry firing will also greatly help the new shooter.

Draw some cutouts of the four types of targets on a sheet of plain paper, trying to match the scale of the targets at the various ranges. Go to the range, and try to draw the targets to scale on a piece of paper and use this as a dry fire target to practice with at home.

Breathing techniques will also help out greatly. Breathing techniques combined with proper trigger control will be essential for accurate shooting at long range. The shooter needs to learn the concept "minimum arc of movement." This is where the amount of movement in the sights or dot of a handgun is at the lowest point. In preparing to deliver a shot, the shooter normally takes in a deep breath or two. At this point, the firearm is extended and another deep breath is taken and the sights are settled onto the target. The shooter will normally notice that the sights are moving around, but the amount of movement will slowly decrease after about 2-3 seconds. The amount of movement will be at the lowest for only about 5-7 seconds, and this is the period that the shooter should be applying direct trigger pressure to the trigger in order to fire the shot. If the shooter is reacting to the amount of movement and is hesitating on applying trigger pressure, it usually results in holding the gun too long. At this point, the shooter will begin to experience the amount of movement of the sights to the target greatly increase, and at this point the shooter usually yanks the shot in order to get rid of it, almost always resulting in a poor shot. Alternately, the shooter will put the gun down to the low ready position, or down from the target, and start over, and this is the correct approach.

One of the best ways to overcome these impediments is to have a plan of approach to each shot. For example, the plan might be to take three deep breaths, raise the pistol slightly over the back of the target, then take one more deep breath, settle into the center of the target, and immediately start applying trigger pressure. By the time the pistol goes off, the shooter should have attained the minimum arc of movement and the shot should be a surprise break. Whatever the plan is, there should be a plan for each and every shot. The key to success is to actually have a plan and stick to it. Another key is that if the concentration is broken for any reason, or if the sequence of delivering a shot is interrupted by a break in the shot sequence or the thought process, the sequence of delivering a single accurate shot should be started over. Remember, there are time limits to the shot string, but these are usually pretty generous, so if the shooter is experiencing difficulty in delivering the shot, it's always better to stop the shot sequence and start over than deliver a shot in haste, just to get rid of it and going on to the next shot. Another key point to remember with optical or electronic sight is to not react to the amount of movement to the reticle or the electronic dot.

LOADING PROCEDURE ON THE FIRING LINE

Some malfunctions are caused by not utilizing a proper loading procedure on the firing line prior to the start of the shooting string. The following procedure is for the 1911-style handgun, since they are so popular for action shooting sports, you may need to modify this procedure based on your pistol or the type of action shooting game you are participating in.

When the range officer gives the command to load and make ready, you will be on the firing line or in the starting box with an appropriate number of loaded magazines and an empty pistol. The procedure is to draw the pistol from the holster with the strong hand, otherwise known as the firing hand, keeping the finger out of the trigger guard, and preferably, well out of the trigger guard so it's easy for the RO to see, with the handgun pointed downrange. With the weak, or non-firing hand, pull the slide to the rear and, with the thumb of the firing hand, push up the slide stop to lock the slide to the rear. Once the slide is locked open, draw a spare magazine that is loaded with two or three live rounds.

I keep this magazine in my magazine pouch, in a back pocket, or in my side pocket of my cargo shorts, or somewhere on my person, and it is used just for this purpose. Usually, it's a magazine that may have given me a feeding malfunction at some point, where I feel that the magazine is not 100% reliable, and one that I don't want to use in a match but it's good enough to use to feed a first round into the gun.

Insert the magazine fully into the magazine well with a fair amount of force, until you hear the click. Reach over with the thumb of the non-firing hand and press down on the slide release, letting the slide go forward. This will strip a live round from the top of the magazine, feeding it into the chamber. You should watch the round actually go up the feed ramp and into the pistol.

At this point, you can do what's known as a "pinch-check." This drill is for more advanced shooters, but is a sure way to tell if there is actually a live round in the chamber, so I'll explain it here. To do a pinch check, reach up with the weak hand, and "pinch" the front of the slide, at the same time, pull the slide back about $\frac{1}{2}$ inch or so, just far enough to expose the round in the chamber without ejecting it. Look down into the ejection port opening to verify there is a live round in place, and then let the slide go forward to seat the round.

The downside to this procedure is that, on some tight-fitting custom guns, there is a chance that the slide will not go all the way forward, which will cause the disconnector in the pistol to disengage the trigger mechanism because the slide is slightly out of battery, and the pistol will not fire in this condition. The slide needs to be fully forward for the pistol to be fired.

To counteract this, once you've verified the gun is loaded, let the slide go forward, and then push the slide forward with the thumb on the back of the slide to make sure the slide is fully into battery. Engage the thumb safety, then reholster the pistol. This needs to be done with the trigger finger well outside of the trigger guard.

Some games, like IDPA, state that you cannot start with more than 10 rounds in the magazine, even if the magazine holds more than that. It also states that you can have one in the chamber. So you start with 11 rounds total, even if the magazine holds more than 10 rounds. IPSC is different; you can start with as many rounds as the magazine will hold. You need to check the rules of the game you are playing since they may be different from game to game.

MALFUNCTIONS AND MALFUNCTION DRILLS

In the bullseye game, if the pistol malfunctions it's very easy for the shooter to simply stop shooting, keep the pistol downrange, and raise the hand and call for an alibi. A referee will come over and verify that it's a legitimate malfunction, i.e., the primer failed to detonate, the cartridge failed to feed or chamber, the gun misfired. If the shooter just failed to reset the trigger in a rapid fire event, or something that looked like a malfunction but in reality, the pistol really didn't malfunction, the alibi is not allowed and the shooter loses however many rounds were left in the gun. If the malfunction is allowed, the shooter gets to shoot an alibi string, and all shooters that had an alibi will be allowed to fire another five round string, with the lowest ten shots counted for score. Reloading is performed at the start of every string and only under the direct supervision of the range officer.

In silhouette, the time limits are so generous that there are no alibis, and reloading is performed at the shooter's discretion, as long as the shooter fires all of his or her rounds under the time allotted. Malfunctions are rare, since most of the firearms are either single shot or single action revolvers. If there's a malfunction, it's usually either caused by the ammunition, usually seating depth of the bullet too long or the case wasn't resized properly in the reloading process, or the firearm is out of commission with a broken internal part.

Cowboy Action shooting is similar to silhouette in that the single action revolvers typically don't have feeding or other of these types of malfunctions since they are single action, loaded at the table and fired all at once. If the guns have a malfunction, and they will sometimes, it's usually of a nature that a gunsmith needs to get involved and the gun is usually out of commission until it can be repaired.

Not so with some of the action shooting sports. Here, since time is critical, the shooter has to take some sort of corrective action when the pistol malfunctions because the clock is running. One of the best ways to overcome a malfunction during a match is to not panic! The two main times shooters have a meltdown are when the pistol malfunctions and trying to run the stage too fast.

There are several types of malfunctions in a semi-auto handgun and the first thing a shooter needs to do identify the type of malfunction. Before we get into the malfunction terms, let me explain the eight cycles of operation that any firearm goes through in the firing cycle. These are fundamental to any firearm. Here are the eight cycles of operation that all firearms follow. It doesn't matter if it's a 155mm Howitzer or a 22 LR Derringer.

- **Feeding -** This cycle starts when the bolt, slide, breechblock, while moving forward, contacts the cartridge in the magazine and gets the cartridge out of the magazine and started into the chamber. In single-shot handguns like the Thompson/Center Contender, feeding is performed by the shooters hand, then chambering is performed when the cartridge is seated by hand into the chamber, which leads to:
- **Chambering** – This is where the cartridge enters and seats into the chamber of the firearm.
- **Locking** – This cycle is where the breechblock (slide, bolt, etc.) is locked with the barrel. This cycle can vary from firearm to firearm, blowback pocket pistols are "locked" at the slide and barrel by the spring tension of the recoil spring, while a recoil operated firearm like an M1911 the barrel is locked to the slide by the top locking lugs, and is also locked to the frame by sitting on the slide stop pin, which is mounted crossways into the frame.
- **Firing** – This is where the cartridge is fired by the firing pin or striker indenting the primer and crushing the primer pellet.
- **Unlocking** – This cycle is where the chamber pressure of the fired cartridge drops to a safe level allowing the slide, or breechblock to unlock from the barrel.
- **Extraction** – The cycle is where the cartridge is extracted by the extractor, and removed from the chamber.
- **Ejection** – This cycle is where the fired case is completely ejected away from the firearm by the ejector.
- **Cocking** – This is the cycle where the firearm's trigger mechanism is reset in order to fire the next cartridge.

Now that we have a basic understanding of how the firearm operates, we can better understand how it can malfunction. Here is some basic handgun malfunction nomenclature:

Failure to feed – This is where the ammunition may start to come out of the magazine, but the slide's forward motion has stopped before the cartridge has fully exited the magazine. There could be several reasons for this. Usually, with a semi-auto pistol, this malfunction is either related to a bad magazine or with the use of reloaded ammunition not assembled correctly.

Failure to chamber – This is where the cartridge has exited the magazine but is not fully seated into the chamber and the slide is not completely closed.

Failure to lock – This is where the cartridge is fully into the chamber, but the slide is just out of battery enough to not fully close, and the trigger mechanism is disconnected, rendering the pistol unable to fire.

Failure to fire – Here, you pull the trigger, the hammer or striker falls and there is no kaboom! There could also be several reasons for this.

Failure to unlock – This is extremely unusual in a semi-auto. Normally if the pistol fires, the slide will move rearward, except in very unusual circumstances.

Failure to extract – The pistol fired, but it left an empty case in the chamber. This is usually a pretty bad condition when it happens on the firing line in a match, but is usually a pretty simple fix back in the shop.

Failure to eject – This is where the cartridge fired and was pulled out of the chamber, but the spent case did not clear the gun. It was not ejected away from the pistol.

Failure to cock – This is where the hammer follows the slide down during the firing cycle. This is always a bad situation. Sometimes, there wasn't enough power in the cartridge to fully push the slide rearward and also not far enough to the rear to cock the hammer. Usually this is a squib load. If it's not a squib load, then there is an issue

with the hammer and/or sear engagement, and a gunsmith needs to get involved. If it is a squib load, you need to immediately get the pistol off the firing line, and get the bullet cleared out of the barrel. Bullets usually get stuck in the barrel from squib loads.

Now that we have a basic understanding of the functioning cycles of a firearm, we can go through some of most common malfunctions that semi-auto firearms will experience, and drills to clear a malfunction and keep you in contention in a match situation. This section will focus on malfunction drills for the competitive shooter, which may or may not be different from a tactical or self-defense drill.

MALFUNCTION DRILLS

Now that we have an understanding of *what* a malfunction is, the next point to learn is how to identify what type of malfunction you are dealing with. Different malfunctions require different clearing steps. The first step in clearing a pistol with a malfunction that happens during a match is to determine as quickly as possible what the nature of problem is, then, also as quickly as possible, apply the proper corrective action.

Failure to feed – If, at the start of the stage, the pistol fired one or more rounds, and you have a failure to feed, this could be either an ammunition or magazine problem. This is why it's important to test the gun at the range with a variety of different handloads and factory loads, with a variety of magazines, not under match conditions. Shoot as much as possible with your match gun, match ammo, match magazines, etc. While testing at the range, try testing the pistol with factory ammunition and see if you can replicate the malfunction. If you can, it's not the ammo, and is therefore likely a magazine issue and you should try changing magazines. If it still malfunctions with different magazines and factory ammo, then it's likely an issue with the pistol. Regardless, you are on the firing line and the pistol fails to feed after firing a round or several rounds and the clock is running. Depending on how far the round tried to feed into the chamber, you can try to clear it quickly by just racking the slide back, and letting it go forward. This is actually best performed as the Tap, Rack Bang Drill.

Tap the bottom of the magazine to make sure it's seated, rack the slide, then try to fire the gun. This will likely eject the offending cartridge and feed in a new one, getting the pistol back into the game. Sometimes, this is caused by reloaded ammo, where the case may not have received enough crimp on the case mouth or the round may be seated a little too long or too deeply. Semi-auto handguns are sometimes a little finicky about seating depth. Ejecting that round and getting a fresh round into the gun will usually get you back in the game.

As a side note, semi-wadcutter ammunition is more finicky than round-nose ball ammo. If you reload for bullseye, semi-wadcutter is almost mandatory, since you want the cleanest hole in the target as possible for scoring purposes. The problem with semi-wadcutter ammunition is that it's sometimes a little hard to feed properly, so many top shooters load their match ammunition with round nose "hardball" bullets for better feeding.

Failure to Feed 2 – This is where you are firing a string and the gun tries to feed a round into the gun but has an empty piece of brass or a live round halfway into the chamber, and is trying to feed another round on top of that one. This is a fairly uncommon but serious malfunction in that the shooter can't just rack the slide and continue shooting. The shooter needs to strip the magazine out of the gun, cycle the slide two or three times quickly, then insert a fresh magazine, cycle the slide and try to continue shooting.

Failure to Feed 3 – This one doesn't happen very often, and is usually an ammunition or cleaning or maintenance problem. This is where the slide feeds the round forward, but doesn't quite go all the way into

Here Mike is showing Kyle how to clear a pistol that has a double fed malfunction. There are two rounds that have been stripped outof the magazine and have tied up the gun. The only way to clear this type of malfunction is to strip the magazine out, cycle the slide several times, and look at the feed ramp quickly to make sure to rounds are still present, then insert a fresh magazine and recharge the pistol and re-engage the targets.

Here, Kyle has identified the malfunction, and instinctively knows how to clear it.

battery, with the slide staying out of battery just enough to activate the disconnector and render the pistol inoperable. Usually, you can bump the slide with the palm of the hand to seat the slide and fire the gun. If not, try cycling the action to remove that round and feed in another one.

Failure to Fire 1 – This is a situation where you have a single action automatic like a 1911 with a thumb safety, or a DA/SA like a Beretta pistol with an external safety. You draw, present to the target, press the trigger and nothing happens. If you have a 1911-type pistol, chances are that the safety is engaged, and you failed to fully disengage the thumb safety. If you have a pistol like the Beretta, you will be pressing the trigger, the trigger will go to the rear, but it will feel like it's disconnected, which it is. If/when it happens, be prepared for some good-natured ribbing from your shooting buddies. You may also have too high of a grip on the gun, thereby activating the grip safety. Funny things can happen when the buzzer goes off, and I've seen this happen more than once. If you press the trigger and the trigger doesn't move and the gun just seems like it's locked up, it's because it is. Disengage the safety, re-acquire the target and commence shooting the string.

Failure to Fire 2 - You are on the firing line getting ready to shoot a stage, your firearm is loaded and in the holster, and you have a plan in your mind on how to complete this stage. You nod to the RO that you are ready. You hear the beep, draw the handgun, get a sight picture, press the trigger and the hammer falls with a sickening click. You have one of two situations: when you were given the command to load, you did not fully seat the magazine, and when the slide was cycled to get the first round in the chamber, it ran over the top of the first cartridge in the magazine and the gun didn't load and chamber the first round; or the cartridge did load and is sitting in the chamber, but the primer, for some reason, did not detonate, either by not being impacted by the firing pin, or if the primer was struck by the firing pin, you have a dead primer.

Regardless, you have a gun that didn't go off, and the timer is ticking, so you have to get the gun back in action. The way to do this is to simply rack the slide. Do this forcefully by taking the finger off the trigger, and then pulling the slide to the rear and letting it go, slingshot-style. This should get the offending round out of the chamber a fresh

Here, the fresh magazine has been inserted and the slide is about to be released, recharging the gun.

round into the gun. Re-acquire the sights and sight picture and engage the target. When doing this, make sure that the ejection port is not covered up by your weak, or non-firing hand to ensure the round has plenty of room to clear the gun. Always remember to check the chamber when you load the gun, this will make sure that a cartridge actually went into the chamber when the gun was loaded.

Failure to extract – This is usually caused by an extremely worn or possibly a broken extractor. Not much you can do with this malfunction other than clear the gun, take it off the firing line and turn it over to a qualified gunsmith.

Failure to eject – This is usually caused by an underpowered cartridge that doesn't have enough recoil energy to fully push the slide to the rear and kick out the empty case. Always check your reloading manuals to make sure you are loading a middle-of-the-road cartridge. You want a Goldilocks round. Not too much power, which will wear out both the gun and the shooter, but not under-powered to where the gun malfunctions.

One form of ejection malfunction is called a stovepipe. It doesn't happen too often, but I've seen it a few times. This is where the empty brass is not fully ejected and is caught by the slide going forward feeding in the next round. This is called a stovepipe jam because the empty cartridge case is poking up out of the ejection port and looks like a stovepipe. This type of malfunction happens from time to time and when it does, the gun is actually in the process of feeding a new round into the chamber and the spent case doesn't clear the ejection port before the slide is starting to close while feeding in the new cartridge. The best way to clear this jam is to simply wipe the brass out of the gun with the non-firing hand from front to back, the slide should then close on the live round and then you begin firing again.

In malfunctions with semi-auto pistols, many times failures to feed and failures to eject are not caused by a mechanical failure. They are actually caused by shooter error. Weak recoil spring and weak magazine spring can cause all types of malfunctions, but a weak grip, or a shooter not having firm resistance in the arms will cause many of the types of the failures discussed here.

When malfunctions happen in a match, like in this photo, malfunction drills allow the shooter to clear the gun and get it back into the game without the shooter going into a panic.

The reason is that the semi-auto pistol has to have a firm surface for the recoil spring to operate against. If the shooter doesn't have a firm grip and tension in the arms, it will take away energy from the recoil spring, making it difficult for the spring to do its work. I've actually demonstrated this on the firing line by taking a bullseye pistol that was functioning normally and, with a weak grip and just enough tension in the arms to keep the gun level, inducing a failure to feed and eject twice out of two, five-round magazines. Granted, the recoil spring on a bullseye gun is very light, usually about four pounds lighter than a stock Colt 1911 spring, so it was easier to take away energy from that system, as opposed to a full strength recoil spring on a stock gun, but the concept is the same. If the recoil spring is a little worn and the gun is dirty, it becomes easier to have these sorts of malfunctions if the shooter doesn't do his or her part.

DRAWING FROM A HOLSTER

WARNING – Drawing a loaded pistol from a holster can be dangerous with a risk of personal injury or death. You should perform this drill with an unloaded pistol until you are absolutely certain you can perform this drill with a loaded pistol at the range

under match pressure conditions.

Some of the action pistol games like steel shooting do not require that the shooter start the string with the pistol in the holster. This is one reason that, if your range has a steel-type competition, it's really the best way to get started in the action shooting sports. These matches usually only require the shooter start from the low ready position. Fortunately, drawing a pistol from a holster is pretty straightforward and can be learned with a few simple drills. These drills are easy to practice at home with an unloaded pistol. In fact, dry firing and drawing from a holster with an unloaded pistol are two activities that you can do at home that will improve your competitive shooting skills exponentially.

Keep in mind that holsters today are very specialized. Take the popular 1911. There are holsters for tactical use, concealed carry, competition and everything in between. Some of these holsters can serve double duty, depending on what type of competition you are engaged in. For example, if you shoot IDPA, IPSC or 3-gun, several of the various types of concealment holsters can be used in these competitions. The exceptions are shoulder holsters, which are not ever allowed, and holsters with thumb breaks.

In IDPA competition, if your holster has a thumb break feature, it must be used during the match. In fact, if the holster has any type of retention feature, it must be used during the match. This will put the competitor at a distinct speed disadvantage. It can be an advantage to have one holster for both concealed carry and competition, since you will only have to learn one holster, and by only having the one holster, you will become very familiar with it under various circumstances.

On the flip side, however, it might be a little more expensive, but if you carry your competition handgun for personal defense and are licensed to carry concealed, it can be a good idea to have one holster for competition, and the other holster for everyday concealment. The downside to this is that you have to learn two holsters, so it takes a little bit of dedication and practice in order to become proficient with both, but the payoff can be worth it. Concealment holsters are very specialized and offer distinct advantages to a holster that is used for both concealment and competition. Regardless of the route you take, once you're ready to start competing with your chosen handgun, you will need to know how to properly and safely draw from the holster as smoothly and efficiently as possible.

Drawing from a holster can be broken down into several easy steps. These steps are pretty simple and can be learned by anyone willing to dedicate some time to the drills. The more you practice these drills, the better, smoother and safer your draw will become. Before I get into the seven steps, let me just say that the key to drawing from a holster in competition is not speed, it's being smooth. Many new shooters attending a match for the first few times will see some of the more professional shooters, or just shooters who have been competing for a long time, draw and run very quickly once the timer starts. These new shooters then feel

that they have to replicate that speed from the holster, and that's when they usually get into trouble. I've seen people drop their pistol coming out of the holster at a match. If this happens, your day as a competitor is done, and the match, for you, is over. Dropping a pistol is an instant disqualification. Again, the key is being SAFE and SMOOTH.

The main point to remember is that during the draw, when the buzzer goes off, there are points where you can go fast and other points where you need to be sure of yourself.

The start position in many of the action pistol sports is from what's known as the surrender position, with the hands up at head level. In IDPA, the hands are down at the side, with a shirt of jacket covering the pistol.

In Cowboy Action shooting, the hands are usually at some start position, either on a bench or a barrel, or some other piece of equipment. In Cowboy Action, the fundamentals of holster design apply to that game as well. The holsters for that game must be period correct. The rules are pretty basic for Cowboy Action, the holster cannot be more than 30 degrees from vertical, and must allow a safe draw. There are also rules for pocket and derringer firearms.

For the action shooting sports, there are a few steps for a safe and smooth draw.

From the start position, the hands can go quickly to the gun. The non-firing hand should go to the front of the body around the stomach area. This is so the hands can come together once the pistol clears the holster. Keep the non-firing hand close to the body so the gun doesn't sweep the hand when coming out of the holster. Sweeping any part of the body with a loaded pistol at any time during the match will usually get you an instant DQ, or at the very least, a warning from the RO, and a second infraction will get you sent home.

The key to the draw is to get a full grip on the pistol, and this is where most people have trouble. This is also a point where you can really practice the technique in dry-fire. Go quickly from the start position to the gun, but once the hand has reached the pistol, slow down to make sure you have a secure, full firing grip on the pistol BEFORE you try to draw the pistol out. Push the web of the hand well into the backstrap of the pistol. What you *do not* want to do is to have to adjust the grip between the point of obtaining the grip and drawing the pistol out of the holster. This not only wastes time, but is also a good way to drop the pistol.

Make sure the trigger finger is well outside the holster and pointed straight to the ground. This way, the finger will be straight and away from the pistol when the handgun is drawn from the holster. Range officers always appreciate it when the competitor keeps the trigger finger well away from the pistol. Sometimes, the competitor can have the trigger finger out of the trigger guard, but it's so close that the RO may stop the shooter for an unsafe act. Trigger fingers that are well away from the trigger are easy to see when the shooter is drawing quickly or on the move. When you practice, always practice with the trigger finger well away from the gun; it's really a good, safe habit to get into regardless of whether you are a competitive shooter or not.

Also, always make sure that the safety of the pistol is NEVER taken off when the pistol is in the holster. Going back to our 1911-style gun which is in the holster in Condition One, that is, hammer cocked and the thumb safety engaged with a round in the chamber and loaded magazine in place, when obtaining a firing grip, the thumb can naturally fall right on the thumb safety, and in the heat of competition, many newer shooters can simply rest their thumb on the thumb safety and take the gun off safe, while

it's still in the holster. This is something the RO may or may not see since the drawing motion is usually so fast, but if the RO hears a click and the pistol is not out of the holster, that is a safety violation.

On YouTube and there are videos of people on the range who have shot themselves trying to draw a pistol from the holster too quickly with the gun off safe before the gun had cleared the holster and the body.

The hand motion goes quickly but smoothly from the start position, then obtains a secure firing grip on the pistol, with the non-firing hand at or near the stomach. I like to have my weak, or non-firing hand at my stomach with the palm facing my right side, toward the pistol, so it's in a good position to receive the gun when the hands come together during the draw. Remember to keep the head and body still, only the arms are in motion. Keep the feet about shoulder width apart, and the knees flexed. You want to stay in a good, athletic position and be relaxed. A key here is that you want to maintain an "economy of motion." What does that mean? Simply put, it means that you want to move the hands to the pistol, obtain the proper firing grip, and draw the pistol out of the holster with as little extra motion as possible.

Once you have obtained the proper firing grip, lift the pistol straight up and out of the holster; bring the weak hand to the gun, coming together in a two-hand hold at the center of the chest. Once the hands are together, push the pistol forward toward the target. The good thing about this technique is that if the target is close, say three yards or less, the shooter can engage the target without fully extending the arms. I've shot some IDPA matches where the target is three feet away, and time is wasted by fully extending the arms.

There are two common mistakes that new shooters make in their technique when drawing from the holster. They usually are either casting or bowling. If the shooter is casting, that means that they are drawing the pistol, slightly pointing it toward the sky then bringing it down to the target. This is very unsafe and wastes time. The second poor technique is bowling, where the pistol is swung up toward the target in a motion that mimics how you deliver a bowling ball. Remember, we are trying to incorporate an "economy of motion" and these are extraneous motions that are not only unsafe, but waste valuable time and are unnecessary. What you want to do is to have the pistol clear the holster, bring the hands together at the chest and push straight out toward the target.

There are some instructors at tactical schools that teach a different technique for self-defense purposes, and that's fine. Remember, we are concerned here with developing a good technique for the competitive shooter, not tactical. If the shooter wants to develop a technique that's geared more toward defensive purposes, that's fine and that technique may be utilized on the range in competition, as long as it's safe.

Once the hands are together and the gun is started to be pushed toward the target, that's when the sights should be picked up and the safety disengaged. Once the arms are fully extended, the shooter can engage the target. Once the shooter has engaged all targets and has finished firing, the range officer will give the command to unload and show clear. This means that the shooter needs to unload the pistol and show the RO that the pistol is actually unloaded, including both the magazine and the chamber. The proper way to do this with a semi-auto pistol is to keep the pistol pointed downrange, with the finger well out of the trigger guard, and remove the magazine. With the revolver, swing out the cylinder and dump out the cartridges or spent shell casing from the cylinder.

Most shooters take the magazine out of the handgun and place it back in their maga-

zine pouch on their belt, but there's nothing to say you can't press the magazine release button and let it fall to the ground. Once the magazine is out, pull the slide to the rear and lock the slide open with the slide stop. Show the RO that the chamber is empty, they will physically look at it. Once the RO has looked into the chamber and verified that the chamber is empty, the RO will give the command, "If clear, slide down, hammer down and holster." What this means is that the RO is telling the shooter to let the slide go down. With a revolver, swing out the cylinder and show the RO the empty cylinder, then close the cylinder and holster the revolver. With the semi-auto pistol, let the slide down by pulling the slide back slightly, letting the slide stop release from the slide, and easing it down quickly.

Never let the slide slam down on an empty chamber. It doesn't really hurt service-type pistol like the Glock, Springfield XD, Smith and Wesson M&P, or various Sigs, Berettas, and such, but with a match pistol like the 1911 that's had a trigger job, letting the slide slam down on an empty chamber by releasing the slide stop, and slamming it home is the fastest way to ruin that expensive trigger job you paid for. The reason is that when the slide slams home, inertia also forces the hammer forward and down onto the sear. The hammer hooks, which are resting on the sear nose, are driven hard onto the sear nose and damage the carefully honed primary and secondary sear angles. This destroys the trigger job in short order.

Simply guide the slide down by hand, and then, with the pistol pointed downrange, pull the trigger to let the hammer down and holster the pistol. Again, letting the slide slam forward on an empty chamber is never a good idea with any gun, it just needlessly accelerates the wear and tear on a gun, and as mentioned, service-type guns can take it, but a Match grade 1911 cannot. Also, remember that dry firing the pistol will not hurt either the 1911-type guns, or the striker-fired, or other service pistol type guns. Once you've holstered the pistol, the RO will announce "range is clear" and at this point you can move forward of the firing line and check and score the target with the RO.

RELOAD DRILLS

If you are interested in becoming more proficient in the action shooting sports, practicing the reloads is essential. All of the action sports (IPSC, IDPA, GSSF, 3-gun) require that the shooter fire a certain number of rounds, then either advance to another shooting position or engage a different set of targets, reloading in between or, sometimes, reloading either before or after the shooter

moves from one position or another. Again, different games have different rules, and all while the clock is running. Fortunately, this is a skill that can be learned since it's all about fundamentals and muscle memory. Once the shooter understands the physical mechanics, it's really just a matter of practicing and being able to repeat the drills on command in a match situation.

One point to remember when reloading the semi-auto pistol is to keep the finger out of the trigger guard, and keep the pistol at eye level and bring the pistol closer to the face. Watch the magazine go into the magazine well, and into the pistol. Seat the magazine, then extend the arms, pick up the sights and continue firing.

The type of competition you are engaged

Here, my son Kyle fires a series of modified Bill Drills at the silhouette target, where he fires two rounds, reloads and fires two more.

Here, the magazine is inserted into the pistol, with the pistol held at eye level as the shooter "looks" the magazine into the gun.

While walking the figure eight around the barrels and engaging the target at close range, Mike shows how to use good footwork while executing a reload on the move. These types of drills are shot at close range since the idea is to reinforce how to use good footwork and reloading skills, without needing to concentrate on marksmanship as much since the targets are close.

in will determine what type of reloading you will perform. In USPSA, the type of reload performed is the emergency reload, where the targets are engaged and at a convenient point, the magazine in the firearm is dumped on the ground while the pistol is recharged with a fresh magazine.

In IDPA, there are two reloads permitted, the emergency reload and the tactical reload, or reload with retention. In this scenario, the magazine is not just dumped on the ground, but has to be retained on the shooter during the entire string. Additionally, all reloading of the firearm needs to be performed behind cover, not so in USPSA. Always consult the rulebook of the form of competition you are engaged in for specifics.

Footwork when reloading is critical, the shooter needs to be able to move and reload at the same time.

Regardless of the type of competitive shooting you are engaged in, there are some fundamentals of reloading the pistol that are common to any type of practical shooting.

The main point is that the finger must come out of the trigger guard as soon as the reload is initiated. The second is the pistol is held at eye level and drawn close to the face. The thumb presses the magazine release button and at the same time the weak hand moves toward the fresh magazine, assuming this is an emergency reload.

CHAPTER TWELVE

HANDLOADING

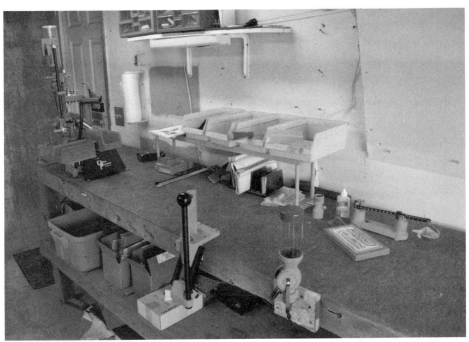

Reloading can lower the cost of shooting, and allows the shooter to tailor the load to the particular gun or shooting sport.

In order to become proficient at any sport, the participant needs to practice, and shooting is no different. This practice is a good news / bad news relationship. There's a correlation between the amount of good practice and the rise in skill level. That's the good news. The bad news is that live fire practice tends to get expensive fairly quickly. There are some things we can do to help alleviate the pain in the wallet created by hours of practice and thousands of rounds of downrange.

One way to help lower the cost of practice doesn't cost a dime; it's dry fire. We

talked about that in the chapter on marksmanship, and it's so critical to improving one's skill with a handgun that I wanted to mention it in this chapter as well.

The other way to get in a large amount of practice at a low cost is to acquire a handgun that is similar to the firearm that you intend to use in competition, but in .22 LR chambering. A box of .22 rimfire is about $6 for 50 rounds, whereas, a box of 50 centerfire ammunition is about five times that amount. So, to equate the two, we can get five times the amount of practice with a .22 rimfire that we can with the centerfire gun. Again, it's

The Redding micrometer dies and the Redding competition press make an excellent combination for single stage reloading for games like silhouette, where it's about creating small amounts of precision ammunition and not about volume.

not an exact comparison, but the fundamentals that we can practice are similar between the centerfire and the rimfire, all things being equal.

The third way to get more practice and lower the cost of ammunition is what most shooters eventually do, and that is to reload their spent brass. Reloading has many benefits to the shooter besides just lowering the cost of shooting. It also allows the shooter to tailor the load to the particular gun or shooting sport.

Ammunition is manufactured in batches, or lots. These lots are numbered at the factory for quality control and liability purposes. If there is an issue with a single loaded round, the factory can trace the round back to the lot and the date and time it was manufactured.

Our pistolsmith had access to his ammo bunker, which contained tens of thousands of rounds of factory ammunition stacked on wooden pallets, each divided into lots by lot numbers. Each gun was tested in the off season to determine which lot produced the best group out of a particular pistol. All of the service teams do this. The civilian shooter doesn't have the luxury of being able to test two or three dozen different of lots of factory ammunition, then once they find the lot that shoots the best, having thousands of

rounds of loaded ammo available for that gun. However, the civilian shooter can do something similar, but on a smaller scale, and this is where reloading comes in.

Another benefit of reloading, besides allowing the shooter to save money and practice more, and besides tailoring the load to the individual gun for best accuracy, is that it is a great hobby to get into, is easy to learn

The Hornady single stage reloading press is also a very good choice for the single stage reloader.
Image courtesy Hornady Mfg.

and once the initial expense of equipment is purchased, can last for decades. It gets the shooter more involved in the shooting sports and increases the shooter's knowledge of two of the four areas of ballistics: internal and external (the other two being terminal and forensic ballistics). The last benefit of reloading is cost savings. Most new shooters are unaware of how much money they can actually save by reloading. As an example, a typical 30-06 cartridge costs around a dollar a shot for factory ammunition. The most expensive cost of the cartridge is the brass case because of the steps and tooling needed to manufacture the component. A little over half of the cost of that loaded cartridge is the brass, so by reloading and reusing that component, about 54% of the price of the cartridge is saved by reloading, so the shooter saves over half of the cost of the box of ammunition.

By reloading your own ammunition, you can custom craft the ammo to tailor it for the individual pistol, can gain knowledge about firearms in general, can actually make better than factory ammo as far as accuracy is concerned, and can save a ton of money to boot. What's not to love?

So, now that I have you excited about getting into reloading and have convinced you of the benefits of "rolling your own" ammunition, let's get started on the fundamentals of how to create good quality ammunition on your own.

The first thing to know about reloading is that it's safe, as long as certain rules are followed. Safety is paramount with anything, and loading ammunition is no different. Modern smokeless powder has enormous energy potential and burns at a very fast rate, but does not explode, and is very safe to handle, much safer, in fact, than older black powders. Primers are explosive by their very nature, but are only really dangerous if set off all at once, so careful handling, including safety glasses, is mandatory. Having said that, I would guess that there are tens of millions of rounds of ammunition handloaded by shooters across the country every year without incident. Handloading is a very safe and enjoyable hobby

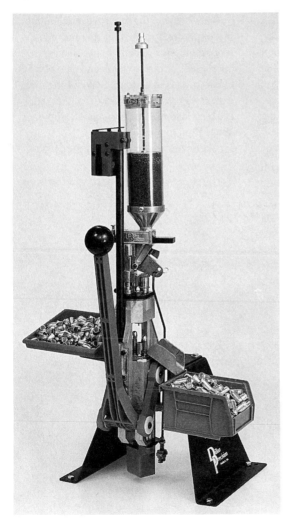

The Dillon Square Deal is an economical reloader capable of cranking out 350 rounds an hour. Image courtesy Dillon Reloading.

where common sense and a few simple safety precautions will go a very long way.

There are two types of reloading presses that reloaders use, the single stage press and the progressive press. These are two different machines although, fundamentally, they both perform the same steps. The progressive reloading press is a little more automated and can reload much more ammunition per hour than a single stage press.

The type of press you choose will be determined by the type of shooting game you get into. For most handgun competitors, the progressive reloading press will be the one to use, because competitive handgunners, even those who compete at local weekend matches, consume a large amount of ammunition, especially when you include practice ammo and match ammo.

For example, a typical steel-type match will require around 250 rounds. To load that much ammunition on a single stage press would take a full day. Add weekly practice ammo on top of that, and the ammunition requirements for even a casual weekend shooter skyrockets to maybe a 500-600 rounds a week. Serious IPSC, IDPA, 3-gun, steel shooters, and action pistol competitors will shoot many times that. When I shot bullseye with the Army team, we would shoot about 200 rounds a day, and then a match of 300 rounds on the weekend, not including team matches. To load that much ammunition on a single stage press would take more time to reload than it would to shoot, so we need a faster way to make a large quantity of high quality ammunition.

This is where the progressive reloading machine comes in. A basic and inexpensive progressive reloading machine can be purchased for around $500 and can load 500 to 600 rounds in an hour. Some of the more expensive presses can cost twice that, but can also load over twice as much ammo, or about 1200 rounds in an hour.

There are several brands of progressive

You can buy the Hornady Lock and Load Kit that includes virtually everything you need to get started in the hobby of reloading. Image courtesy Hornady Mfg.

reloading presses available on the market. They are made by Lee Precision, RCBS, Hornady, and the one that started it all, Dillon Precision. One thing to remember about progressive reloading presses is that just because they are used mostly by competitive handgunners to load a large quantity of ammunition, the machine is not restricted to just loading handgun ammunition. It can load a wide variety of bottlenecked rifle ammo as well. If you have an AK or AR style rifle, or a rifle that you just want to go out and bang away with, as well as a handgun or three for competition, it just makes sense, unless you are independently wealthy, to reload in order to feed these hungry beasts.

The progressive reloading press employs a turret system in order to put the required dies into a specific order. Also attached to the press is a powder measure, and a long primer tube to feed the primers to the system. I'll discuss progressive presses more a bit later.

The second method of reloading is primarily reserved for rifle shooters. The single stage reloading press is designed to create a very uniform and consistent reloaded cartridge. In the precision rifle game, cartridge case necks are measured and trimmed for length and runout, primer pockets are reamed, and a host of other case preparation techniques are used in order to create the most absolute uniform loaded round possible. In the rifle game, the shooter may need only a few dozen rounds or less. In the benchrest game, the cartridge is reloading right at the shooting bench. Rifles are used more for precision, and therefore, there is more emphasis on making every cartridge as perfect and consistent as humanly possible.

Where the single stage press comes into play in the pistol game is silhouette shoot-

The Dillon RL550b is the workhorse in progressive reloading presses. This press will run about $500 and can load around 500 rounds in a single hour. Image courtesy Dillon Reloading.

This Hornady ultrasonic cartridge case cleaner is a great way to get the fired cases cleaned and prepped for reloading. Image courtesy Hornady Mfg.

ing, where there may be only a hundred rounds fired in a day, and those rounds have to be as consistent and accurate as possible because of the nature of the targets and the distances involved. Silhouette shooing is like the slow fire stage of a bullseye course; time limits are generally very generous, the target is small, and the precise accuracy needed to knock down the chickens, pigs, turkeys and rams is substantial.

So, getting started with reloading equipment depends largely on the type of competitive shooting you will be doing. Let's take a look at getting started with the progressive reloading machine, assuming you are interested in competing in one of the action shooting events, such as IPSC, IDPA, steel challenge or NRA action pistol.

One caveat to this chapter, if you are interested in getting into bullseye, I would reload for timed and rapid fire stages, and for practice at fifty yard for the slow fire match. If actually in a match, I would use factory ammunition at the 50-yard line, and have the pistol zeroed for that ammunition prior to the match. Know what the scope or iron sight settings are for that load, keeping in mind that a change in ammunition lot numbers, even within manufacturers of the same ammunition, bullet weight, etc., can make a huge different in the gun's point of aim and subsequent zero. You don't want to get up to the firing line and being the slow fire match using a different lot number of factory ammunition and realize the first shot out of the gun is a high left six. The reason you want to use factory ammo for the slow fire stage is that it's difficult to get the kind of *consistent* accuracy needed at the 50-yard line from handloaded ammunition. With the factory ammo, if a shot is bad and you didn't call it, it was probably you that broke your concentration and weren't able to call the shot. If you shoot reloaded ammo and the shot is bad and you can't call it, was it you

breaking your concentration, or was it the fault of the ammo, as flyers are more prevalent with reloaded ammunition?

So, you want to get started in the action sports and you want to shoot a lot of ammo – good! There are several companies and reloaders to get you started. In basic terms, and regardless of the manufacturer, the progressive reloader basically works like this: The turret on the press is at the heart of the system, and is analogous to a little assembly line. I'll use the popular Dillon RL550b, which is an excellent starter system, as an example, but other manufacturers like RCBS, Hornady and Lee, also make great products.

The Dillon has four stations. Station #1 is where the pistol case is deprimed and resized. In this operation, a cleaned and empty spent case is placed onto the turret tray.

The Hornady single stage reloading press is also a very good choice for the single stage reloader.

The Dillon D-Terminator electronic scale really speeds up the time it takes to measure individual powder charges, or to calibrate the powder measure for either a progressive press or on a single stage system. Image courtesy Dillon Reloading.

The sizing die deprimes the case, sizes the case back to factory specifications, and gets the case ready for the next step. Image courtesy Dillon Reloading.

The seating die seats the bullet after the case has been charged with powder. Image courtesy Dillon Reloading.

When the handle of the press is lowered, simultaneously the ram, or turret is raised, the empty case is run up into the resizing die, and at the same time the spent primer is punched out of the case. This operation, besides punching out the primer, resizes the case walls back down to factory SAAMI specifications. The press handle is lowered and the fresh primer is seated into the case. The turret is then rotated clockwise, and now, the primed and resized case from Station #1 is moved over to Station #2, and a new, spent case is placed onto the tray at Station #1.

The press handle is lowered, raising the ram and turret back up, which deprimes the case in Station #1; the case at Station #2 gets the case mouth flared and the powder charge dumped into the empty case. So this time there were two operations performed simultaneously, instead of just one operation as with a single stage press. When the handle is lowered, the case in Station #2 is now primed, charged with powder and the case mouth slightly flared in order to more easily seat the bullet, while the case in Station #1 is deprimed, resized and re-primed with a new

primer. The turret is rotated again clockwise, and a new, cleaned case is inserted into Station #1, and a bullet is seated onto the case mouth at Station #3. Now, when the ram handle is raised, the case in Station #1, is resized, and deprimed, the case in Station #2 is charged with powder, and the case mouth is flared, and the case in Station #3 has the bullet seated to the proper depth.

When the turret handle is lowered, the case in Station #1 is reprimed. Now we have performed three operations on three different cartridge cases with just one cycle of the handle. We rotate the turret clockwise again, and place an empty case in Station #1, and a bullet onto the case mouth at Station #3 and lower the turret handle again. Now, the case at Station #4 has its case mouth slightly crimped, the case at Station #3 has the bullet seated, the case at Station #2 has the case mouth flared and a powder charge dumped into it, and the case at Station #1 has its case resized and deprimed. On lowering the handle all the way, the case at Station #1 has the primer seated.

We now have all four stations going and each station is performing an operation with a single pull of the handle. Additionally, now that we have all four stations going, remember that every pull of the handle produces a high quality loaded round of ammunition. As long as we have powder in the powder measure, primers in the primer tube, empty cases and bullets to seat, we can load very high quality ammunition all day long. This is why these machines can produce 5-600 rounds an hour.

I should mention a few details about the operation at Station #4, however. In this operation, when the loaded cartridge is run up into the die, the case mouth is crimped slightly in order to properly grip the bullet

The crimping die closes, or crimps, the case mouth to lock the bullet into the case. Image courtesy Dillon Reloading.

and provide enough tension to hold the bullet in place. This operation is extremely critical, especially when the cartridge is used in a semi-auto handgun. Cartridges like the .45 ACP, 9mm and others in the same class, are straight-walled rimless cases. This means that the rim on the base of the cartridge does not extend out past the body of the case, so this makes it a "rimless" case. These types of cases headspace on the mouth of the case. There are four types of cartridge cases: rimmed, rimless, semi-rimmed and belted. All cartridges cases, from the .22 LR up to the 40mm, fall into one category or the other. Rimless cases, like the .45 ACP and all others in this category, headspace on the mouth of the case. This means that the chamber dimension is measured from the breech face, to the case mouth. What is headspace? Simply the distance from the breechface of the firearm, to the point of the chamber that stops the forward movement of the cartridge. In the case of the straight-walled rimless case like the .45 ACP, the case mouth is the point where the cartridge stops when the round is chambered. It's for this reason that you have to be careful when setting the crimp on these types of cartridges. If there is too much crimp applied to the case, it has too effects. One is the chamber pressure goes up because the bullet is being held too tightly, and for too long for the burn rate of the powder. The second and more important point is since this case headspaces on the case mouth, we can have an effect on the way the case is chambered. It will seat too deeply into the chamber, causing failures to fire, or if the gun does fire, the cartridge case will slam back against the breechface, the primer will flatten out, and a host of other very bad things could happen. So, we want to make sure the case mouth is crimped slightly, but not excessively.

So, now that you have an understanding of how a progressive reloading press reloads hundreds of rounds in an hour, let's turn our attention to the single stage presses and how they work. This section will be useful for the silhouette shooters or those who would like to get involved in the sport. Shooters wanting to get into silhouette can get involved with nothing more than the right firearms chambered for the lowly but mighty .22 LR, but for those who want to step up their

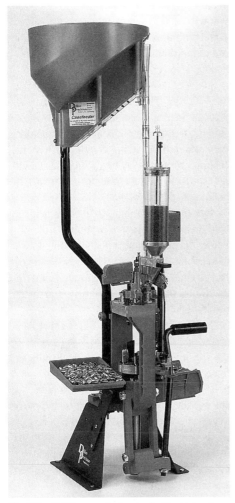

The Dillon 650 is a great reloader for the high volume club shooter that may shoot several practical shooting disciplines. This reloader is capable of putting out 800-1000 high quality rounds an hour. Image courtesy Dillon Reloading.

game, the unlimited class is where it's at.

In order to compete in the unlimited class of silhouette, you will need to reload rimless bottlenecked cartridges like the 7BR, 6BR, & TCU and other exotic calibers, and this will mean substituting the progressive press for a single stage press. Just like there is more than one company making progressive presses, there are more companies producing single stage presses. When I first got started in reloading, I was loading .223 cases in my Thompson Contender on an RCBS Rockchucker press, and this is still one of the oldest and most popular presses available. Fun fact: RCBS actually stands for Rock Chucker Bullet Swage, and the press was initially manufactured to swage lead cores into bullet jackets for shooting rockchucks at long range, a cousin of the Eastern woodchuck, out in the Western states. For my money, though, I use a single stage press from Redding Reloading. Other great manufacturers of single stage reloading presses are Lee and Hornady. These days, you really can't go wrong with any of these companies' products, either for progressive or single stage presses as they have been in business for decades, and make very solid products. It really comes down to personal preference.

For single stage presses, look ahead at the type of reloading you will be doing now and what you might be reloading for in the future. For example, if at get a starter press and decide to get into shooting some of the big belted magnums, or you decide to get into case forming or some other type of high pressure use of a reloading press, you will need a more powerful press in order to handle these heavy duty chores, so get one of the sturdiest ones you can. For now though, we'll concentrate on the standard "O" style presses, and look at the reloading process.

Regardless who made the press, all metallic cartridge reloading follows the same basic steps. Step number one, is to check the cases and clean them. If you are working with unfired brass, you will still need to check the cases for any defects and wipe off any residue. You want to keep cases clean so you don't damage the dies. Use a soft clean cloth to wipe them down. If using once-fired brass, then you'll need to tumble them in a case tumbler in order to remove the powder residue and to polish the case. When inspecting the cases, look for split necks, large bulges, dents, and other defects. Look for signs of excessive pressure, like flattened primers and swelling at the case head.

Any case that has defects such as these should be discarded. Small dents around the case mouth are inconsequential, as the expander ball on the sizing die should iron these out.

Once the cases have been cleaned and inspected, the next step is to lubricate the cases. A lack of case lube will result in a stuck case, but too much case lube is not good either. Try not to get lube on the necks as it will cause dents in the case shoulder. Note that we are reloading bottlenecked cases here. If you are reloading straight-walled cases with carbide dies, you will not need to lube the cases, as the carbide is slippery enough as it is. You will also need to clean out the case necks and place a little lube on the inside of the neck as well. This will perform two functions; it will make it easier to operate the press when sizing the cases, and it will prevent excess working on the brass, which will increase the life of the case. I usually lube inside every two or three cases inside the necks for easy reloading.

There are many types of case lube on the market, and try some different ones to see which you like. I like the original liquid lube and the case lube pads, but some people like the newer aerosol case lubes. I've used both and either will work well. Remember, the rule with case lube is the same as with most lubricants – a little goes a long way.

The next step is to install the shell holder onto the ram of the press. Make sure you are using the correct shell holder for the caliber you are loading. Most reloading press manufacturers make a quick reference chart showing which shell holder to use for each caliber. Next we need to install the sizer die. Lower the ram handle all the way to the down position, which raises the ram all the way to the top. Since we are talking about using steel dies, and not carbide dies, you will need to screw the die all the way down until the bottom of the die touches the top of the shell holder, then raise the press handle to lower the ram and screw the die in another $\frac{1}{4}$ to $\frac{1}{8}$th of a turn and secure the die lock ring. The die is now in the correct position to properly resize the case. Make sure the decapping pin is protruding below the bottom of the sizing die. So, we have the cases lubed and ready to go, and the sizing die is mounted on the press and correctly positioned.

I usually have about 30-50 cases that I'm loading at a time, just to make it worth my while. I keep them set up in a loading block to keep them organized. This way, I can do each step in order to all of the cases and I'll make sure that no case gets missed in the process.

Now, take the case, set it in the shellholder and run the ram up so the case goes all the way up into the die. Raise the handle and lower the case, all the way. The case has now been resized and deprimed, At this point, we can use the priming attachment on the press to reprime the case, and many shooters do it this way, but I prefer to re-prime the cases in a separate step. I use a handheld priming tool as this give me a better "feel" when seating the primer.

Remember, rifle accuracy is all about consistency, and primer seating is a very critical step in achieving that consistency. The reason for that is the primer is made

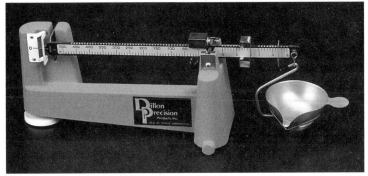

The Dillon eliminator scale uses a balance beam to set the powder charge. This is a slower but less expensive alternative to the electronic scales. Image courtesy Dillon Reloading.

up of multiple parts. One of those parts is a little anvil, on top of which rests the primer pellet. The anvil has feet on it, which rests on the bottom of the primer cup. When the firing pin or striker impacts the primer cup, it slams the anvil and the priming pellet together, and the priming pellet detonates, creating a flame that rushes through the flash hole into the cartridge case and igniting the powder charge. The reason to prime by hand is that seating the primer is very much a process that is accomplished by feel. The primer MUST be seated on the bottom of the primer pocket. Not only seated, but seated with a little bit of force, to make sure the feet of the primer anvil are making contact with the primer pocket and that the primer anvil is slightly "cocked" or exerting a little pressure on the priming pellet. This ensures that the pellet is crushed with the same consistency every time. Many reloaders don't think they get the same feel of the seating pressure that's applied to the primer with the large, heavy ram and with the camming power of the press handle. It's a little like hammering a nail with a sledgehammer. The hand held priming tools gives the reloader the feel necessary to get the prime seated *properly* and with consistency.

If this is the first time we've reloaded this case, we probably don't need to check the overall case length. If the case has been reloaded more than a few times, especially if we are loading with close to max loads, the cases have a tendency to stretch, so it's always a good idea to check the overall length of the case after sizing them. Look at the reloading book you are using to develop your loads and, with a good micrometer, check the case to make sure it's under the maximum length. If it isn't, then you need to trim the cases. There are several good trimmers on the market, some of them are manual type trimmers that you crank by hand that are available for less than a hundred bucks, up to deluxe models that are powered by electric motors that can trim hundreds of rounds an hour, and cost upwards of $300.

Once the cases are the proper length, the case mouths need to be chamfered and deburred. There's a small hand tool that does this job quickly and cleanly. The case mouths, after being trimmed, will be left with burrs and sharp edges on the case mouth. These burrs and sharp edges need to be removed in order for the bullet to slide easily into the case when we get to bullet seating. Scratches on the bullet jackets can actually upset the balance and spin characteristics, and impact the flight dynamics of the bullet slightly. If you are loading straight-walled pistol cases in your single stage press, you'll need to expand the case mouth prior to bullet seating, but since we're talking about bottlenecked cases for silhouette competition, we can skip this step, since the expander ball on the decapping pin has already performed this step for us.

The next step in the process is to prime the case. There are a couple of ways to accomplish this. I've already discussed how to reprime the case with the priming attachment on the press itself, but a better way is to use a dedicated hand-held or bench-mounted priming tool. Use the primer tray to flip the primers so they are anvil side up. Take care when handling primers, especially ensure that your fingers are free of oil or dirt. Oil can affect the detonating properties of the primer pellet, and can be the cause of misfires if too much oil gets into the primer. Once the primers have been flipped in the primer tray, set the primer in the hand-priming tool and seat the primer.

Remember, the hand tool will be much faster and do a better job at priming than using the primer attachment on the press itself. It also helps with getting the proper primer sensitivity when the primer is seated by feel with the hand-priming tool. I recently picked up a new RCBS hand-priming tool that I really like. This tool makes the job quick and easy.

Once the primer has been seated, do a quick check that the primer has been seated slightly below flush with the bottom of the case by running your finger over the case head. If the primer is above the case head, the primer needs to be reseated.

WARNING – DO NOT reseat a high primer on a loaded cartridge!! If the case has powder, a seated bullet and the primer needs to be reseated, the reloader MUST pull the bullet, dump the powder and THEN reseat the primer, recharge the case with powder, and reseat the bullet.

Another good reason for using the hand primer is that is the reloader has a tight primer pocket, or if the primer is slightly larger in diameter, it might be difficult to seat. In this case, if the primer simply cannot be seated between flush and .005 inch below flush with the case head, deprime the case and put the primer in a coffee can with motor oil, which will neutralize the primer. We will need to perform a separate step to these cases, which will be to ream out the primer pocket to make the dimensions of the primer pocket absolutely uniform. In fact, the tool used to do this procedure is called a primer pocket uniformer. Modern cartridge cases are made with such quality control measures that this step is usually not needed, but it does happen. Some precision shooters who are obsessed with accuracy, like the benchrest shooting crowd, perform this step routinely on all of their cases. Several companies make primer pocket reamers to do this step, and it only takes a minute and a couple of quick swipes with this tool. Look for primer pocket uniforming tools where you buy your reloading supplies. It only takes a second with a quick twist of the wrist to make the primer pocket uniform to SAAMI specification, and it can really help with proper primer seating.

The cases are now sized, trimmed, if necessary, and the primers are seated properly. The next step is to charge the case with powder. To do this, we need to consult the reloading manual to see which powder to use and what charge to start with. Remember, always start at 10 percent BELOW what the manual calls for and work your way up. I usually pick something a little below a max charge then start 10-12 percent below that. Or you can pick a mid-range load and go with that. One other rule when reloading is to only have one type of bullet/primer/powder on the reloading bench at a time. It's a good idea to put away all of the components except the ones being used at that time. That way, there's a reduced chance of getting components mixed up.

Once you've selected a powder and a powder charge, fill the powder measure with powder and get the scale ready. There are two kinds of scales: the manual, or beam-type scale, and electronic.

Electronic scales are much faster and some are programmable, where the reloader simply types in the desired charge, and the electronic scale and attached powder measure dispenses the exact amount of powder. As good as the electronic scales are, and I do like them, the beam-type scale is still very useful to double check the charges being dispensed, whether from an electronic scale or, especially, straight from the powder measure.

Assuming we are using the beam-type scale with the powder measure, I use the scale to set the proper charge with coming out of the measure, and triple-check it, and then I usually use the scale to double check every 10-12 rounds or so, that the measure is still dispensing the correct amount. If there is a discrepancy of more than a tenth of a grain or so, I'll need to dump all of the charges and start over. Better to take a little time to re-charge the cases, rather than have a catastrophic accident with an over-charge or, worse, a double charge. Not only that, but remember, accuracy with reloaded ammunition is all about consistency, and powder weight variations make a huge difference in velocity and point of impact.

Now that we have the cases sized, primed, and charged, the next step is to seat the bullet. To do this, we should have already removed the sizing die from the press. We now need to install the bullet seating die. There are two basic types of seating dies: a basic stem seater and a micrometer seating die. The basic stem seating dies do a great job in doing what they're supposed to: that is, seat the bullet to the proper depth. A micrometer seating die does the same thing, but adds a micrometer on top of the die. This gives the reloader the ability to precisely seat the bullet in .001-inch increments. Why is this important? Because seating depth has a huge influence on bullet accuracy. The chamber of the barrel has a section called the throat, sometimes called the "leade." This section of the chamber is located just ahead of the neck, and is a section just wider than bullet diameter, and has no rifling which is called "freebore." It usually extends for .010 to .020 inch and then the rifling will gradually start, reaching full depth in about .030 or so, depending on caliber.

The distance between the curve of the bullet and the spot on the rifling where the bullet touches is critical to accuracy. The longer the bullet "jumps" before it hits and engages the rifling, the more chances that the bullet will not enter exactly on center. If the bullet enters the rifling and the barrel off-center, it will surely exit off center. There

The Dillon stainless steel case gauges are a quick way to check the overall length of the cases. It's a good way to QC your cases. Image courtesy Dillon Reloading.

is a reason there is a freebore area and a long leade angle. There has to be ample time for the case to expand, and the bullet to exit the case mouth and gas needs to escape in order for pressures to drop to safe levels. Adjusting the distance of this bullet jump is one of the ways reloaders can affect bullet accuracy.

For every rifle/bullet/powder combination, there is a sweet spot where the bullet jump is the smallest and accuracy is the best. Some benchrest shooters actually have the bullet making slight contact with the rifling as the bolt is closed. These shooters are highly advanced at reloading and this technique should not be tried by the average reloading enthusiast. All of this brings us back to the micrometer seating die. By experimenting with the seating depth of the bullet, we can influence the accuracy of the rifle/load combination and find that sweet spot. Sometimes, just a few thousandths of an inch one way or another can have a huge effect on accuracy of a particular load in a particular rifle. Naturally, since we are making precise measurements, we need precise tools, and the reloader has no shortage of measuring instruments.

A good set of calipers, either mechanical or digital, is essential, and there are all manner of other types of tools to help make finding the right depth simple and easy. A good way to find out about what tools are worth the money is to talk with your reloading buddies at the range. Also, remember that a good set of micrometer dies is not just for bottle-necked rifle type cases. Handgun cases also benefit from precise bullet seating, especially with heavy recoiling rounds like the .44 MAG and others that need precise crimping to keep the bullet in place during heavy recoil.

One thing that a reloader needs to have is a good notebook. The best reloaders are great at taking and keeping notes. If you can keep track of all of the variables, and how you made adjustments to those variables, and what results those adjustments did to the size of the group, the better and more enjoyable your shooting will be. You don't even need to keep track of all of the variables, just the most important ones.

But keep in mind that the more detailed the notes, the more you can spot trends and see what affect the changes are having in group sizes. By keeping track of things like bullet type and weight and lot number, power type, charge and lot number, type of brass, seating depth, primer type, and other important data, and what the group size was for these combinations, the reloader will soon find combinations that work for a particular rifle, or even type of rifle. If you are a silhouette competitor, long-range accuracy is the name of the game, so the more accurate the load, the better your results will be, all thing being equal. The more successful competitors will keep track of their reloading data and refer to it often. Also, remem-

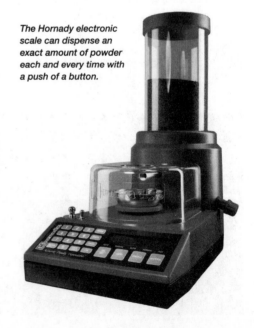

The Hornady electronic scale can dispense an exact amount of powder each and every time with a push of a button.

ber to include atmospheric conditions that were present at the range during shooting, as barometric pressure and temperature can have a huge effect on velocity and subsequent group size.

So the next step in the reloading process is to seat the bullet, and we have decided to use the micrometer seating die. Put the seating die into the press and, with a case in the shellholder, run the ram up to the top of the stroke. Next, screw the die body down into the press until it stops. At this point,

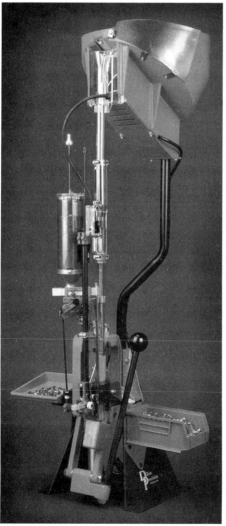

the crimping shoulder of the die is making contact with the top of the case mouth. We don't want to crimp the case, so back off the die about a full turn, and set the die in place with the lock ring. Next, back out the micrometer seating plug so we don't accidently seat a bullet in too deeply, and lower the ram. Set a primed and charged case into the shellholder, and lower the ram handle slightly, place a bullet onto the case mouth, and hold it in place while lowering the ram handle, raising the ram up into the seating die. Lower the ram, take the cartridge off of the shellholder and measure the overall length of the case. Look to your reloading manual to see what the maximum overall length should be. If you have data that gives a recommended seating depth, use the micrometer adjustments on the seating die to get the loaded cartridge to the optimal overall length.

If you, as a silhouette competitor, are reloading and competing with a bottle-necked cartridge, like the 6 and 7 BR, check out the neck sizing dies that are available from many manufacturers. What these dies do is, when the fired case is run up into the die, the case is only sized, or squeezed down in the neck area. This leaves the shoulder and the case body virtually the exact size of the firearms' chamber. Why is this important? Because when the case is full length resized, it tends to work the case by expanding during firing, and then squeezing it down, expanding and squeezing. This will cause the brass to flow towards the front of the case, and is what leads to case head separation. Neck sizing only works the case neck, and will give longer case life. The downside is that the cases, since they are exactly the same size as

The Dillon RL-550 is a very popular and economical way to load a large quantity of high quality ammunition needed to compete in practical shooting events like IDPA, USPSA, or even 25-yard ammunition for bullseye. Image courtesy Dillon Reloading.

the chamber, can only be used in the firearm they were formed in; they are not interchangeable with other firearms in the same chambering. There is a huge upside by using this technique, though. The cases, since they are sized exactly with the chamber, will be positioned in the chamber exactly on center with the bore, assuming the chamber is centered. With a case that is unfired, or full-length resized, the case, because it's a loose fit, will not be sitting on center with the axis of the barrel, so the bullet will get be a little off-center when entering the rifling. With a case that is neck sized, the case is already expanded and the case and bullet should be centered up with the bore. So, with neck sizing, you get longer case life and better accuracy. Sounds like a win-win.

Along with the reloading process, there are some tools that have been developed by some ingenious people to help measure, test and verify the accuracy and velocity our firearms, and factory and hand loaded ammunition.

The first of these tools is the Ransom rest. In a former life, I was a chief gunsmith for a classified DoD facility where I was responsible for building and testing various small arms for U.S. Special Operations. One of those small arms systems was the 1911. Every pistol that we built, I, and a small team were building them for over a decade, was individually tested using a Ransom rest. I personally built and tested over 500 custom 1911 handguns for those units, and we literally could not have done our job without the Ransom rest since the customer had very specific accuracy requirements.

The Ransom rest is a very well-engineered tool that enables the gunsmith, reloader or hobbyist to determine the accuracy level of a particular handgun, ammunition or handgun/ammunition combination. If you need to test ammunition, the reloader will get best results by using a gun of known accuracy in the rest. Using a handgun with a well-fitted, match-grade barrel will produce excellent results. The Ransom rest works by taking out the element of human error when test handguns and ammunition. The handgun is clamped into the padded rest, and the trigger is pressed by an actuator bar. The rest has a spring loaded dampening system that works very well. It can handle the largest magnums with very consistent results. The handgun inserts are molded for individual handguns, and for some custom guns they will need to be trimmed, for things

Here I'm testing a batch of Black Hills ammunition through my bullseye pistol for accuracy the only way it should be tested, over a Ransom rest. This device takes out the human factor of accuracy testing. Also note the Oehler 35P chronograph. This is a great way to test both accuracy and velocity of a cartridge/gun combination at the same time.

like extended thumb safeties on 1911s, for example.

To use the system, the rest needs to be mounted onto a piece of plywood and elevated off of the shooting table. I use C-clamps to attach the plywood base to the shooting bench, which must be solidly mounted to the ground. In my days as a DoD contractor, our shooting bench was portable, but the tabletop was made from a steel plate and weighted down with rectangular steel bars, and weighed close to a hundred pounds. The legs had four-inch spikes on the feet to help anchor it into the ground. Currently, at my local range, we have typical T-shaped concrete shooting benches that the plywood can be C-clamped onto. The plywood base that the rest is screwed into needs to be elevated off of the shooting bench. The instructions for setting up the plywood base for the Ransom rest come with the unit and work very well.

Once the Ransom rest and plywood base is clamped onto the shooting table, the handgun gets mounted into the rest inserts, and the three star knobs labeled A, B and C, get tightened in AB, AB, then C order. These star knobs need to be only tightened with the fingers, never tighten with tools.

With the 1911 pistol, make sure all safeties are depressed before final tightening or the gun won't fire. I always cycle the gun a few times, dryfiring the pistol a few times prior to loading any ammunition. Also, when using the Ransom rest, make sure that the gun is not raised or lowered by handling the gun, always use the ledge cast in the Ransom rest provided for that purpose. The actuator bar needs to be placed into the center of the trigger for best results, and with DA revolvers, make sure that the trigger returns fully after firing. This is where dryfiring the pistol becomes crucial.

Once the pistol is set up and ready to go, and has been dryfired and cycled in the rest to make sure it will function properly, the next step is to actually load the pistol and send some rounds downrange. With the semi-auto pistol, raise the pistol, lock the slide back, and insert the loaded magazine into the pistol. Before you lower the pistol, let the slide go forward chambering the first round, and then push the pistol down by using the ledge, until it hits the elevation stop. Start firing, if you are using a 7-round magazine, fire five rounds, and lift the pistol and insert a fresh magazine. This does a couple of things. First, the very first round was

Another shot of the Ransom rest where I'm getting ready to accuracy test some of my handloads.

chambered from a slide open position, and wasn't cycled through the gun like it subsequent rounds are. This round will have a slightly different point of impact because of the way the round is fed into the gun. Also, when the first magazine of ammunition is run through the gun, it will "settle" into the rest inserts. The gun's point of impact will rise up about an inch per shot at 25 yards as the gun is settling in.

Once the gun starts to produce a nice, round group, then we can start to test the ammunition or the gun for accuracy. At this point, I'll place a fresh target on the target frame with the center of the target over the group we just shot. Another point to remember about the Ransom rest is to not shoot the gun dry when firing groups. I always fire five-shot groups with a seven or eight shot magazine. If the gun is shot dry and a fresh magazine inserted to continue the group, nine times out of ten that shot will be a flyer.

Two last points when using the Ransom rest are that, when discussing accuracy, consistency is the key. Pushing down the rest after each shot with the same pressure, and actuating the trigger with the same pressure and touch, will yield consistent results. The last point of the Ransom rest is that if the handgun has had ANY trigger work done to it, the gun should be fired with only two rounds at a time until you are sure that the gun is safe to fire. If the gun doubles, that is, fires two rounds at once, or the hammer won't stay cocked when the slide is returned to battery, take the pistol out of the Ransom rest and have the pistol checked by a competent gunsmith. Never stand over the top of the Ransom rest while firing, always stand off to the side in case the gun doubles.

We ran into instances with older National Match frames where the inserts were tightened so firmly that the trigger would not return to the forward position, and we had to back out the star knobs slightly until the trig-

ger popped forward. The Ransom rest is an outstanding tool and can really demonstrate real accuracy from any gun and ammunition. There are a wide variety of inserts for most of the popular pistols, including the polymer-framed guns. These polymer guns need to be handled a little differently. Since the guns' frames can be squeezed much more than a steel or alloy framed gun, the answer is to tighten these guns almost, but not quite as tight as a steel gun, but also, these guns need to be shot many more rounds than a steel framed gun to "settle" it into the inserts. A steel gun may take 8-10 rounds to settle it in, but the polymer-framed guns may need to have 25 rounds before they are fully settled in and ready to begin testing. The shooter will know when to start testing when the settling groups are nice and round, not stringing vertically.

The next item I feel should be on every

Here I'm testing the excellent Federal 357 Hydra-Shok round through the S&W 686.

Another shot of the S&W 686 where I'm testing the Federal 38 Spl +P Hydra Shok.

tor. The M85 has replaced the M82, and can calculate functions like ballistic coefficients and rates of fire for machine guns. I was also fortunate enough to attend Dr. Oehler's two week ballistics course where he demonstrated and discussed not only the intricacies of the M35P, but also the discontinued M43, and the older industrial M82. He also talked at length about interior and exterior ballistics, and the properties of projectiles in flight. It was an eye-opening and an unbelievable experience for anyone into shooting, reloading and firearms.

shooter's short wish list would be a chronograph, and when it comes to discussing the state of the art for chronographs, it doesn't get any better than the iconic Oehler Model 35P from Dr, Ken Oehler.

I've owned two M35Ps over many years. I've also worked with the M82, which is the industrial version that I had available when I was the chief gunsmith for a DoD contrac-

The M43 also measures pressure, using a strain gauge. Dr. Oehler, a PhD in Electrical Engineering, invented the modern chronograph. He holds several patents for the chronograph, and his instruments are used by governments, commercial ballistics labs, and arsenals for over 40 years. There simply is none better. My 35P is indispensable for ammunition testing and load development.

Many of the action shooting games have what's called a "power factor" discussed in other sections of the book. This is where the ammunition has to have a minimum bullet weight and velocity. Can you just go by the velocity tables in a given reloading book to see if your handload meets this minimum velocity? Sure you could, but as you advance in ability and go to the

Here I'm testing a batch of factory Black Hills .45 ACP ammunition for accuracy and velocity using the Oehler 35P chronograph.

larger matches, they will test your ammunition to ensure it meets this minimum. Also, if your handload has too much velocity, you are burning excess powder and generating too much recoil, which translates into slower recovery times. Thus, your competition will have an advantage. It's in your best interest to gain every advantage you can in these fiercely competitive events.

One last point, the more velocity you generate, the more wear and tear there will be on you and your firearm. At the end of the day, fatigue will set in from the effects of recoil. Believe me, it makes a difference. A softer-shooting gun will not wear you out after a long day of shooting as will a harder recoiling pistol. So it's to a shooter's advantage to get the velocity as close to the lower limit as possible, without going below it.

Back to the 35P. The 35P and, for that matter, all chronographs work on a very simple principle. A bullet is fired through what's called photovoltaic sensors, which have diffusers mounted over the top of the sensors. In the 35Ps these diffusers are called skyscreens. The skyscreens actually function as diffusors, as they diffuse the sunlight coming down onto the sensors. The sensors detects the dark shadow of the bullet against the skyscreen as the bullet passes through the first screen, which is placed about 10 feet from the muzzle of the gun. When the bullet passes through the first screen, it starts an internal clock in the computer. The bullet keeps moving and is detected by a second screen, which placed a known distance apart from the first screen. Usually they are spaced four feet apart. When the bullet passes through the second screen the internal clock stops. The computer has a known distance between the two screens and calculates the velocity based on the time it took the bullet to travel the distance between the two screens. The Model 35P also has a third screen, located midway between the start

and stop screens. This is a Proof Screen or Proof Channel. It acts as a quality assurance check to make sure that the velocity reading you are receiving is relevant. So, if you get a reading of 9999 fps, then the 35P knows that this is wrong and the unit will automatically omit the reading and you can then fire another shot and continue testing.

So the chronograph not only allows the competitive shooter the ability to develop loads that comply with the rules of the game, it also allows the shooter to develop very consistent and accurate loads. For the bullseye shooter, this is extremely important. Most shooters use factory ammunition at 50 yards, but the competitor still needs to develop very accurate handloads for the 25-yard timed and rapid fire stages; otherwise it gets pretty expensive shooting factory ammunition at both yardages. For the practical pistol sports like IPSC, IDPA and others, accuracy is still important, as some of the shots may be longer, especially in IPSC, but also economy and reliability is also important. The chronograph allows the shooter to develop loads that deliver consistent velocity, which translates into improved accuracy. Also remember, manufacturing variations can cause unexpected results when handloading, and the chronograph allows the shooter to verify loads developed using data from the reloading manuals. All of the manufacturers that develop load data and publish loading books do a fantastic job of testing components before they put the loading data in the reloading manuals. However, all firearms and ammunition is manufactured with tolerances of plus or minus a certain amount. So, the chamber dimensions, the barrels' bore and groove dimensions, the dimensions of the case wall thickness, bullet jacket thickness, bullet hardness, and a hundred other factors are all variables that affect the chamber velocity and pressure readings. So the velocity of a given load in a manual is approximate, and is what the testing lab generated *in their firearm under controlled conditions.* This is why the manuals and a little common sense tells the reloader to begin load development by picking a load and backing off 10 percent and slowly working up to that load while watching for signs of pressure.

The chronograph is extremely useful for load development in finding the highest velocity, and the best accuracy from a given set of cartridge components and the individual firearm because all firearms are not created equal. They are close, but again, manufacturing tolerances being what they are, there are literally hundreds of variables that can affect velocity, pressure and accuracy in an individual firearm. So the chronograph becomes a very crucial tool in the process of load development, regardless of the shooting game the reloader is involved in. So now that I have you convinced you need a chronograph and what it does, let's get down to the nitty gritty. What does the output from the chronograph actually tell me?

When the reloader fires a series of shots, the 35P will show the Proof velocity, the Shot number, and the Primary Velocity, all on a single line. If the 35P detects an erroneous shot, it will print out an X, and the data is omitted. Notice I didn't say the data is erased. No load readings are ever erased from the memory. The X removes the data from the statistical summary, but it the data remains. When the Summary button is pressed, the 35P totals up the shot data and summarizes it. You will be given a printed display showing: Highest Velocity, Lowest Velocity, Extreme Velocity Spread, Mean or Average Velocity, and the Standard Deviation. For those shooters like myself who are mathematically challenged, this data provides important information about the load being tested. Of the information presented, I like to use the Mean as to whether or not the load I've selected and loaded for, is close to

High quality reloading dies like these will give excellent results for decades

what the velocity was in the manual I was using when developing the load. In other words, have I hit my target velocity? I try to start a little low from the manuals and work my way up to a max load, and this is where the chronograph really shines. The Extreme Spread tells me how consistent my reloading technique is, how good I am at throwing a powder charge. But the Standard Deviation really tells me how good the load is. The group shot with the load having the smallest SD may not be the smallest group size, but it is definitely the most consistent, and consistency is one of the fundamentals of accuracy. Standard Deviation is used in math to express confidence in the statistical conclusions.

To summarize, the two main tools for the serious reloader and competitor are the Ransom rest and Oehler 35P chronograph. The Ransom rest lets us test firearms using handloads and factory loads to see what the accuracy potential is with each of these components separately or together, and the chronograph lets us test those same factory loads and handloads for consistency and velocity using a statistical methodology.

CHAPTER THIRTEEN

CUSTOMIZING GUNS FOR COMPETITIVE SHOOTING

Proper eye safety is key anytime you are at the range. It needs to be comfortable and offer full protection, and should be designed specifically for shooting. These Wiley X glasses are an excellent choice. Image courtesy Brownells, Inc.

One of the great things about competitive pistol shooting is the fact that you can get into it with very little initial expense, depending on the game you choose. For example, I can go to my local range and shoot a monthly steel match with virtually any firearm I own. It could be an inexpensive used .22 pistol and five magazines and 250 rounds of ammunition, and I could literally shoot for the entire day with nothing else. I don't even need a holster, just a good, reliable firearm, ammunition, magazines and eye and ear protection.

Some other shooting games might take a bit more equipment, but still you need not much more than a good, reliable handgun in 9mm and above, reliable magazines, ammunition, a good quality holster and magazine pouches, and eye and ear protection to compete in IPSC, IDPA, and if the gun is a Glock, you can also shoot in the Glock Shooting Sports Foundation matches, as well as the aforementioned steel matches.

That's four shooting games with a single firearm, and if you have a good shotgun and an AR-15 type rifle, you can also shoot 3-gun matches, which are one of the most popular and fastest growing matches in the country. For Cowboy Action shooting, a good, stock Old West type revolver like a Ruger Blackhawk or a Uberti/Colt clone, a good, inexpensive double barreled shotgun, and a lever type rifle and you are good to go. This is not to say that there are no modifications allowed in SASS. Far from it, rather the type of modifications that are allowed are normally small, and that do not alter the basic stock configuration of the gun. Remember, in SASS, it's all about authenticity, down to the smallest detail on the costumes worn. For example, the screws on a revolver can be replaced from normal slot-type screws to more modern socket head screws, because that modification doesn't alter the outline and general authenticity of the gun. Looking at the pistol, you would probably not notice that the gun even had modern Allen head type cap screws. You can also perform what's known as a Manhattan Modification, where the percussion revolv-

Hearing protection is mandatory and these Peltors work great. Electronic hearing protection allows normal conversation while blocking out loud noises like gunfire. Image courtesy Brownells, Inc.

Custom guns like this Caspian 1911 pistol I built for my son has all the bells and whistles a good gun for many types of competition, such as IDPA, USPSA in the single stack class, steel shooting, and even bullseye. The gun has a match barrel, checkering on the frontstrap and under the trigger guard, BoMar adjustable sight, ambi safety, and shoots five shots under an inch out of a Ransom rest at 25 yards.

Some people like to wear ear plugs and not ear muffs. For competitive bullseye shooting, there can be quite a bit of noise from 30-50 shooters on the line firing at once, so ear muffs along with plugs make a big difference. Image courtesy Brownells, Inc.

The shot timer works as a great training aid while at the range. Having a buddy to start the timer when going through some of the shooting drills is a great way to improve your shooting skills. Image courtesy Brownells, Inc.

er's firing mechanism is modified to accommodate cartridge firing which was common to the period. Sights for the revolvers are normally just blade or post, without paint or other embellishments.

The shooter can alter the grips with checkering, inlays, carving or other types of modifications, but they cannot be modified into a "target" type of grip with a thumbrest, for example. The shooter can install trigger stops, but barrels cannot be heavy type "bull" barrels.

For silhouette shooting, a basic Thompson/Center Contender in a single caliber like .22 LR and, with either iron sights or an inexpensive pistol scope, can be used to compete in certain classes at a high level. But at some point, you may want to compete in silhouette unlimited class, and that

would take a whole other set of handguns and sights. So, after some time, shooting a Plain Jane semi-auto handgun, some people will want to up their game. What to do? The modifications you can make to a handgun will depend on the game you are shooting. In other words, a modification to a pistol might be allowed in one sport but not in another. This chapter will list the modifications that you CAN do to your gun, but you will need to check the rules to see what's allowed and what's not in the particular sport you choose. Many times, a modification will be allowed, but it will put the shooter into a higher category.

For example, if you are shooting a 1911 style handgun in IDPA, and you install a Match barrel and aftermarket sights, you may move from stock service pistol to enhanced service pistol or possibly custom defensive pistol. Glock Shooting Sports Foundation (GSSF) matches may have other rules. The best approach is to check out the rulebooks for the individual types of competitions you are interested in competing in.

Also, check with established competitors to see what they are shooting. Now that we've established that we want to move up our game and enhance our equipment, let's go through some of the modifications available for the various firearms for the different shooting games that are popular in competitive shooting today.

SIGHTS

Enhancing the firearm for competitive shooting really comes down to four areas: sights, triggers, barrels and miscellaneous. Miscellaneous modifications address grips, magazine wells, extended safeties, etc., and many of these modifications depend on the pistol. The 1911 has been used in competitive pistol shooting longer than just about any other handgun, and lends itself to many enhancements. But let's focus on the Big Four. Sights can be broken down into two main types – optical and iron. Optical sights include battery-powered sights like Aim-point, Leupold Delta Point and others. The other types of optical sights are telescopic sights, and these are used in silhouette shooting. The leader in optics for metallic silhouette shooting is the Leupold Extended eye relief scopes, but electronic sights like the Aimpoint are also popular depending on the category you are competing in.

For bullseye, I believe the beginning shooter really needs to get a good handle on the fundamentals of marksmanship before transitioning to optical sights. Unless the shooter is of a certain age, then iron sights should be used until the shooter is achieving a score of 2600 or so, then they should stick with iron sights. Once that level has been achieved, the shooter can transition over to an electronic sight, and for bullseye, the Ultradot and Aimpoint dominate the firing line from the local matches up to the National Championships at Camp Perry. The Aimpoint CompC , the T-2 and the Ultradot are the current favorites.

There are two types of optical sights: tube style and open style sights. The tube type sights are excellent for bullseye, and NRA action pistol, whereas the open type sights are great for a fast game like Open Class USPSA and steel matches. The tube style sights are great for the precision game because they are precise and durable, their windage and elevation adjustments are repeatable, and they hold their zero very well.

If you shoot bullseye for any length of time, you want to install an optical sight at some point. This base for the 1911 pistol will allow the shooter to mount a variety of optics. This could even work on a 1911 for steel competition as well. Image courtesy Brownells, Inc.

Electronic sights usually have a dot reticle, although the Ultradot sight has three types of different reticles, the dot and two others. Additionally, the dots of the Ultradot are adjustable for size and intensity.

So if you want a larger size dot when moving from the 50-yard line to the 25-yard line, for example, you can do that. Some shooters feel that making the size of the dot smaller, going from the farther distance to the short line at 25 yards, makes the wobble of the dot more manageable. Also, remember that most dot sights have a fixed dot size, usually expressed in MOA, or Minutes of Angle. What this means is that the 3- or 4-minute dot will approximately cover 3 or 4 inches at 100 yards (1 MOA being about 1 inch at 100 yards). So a 3 MOA dot would cover about 1.5 inches at 50 yards.

The nice thing about optical sights on the centerfire gun is that, when paired with the .22 LR pistol, both guns can be fitted with the same sight, which makes it easy to shoot a full 2700 match using two firearms with the same type of sight mounted on each gun. This is how the Army Blue team did back in the 80s and how most shooters do it today: two guns, with either an Aimpoint or Ultradot attached to each gun. One other advantage of an optical sight is that is allows the shooter to keep the eyes focused on a single focal plane, rather than having to keep the focus on the front sight and disregarding the rear sight and the target, as with iron sights. This makes shooting with optical sights much faster than with iron sights, all things being equal.

Steel shooting is where an optical sight can really speed things up. Remember, the targets are fairly large, and the range is generally fairly short, so speed rules, and it simply takes too long to acquire iron sights fast enough to be able to compete. Fortunately, there are normally different divisions in steel shooting: limited,

open, single stack, which is 1911-style handguns, as well as production, and IPSC production. If you are shooting an optical sight of any kind, you are normally automatically put into an open class where pretty much any legal firearm is allowed. Even at the local club-level, this rule pretty much holds true. Optical sights will however, get put into a more advanced category. The good news is that you will be competing with other shooters firing the same equipment. Since an optical sight gives the shooter such a tremendous speed advantage, the shooters will always be competing in the same category. This rule pretty much holds true throughout virtually all forms of competitive shooting, not just with handguns.

In IPSC competition, optical sights like the C-MORE and other are restricted to open class, and this is where the shooting gets fast and furious. Pretty much anything goes, from high capacity magazines, to compensators, and just about any other safe modification you can think of. Most shooters start out in limited class with a box stock pistol, and then apply the legal modifications that are allowed in the limited category, and finally, step up to open class as their skills and interest in the game goes up.

The other sub-category of sight is iron sights, and within iron sights there are two subcategories, fixed and adjustable. For a

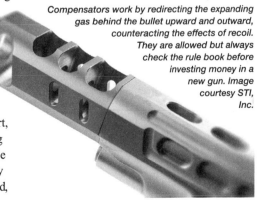

Compensators work by redirecting the expanding gas behind the bullet upward and outward, counteracting the effects of recoil. They are allowed but always check the rule book before investing money in a new gun. Image courtesy STI, Inc.

precision game like bullseye, the adjustable sights are mandatory.

The reason for this is because during the slow fire match, fired at 50 yards, changes in the point of impact, or zero, can change based on various factors. With factory ammunition, different lots will shoot to widely changing points of impact from one lot to another. The adjustable sight allows the shooter to make the adjustments prior to the match by zeroing the pistol prior to the match.

The Bomar adjustable sight was the gold standard for decades, and I shot a Bomar rib with an extended front sight for several years when I shot bullseye. Adjustable sights also allow the shooter to make adjustments based on lighting conditions prevailing at the time of the match. In other words, the zero I have on the bullseye pistol when I shot an outdoor match with no overhead cover last week may be much different than the zero I have on the pistol now that I'm shooting on a different range, with a firing line with overhead cover. The difference is even more striking when going from an outdoor range to an indoor range. Throw in going from the 50-yard line to the 25-yard line, and this poses even more sight adjustment changes. Click values for the Bomar sights are 1 click = .4 inches at 50 yards for elevation, so the adjustments are pretty fine and give the shooter a wide range to make adjustments.

For steel shooting, adjustable sights are normally not necessary because, again, the ranges are short and the targets pretty large. As long as the pistol is shooting pretty close to center mass on a silhouette-type target at 25 yards, the shooter should be good to go. By "pretty close" I mean with a couple of inches from point of aim to point of impact. Any more than that and the shooter should really go to some type of adjustable sight to make sure the shots are accurate. I always like adjustable sights regardless of what game I'm shooting, because if I change am-

One of the most popular improvements of any competitive gun is the addition of fiber optic sights. These come in either red or green.

munition, I want to be able to make adjustments. Although, fixed sights are not a bad choice if I consistently use the same loads. So if I have a gun for single stack USPSA and I use that gun exclusively, then I can work up a good, accurate load for the gun and once the gun has been zeroed with the load, adjustable sights are not needed and a good, fixed sight will give a good sight picture and excellent performance.

Always make adjustments to the sights to make sure that the gun is shooting point of aim/point of impact and not use "Kentucky windage." This term means that the pistol's point of aim and the bullet's point of impact do not coincide. In other words, let's say we are shooting at a tin can at whatever distance, and we aim at the center of the can, but the bullet goes four inches high and four inches to the right of the can. We can see that we will never be able to hit the can unless we compensate for the offset. The point we are aiming at and the impact of the projectile do not converge. So in order to hit the can we need to either adjust the sights, or if we are shooting a pistol with fixed sights, we need to align the front sight to the rear sight, we need good sight alignment, but that alignment needs to be placed four inches below the can and four inches to the left of the can.

If we have to hold to the left or right of the target to compensate, that is what's known as "Kentucky windage," and if we have to hold high or low in order to hit the target, that's known as "Tennessee elevation."

Speaking of fixed sights, they are not always absolutely fixed in place. There are adjustments we can make to get the point of aim and point of impact to coincide so we don't have to resort to Kentucky windage. The point of impact in relation to the point of aim will determine how we make adjustments. Front sights can be adjusted by either replacing the sight with a higher front sight, if the point of impact needs to be lowered, because by raising the front sight, we are effectively lowering the muzzle of the gun, lowering the point of impact. This can only be done if the sight has a removable front sight, like a S&W revolver, a 1911-style gun, or another pistol with a removable front sight. Replacement sights are available at placed like Brownell's Inc, which is one of the oldest and most comprehensive places to get gunsmithing and shooting supplies in the country. If the point of impact needs to be raised, we can shave down the front sight. Gunsmiths do this by placing the slide of pistol in a milling machine, but the front sight can be shaved down by hand with fine files if done carefully. The downside to this is that the shooter will need to make several trips back and forth to the range in order to get the adjustment correct, and there's a risk of taking too much material off the front sight and ruining the sight. Also, if the sight is not taken down level with the rear sight, it will make aiming difficult because the top of the sight blade will be slanted.

One way to reduce the number of trips to the range is to take a portable vise to the range to hold the gun and use a very fine file to carefully make the adjustments. The key is to go slow and check your work by firing the pistol at the distance you are trying to zero the gun at as you go. Since this is a fixed sight gun, you may be asking, "At what distance should I zero the pistol" If this is a competition pistol and the game is IPSC, IDPA, steel, 3-gun or similar action pistol type match, I would zero the gun at 15-20 yards. This will give a good point of aim/point of impact from point blank out to about 30-40 yards.

So, we've made adjustments to the front sight in order to correct for elevation adjustments, but what if the pistol is shooting to the left or right of our aiming point? When adjusting the front sight, we moved the sight in the opposite direction that we want the point of impact to be. In other words, to raise the point of impact, we needed to lower the front sight. With the rear sight (to make left/right adjustments), we need to do the opposite. We move the rear sight in the direction we want to move the point of impact. Some fixed rear sights have no provision for making adjustments and that's just fine. Firearms like the S&W compact revolvers have a groove running through the topstrap of the frame which serves as the rear sight notch. Guns like that are not meant to be used in competition, although they can be used in BUG matches in IDPA (BUG meaning backup gun). But for the most part, guns like the S&W revolvers with the groove rear sights are meant for purely defensive purposes where the distances that the pistol will be used is measured in feet and not yards, and the gun can be effectively used with this type of sighting system.

So, assuming that we have a pistol that has a fixed sight that is mounted in a dovetail arrangement, we can make adjustments to the sights in order to bring the point of impact to where we need it to be. As I mentioned, the rear sight needs to be moved in the direction we want the point of impact to go. So, if the pistol is grouping its shots to the left of the point of aim, then we need to move the rear sight to the right, to move the

A range bag keeps things organized and at the ready while at the range. Nothing rattles a shooter more than not being able to find something when it's needed during a match. Image courtesy Blackhawk! Inc.

impact of the group to the right.

Many of these types of fixed sights have a small set screw that helps secure them in the slide dovetail, but another way these sights are secured is by the tight fit of the sight into the slide dovetail. On a pistol like the Glock, for example, there is a stiff blade spring underneath the sight that applies pressure on the sight to enable a tight fit. It takes a special tool to compress these sights in order to move or remove them. So, with the typical rear sight that's fitted to the dovetail, how can we make small adjustments needed to move the sight in order to get the point of impact to coincide with the point of aim? We need some tools for this and again, Brownell's comes to the rescue. We need a small hammer, and both a nylon and a brass drift punch. If the rear sight has a set screw, we will need an appropriate Allen wrench in order to loosen the screw before we can move the sight. Again, we'll need a small vise to hold the gun while we make adjustments if we are making these adjustments at the range. Otherwise, it will be similar to making the adjustments to the

front sight where we make an adjustment, go to the range and test it, then go back to the shop and make another adjustment. This takes a lot of back and forth, so a good way to overcome this is to take a small vise with padded jaws and mount it to a piece of plywood, which can, in turn, be clamped to a shooting bench or to the tail gate of a pickup truck. We need to have a way to hold the slide of the pistol securely in order to tap the rear sight in the direction we need it to go in order to make the adjustment we need.

Once we have the slide secured and the set screw loosened, if there is one, using the nylon or brass drift punch, tap the rear sight in the direction we want to move the point of impact. Nylon drifts won't mar the finish of the gun, but may not have enough inertia to move a tight rear sight, and that's where the brass drift comes in. Brass will leave brass marks behind, but they can be removed. Be advised, brass can leave impact marks on the sight, but if you want to move the sight, you may have to trade off having a few marks on the sight in exchange for getting the gun zeroed. We can sometimes place a rag over the sight to lessen the chance of impact marks from the brass drift punches. Once I've moved the sight the require amount, I always reset the set screw with some blue Loctite thread adhesive to keep it in place.

Because of the precise nature and small targets of bullseye competition, if shooting iron sights, then adjustable sights are mandatory. Also, shooting at the longer distances of 50 yards means that lighting will also have an effect on the pistol's zero, so the sights should have a small amount of adjustment. When travelling with the Army team, we would finish one match and travel to another city and shoot another match, outdoor lighting conditions would always have a dramatic effect on the gun's zero. I remember shooting the National Mid-Winter matches in Tampa, Florida, with overcast conditions, then driving back to the Ft. Benning range for a practice match in the blistering Georgia sun, and having to make three or four clicks of adjustment on the sights. This is why we would always try to get to a match early in order to make sight adjustments, see how fast or slow the targets were turning, and just get a feel of the range, because every bullseye range is different.

If you are going from indoor lighting to outdoor range lighting conditions, the pistol's zero will be dramatically affected. Since the fixed sights are harder to adjust if we need to move the point of impact, the question becomes, why use them? It's precisely because they are difficult to move that makes them so desirable in a dedicated competition pistol, as well as a defensive pistol. Once the sights are set with a particular brand and bullet weight of ammunition, they usually will stay that way. Fixed sights are very durable and give a good sight picture. So they are useful for IPSC, IDPA, 3-gun and GSSF matches.

One recent trend is the rise of fiber optic sight inserts on front and rear pistol sights. Once these sights were the domain of archery and shotgun competitors, but eventually the technology worked its way over to the pistol games. The benefits are clear, they are inexpensive to manufacture, and they provide high visibility in virtually any lighting conditions. In sunlight, the high visibility fiber optic sights absolutely glow, making the speed shooting games easier.

TRIGGERS

This is not replacing the triggers per se, but performing what's known as a "trigger job" on the guns to lower the weight of the trigger pull, and in some cases, install and set a trigger stop. The trigger is one of the most important areas of the pistol, since it's a main point of interaction between the gun and the shooter.

Get a group of shooters around a campfire and ask them which is more important, sight alignment or trigger control. The answer is that it depends on the game we are shooting. Both are important, but I can be fairly accurate shooting a gun with even a rudimentary set of sights. But if the trigger is extremely heavy, spongy, has excessive creep, or is otherwise of poor quality, it takes some time to overcome those shortcomings. Again, it depends on the game. If I'm shooting bullseye, then both good quality, finely adjustable sights, and a great trigger are equally important since bullseye is such as precise game. IDPA or steel shooting? The ranges are so close and the targets are relatively large, that even a halfway decent set of sights will do, and the trigger quality becomes more important. Does that mean that the action shooting sports are less demanding than bullseye? Not at all, it's just a different game.

The action sports emphasize speed and shooting up close. In the practical pistol matches, trigger quality has preference over sight alignment since the ranges are so close.

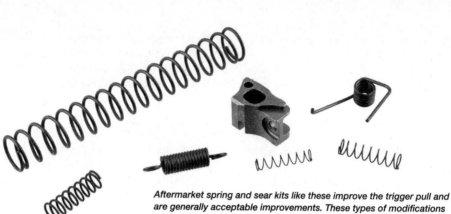

Aftermarket spring and sear kits like these improve the trigger pull and are generally acceptable improvements. These types of modifications make the gun easier to shoot accurately. Image courtesy Brownells, Inc.

We can have poor sight alignment and still make a good shot since the ranges are short and the targets fairly large.

When talking about handgun triggers, it's important to know some of the terminology. One aspect to understand is just how sensitive the human finger and the sense of touch actually is. Groundbreaking new research by Swedish scientists has discovered that the human finger can detect wrinkles on a smooth surface down to nano-scale. (http://www.sciencedaily.com/releases/2013/09/130916110853.htm) This means that humans have the ability to feel objects just a little larger than a molecule, or put another way, if your finger was the size of the Earth, you could feel the difference between a car and a house.

This incredible level of sensitivity means that the interface between the gun and our hands, the trigger, can give the shooter an enormous amount of feedback. This is where trigger terms like rolloff, creepy, spongy, crisp, takeup and overtravel start to have meaning. So let's dive into these terms and provide some definitions and context.

If we are talking about the act of pressing the trigger, the preferred term is "pressing," not "squeezing," because squeezing implies squeezing the entire hand. The fundamentals of pistol marksmanship say the finger must move independently of the shooting hand,

so if we talk about "squeezing" the trigger, people may think in terms of squeezing the whole hand, something we do not want to do. So, the term "pressing" the trigger came about. Before we can actually begin to press the trigger, we run into the term "takeup," and some guns have this feature and some guns do not. Takeup is nothing more than the free travel of the trigger before is meets resistance and starts the process of disengaging the sear from hammer or striker. Some guns have more takeup than others.

As an example of the difference in takeup, look at two popular and very different pistols: the 1911 design which has a traditional hammer and sear fire control design, and the Glock, which is a more modern striker-fired design. Using my 1911 style bullseye pistol, the distance between the trigger at rest and the point where the trigger meets resistance from the disconnector bald and feet of the sear and starts the process of firing the gun is .041 inch. On the Glock, the same distance is .183 inch. For a bullseye pistol, takeup is not really an issue, but for an action shooting sport type firearm, takeup means that there is a longer distance for the finger to travel before that first shot is sent downrange. This is one of several reasons that the 1911 design is so popular with competitive shooters; it's the short, crisp, and fast resetting trigger mechanism that gives it a huge advantage. Notice that we are talking about semi-auto pistols, revolvers do not have takeup in single action mode.

Once we have the trigger started and engaged with the fire control system, two terms come into play: creepy and spongy. Trigger creep is a condition that is very detrimental to accurate shooting. Remember, when firing a shot or a series of shots, we are trying to achieve a surprise break, meaning that the shooter should not consciously know when the gun is going to go off. In the 1911 type pistols, with a hammer and sear arrangement, creep happens when the trigger resistance starts to move the sear nose out of engagement with the hammer hooks, and the shooter feels this movement.

There should be absolutely no movement of the trigger and sear once the trigger is pressed and initial resistance is felt. There should only be steady building pressure on the trigger until the sear is disengaged and the hammer falls. This is how we get the desired surprise break that is so critical to accurate shooting. If the trigger and sear are moving and then the gun goes off, the shooter will be able to feel that and will then anticipate the shot. Problems like creep, sponginess, and anything related to the operation of the trigger require the services of a good pistolsmith.

Sometimes, trigger creep is nearly imperceptible. One good way to identify this is by first making sure the pistol is unloaded. Cycle the slide in order to reset the trigger internal parts; do not just pull the hammer back. Once the slide is cycled and the hammer is cocked, press the trigger and but not to the point where the hammer falls. In other words, only pull the trigger about halfway before letoff and release the trigger. Then carefully pull the hammer back and listen for a very slight click. If you hear this click, this is the sear resetting back against the hammer. This means that the sear actually

started to move out of engagement of the hammer hooks, and this is the definition of creep in the trigger mechanism, the sear is slowly creeping out of engagement with the hammer. Obviously, this can only be done with an exposed hammer type pistol, not a striker fired handgun.

Another term often talked about when shooters get together is a trigger that feels spongy. This is a term that is a little hard to define, but I know it when I feel it. Usually, it is associated with striker-fired pistols, and it is the nature of the system. It's really just the trigger mechanism "loading up" once the initial takeup of the trigger is achieved, it's not a case like creep with the 1911 where the sear is actually moving out of engagement with the hammer. Glock pistols used to be a major offender of this condition, but I have a really old G17, and one of the newest G35 MOS pistols from Glock, and the difference in the quality of the triggers is like night and day. Older Glock triggers were very spongy, but that firearm was designed as a military sidearm, and as such, the triggers were "serviceable." Newer Glock triggers are much less spongy than earlier guns and are more crisp.

Another term used when talking about triggers is rolloff. This is usually associated with the 1911 style design and bullseye guns, but even revolvers can benefit. Rolloff is nothing more than a little softer break when the trigger releases the hammer. Again, this is a term associated with a crisp trigger like a 1911, or other exposed hammer design. Revolvers can also have a little rolloff to the trigger, and a good pistolsmith will know how to set this up for all of these guns.

The last trigger term is overtravel. In the beginning of this section I talked about takeup, which is the initial movement of the trigger before it meets resistance. Overtravel is the continuing movement of the trigger AFTER the sear has disengaged and the hammer or striker is falling. Why is this trigger attribute important? Remember in the chapter on marksmanship I talked about the importance of follow-through. The shooter can influence the shot between the time that the sear and hammer is disengaged and the bullet is out of the barrel. If the trigger is still moving rearward during this time, the shooter can adversely influence the shot. In other words, we want to have the trigger stop all movement as soon as the sear and hammer is disengaged. This is why target triggers on handguns and rifles have a set screw to stop this rearward movement. Normally, the screw can be adjusted by the user with a simple turn of an Allen wrench. I like to set the trigger stop close, but not too close as setting the stop too close can render the gun unable to fire if a little dirt or powder fouling gets between the set screw and the part of the gun that the trigger stop butts up against when the trigger is pulled. This is why you normally won't see a trigger stop on a pistol set up for defensive use, or if there is one, it will be set with a fairly large gap in order to ensure that the pistol will fire.

Now that we have an understanding of triggers, what constitutes a good one, and some bad traits that triggers can have, how can we improve this aspect of the gun in order to help us shoot better scores? 1911-style pistols have a wide variety of aftermarket parts available to enhance the fire-control systems of the gun. Aluminum and titanium, along with carbon fiber triggers, make trigger resetting between shots much faster. Lightweight hammers decrease the locktime, crucial for precision shooting at longer ranges. Other types of guns also benefit from these technologies. Look at the latest Brownell's catalogue and you'll see a wide variety of aftermarket trigger parts available for a wide range of firearms. The Ruger MkII and MkIII benefit from several companies that make match grade trigger

parts for the gun, and remember, the Ruger pistol can be used in bullseye and as a beginning steel competitive pistol, so enhancing the gun makes a lot of sense. Trigger spring kits also help reduce trigger pull weights, and get the trigger pull down to manageable levels for competitive shooting. Keep in mind that simply installing reduced power spring kit will lower the trigger pull weight; it will not do anything for poor trigger quality such as creep. It will also normally only reduce the trigger pull a pound or two. These types of issues require a good pistolsmith. Also, if the pistol is meant for both competition *and* defense, it is best to keep it in unmodified condition for liability reasons in case the pistol is used in self-defense. Striker-fired pistols like the Glock, the S&W M&P, and the Springfield XDs benefit from aftermarket trigger connectors that improve trigger quality while reducing the weight of pull. Always consult the rulebook for any modification you want to perform to make sure it doesn't put you into a category that don't want to be shooting in.

BARRELS

The third area we can modify is the barrel. Again, the decision on installing a match grade barrel depends on the shooting game you are involved in and the level of shooting you are at. In bullseye, since the range is long and the targets at 50 yards are small, the more accuracy we can wring out of the gun, the better. Silhouette shooting too will benefit from match barrels because the targets are small. Again, check the rules to see if any modifications are allowed. The Ruger MkII and MkIIIs and the Thompson Center Contender at the silhouette matches are usually perfectly accurate enough to compete out of the box, but generally speaking, more accuracy is not necessarily a bad thing.

In fact, there is an advantage to installing a match grade barrel beyond just provid-

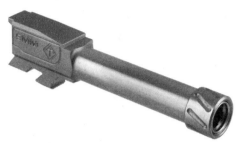

Improvements like this Match grade barrel can really help the accuracy of the pistol, but make sure it's allowed under the rules for the Division you are competing in. Sometimes, these types of improvements can move the gun out of the "stock" category. Image courtesy Brownells, Inc.

Fully supported match barrels like these (bottom) can be more reliable with a variety of ammunition over the traditional type of 1911 barrel (top).

ing the pistol with more inherent accuracy. Confidence is an aspect of shooting that cannot be understated. Installing a match barrel will give the shooter the utmost confidence that the pistol is capable of shooting possibly better than the person holding the gun. When I was a bullseye competitor, I knew that the modifications the Army pistolsmiths made ensured that the guns were capable of shooting perfect scores. This gave me the confidence that if I could raise my skill level, I could shoot a perfect score. Of course, back then and even now no one has ever shot a perfect score in bullseye, but just knowing that the gun was capable of it gave every Army shooter on the firing line a huge boost of confidence.

Match barrels are available from a wide variety of manufacturers and configurations. Basically, match barrels for guns like the 1911, Glock, S&W M&P and the Springfield XD come in two configurations. They are either pre-fit, sometimes known as a drop-in barrel, or oversized in critical areas in order to be fitted by a professional pistolsmith.

Pre-fit match barrels are a great way to get additional accuracy into the pistol, but keep in mind that the barrel may or may not be able to just drop-in. Sometimes, because of manufacturing tolerances, some fitting

may be needed. With the pre-fit barrels, the additional accuracy is provided by the tighter tolerances of the internal bore, groove and chamber dimensions over the factory barrel. Excess tolerances that exist between the barrel and slide are not able to be remedied by the pre-fit barrel. While there will be some gains in accuracy from these pre-fit drop-in style barrels, they do not compare to the oversized match barrel that is fitted to the gun. Using the 1911 as an example, the barrel is fitted via the locking lugs at the top of the barrel to the slide.

The bottoms of the barrel locking lugs are also fitted to the slide stop pin where the barrel sits on lockup when the slide is in battery. The outside diameter of the barrel busing is also fitted to the slide, and the internal diameter of the bushing is fitted to the barrel. These three areas of fitting, top lugs, bottom lugs and barrel bushing, are the reason the 1911 is capable of such phenomenal accuracy.

Other action type pistols also benefit from these gunsmith-fit barrels. I have an oversized Bar-Sto match barrel that I fitted to my Glock 17 over twenty years ago, and it still delivers exceptional accuracy. Bar-Sto Mfg, has been making match grade handgun barrels for decades. I've been to the Bar-Sto facility many years ago and visited with

Irv Stone III over the course of a couple of days and saw the meticulous care they use in making their match grade barrels.

Two downsides to installing any type of match barrel are the expense, and the fact that installing a match barrel will sometimes put the shooter into a higher category, or may not be allowed in the category the shooter is expecting to compete in. in other words, if the pistol has a factory barrel it can be used in production class, but adding a match barrel will get the shooter moved up into limited, or enhanced class. Usually these categories have more proficient shooters, and it's a tougher category to compete in, especially if the shooter is just starting out.

Always consult the rulebooks before performing any modification. As mentioned, these gunsmith-fit barrels are just that, they needed to be installed by a professional gunsmith who has the proper tools and knowledge on how to use them. But whether you decide to have a gunsmith fit barrel installed, or go the pre-fit route, you will experience a much higher level of confidence and accuracy that will take your game to the next level.

The C-More sight is a popular model for a variety of competitive shooting, mostly USPSA open class, steel, and NRA action pistol. Image courtesy STI, Inc.

These night sights are practical for daily use on carry-type pistols, but also work on competitive pistols. Image courtesy Brownell's, Inc.

Popular modifications for the 1911 include the hi-sweep beavertail grip safety with palmswell, a skeleton hammer, and an extended ejector.

Flared magazine wells really help with the speed reloads, but again, the shooter needs to check the rules before installing one on their firearm. Image courtesy STI, Inc.

Extended magazine release buttons are a common accessory for the competitive shooters, but should be avoided on a pistol for guns designed for concealed carry. Image courtesy STI, Inc.

The Gen 4 Glocks have a replaceable backstrap to accommodate any shooter's preferences. These are replaced via a simple retaining pin.

The last area of enhancements that will take your shooting game to another level falls into the category of miscellaneous enhancements. One area to look at is backstraps or grip safeties, depending on the firearm.

Why is this an important modification? It's because getting a high grip on the gun will give the shooter the ability to direct the recoil of the gun up through the arm. Remember, we want to have the axis of the barrel as low as possible in relation to the arm. If the axis of the barrel is high in relation to the arms, the gun will twist in the hand, making recoil management difficult.

Firearms manufacturers are just now catching on to this, with guns like the Glock MOS, S&W M&P, and H&K, and are of-

fering replacement backstraps that let the shooter tailor fit the gun to the hand. The 1911-style guns have had replacement beavertail grip safeties available for the gun for many years that perform the same function; allowing the shooter to get on top of the gun to control recoil.

Large grip safeties offer greater control of the pistol, and for the 1911-style pistols, there are many types and styles available. This part needs to be installed by a professional pistolsmith.

Regardless of the modifications you decide to add to your firearm, always check the rulebook to see if the modifications you want to add are legal for the division and classification you are trying to compete in.

CHAPTER FOURTEEN

NRA WORLD SHOOTING CHAMPIONSHIPS

With any type of competition, there is usually a culmination of the top competitors that come together for a final event that represents the pinnacle of the sport. Shooting has its championships as well, and the shooting sports have been represented in the Olympics for generations.

And each of the competitive pistol shooting sports has their big event. For bullseye, it's the storied ranges of Camp Perry. For action pistol, it's the Bianchi Cup. Cowboy Action or SASS, has the Winter range as their National Championships; and silhouette, GSSF, IPSC, and IDPA all have their championship events. But these events are unique to their individual sport. What if there could be a World Championship that combined some, or many of these disciplines, into one championship in order to find out who was the best overall competitor?

That's what the NRA did when they came up with the NRA World Shooting Championships that were recently held from September 24-26, 2015, at Peacemaker National Training Center in Glengary, West Virginia. The match represented 12 courses of fire, representing various shooting disciplines with handgun, shotgun and rifle. The handgun portion of the match drew from the bullseye, NRA action pistol, Cowboy Action, IPSC and 3-gun competition.

All firearms and ammunition were provided to the competitors, which makes for a level playing field and really tests the overall marksmanship and gunhandling ability of the competitor. Since the firearms are unfamiliar, the shooter has to really rely on good solid shooting fundamentals in order to be successful.

Many professional shooters were there and well as non-pros. One aspect about the match was the prize table, with over $50,000 in cash and awards up for grabs, with the top prize being a check for $25,000 and the title of "World Shooting Champion." The overall winner this year was pro shooter Bruce Piatt, with Diana Muller winning High Lady, and Tim Yackley as High Junior. The reason for the great prize table was the abundance and generosity of the sponsors, with overall match sponsor Magpul contributing greatly to the prize table, and event sponsors such as Leupold, Beretta, Sig, Colt, Nightforce and a host of others contributing big as well.

This made for an event that was rewarding not only for the winners, but also for all of the competitors. This match is a real test of all-around shooting ability and is a unique form of competition. The NRA World Shooting Championship is already a large match with an outstanding list of competitors and sponsors, I predict it will only get bigger and better.

AFTERWORD

This book has been a labor of love for almost a year. During that time I met and talked with a wide variety of handgun shooters and competitors who were passionate about their sport. Hopefully, that enthusiasm has resonated throughout this book, and it will serve to inspire new shooters, or seasoned shooters to take up one of the exciting and fun forms of competitive shooting outlined here.

ACKNOWLEDGEMENTS

There are many people and organizations that I need to thank for their incredible contributions. They include:

Walter, Chuck and Ben at the Bluegrass Sportsman's League in Wilmore, KY where the majority of these images were taken. The Bluegrass Sportsman's League hosts USPSA, IDPA, steel matches, GSSF and 3-gun, along with a variety of shotgun, rifle, blackpowder, dog trials, hiking, camping, fishing and archery events.

Also needing a big thanks are Doug Koenig, Damien Orsinger at NRA HQ, Tex at SASS HQ, Alan Ramsey at GSSF, Mike Foley and others too numerous to list, but you know who you are. Rest assured, every person and organization that contributed to the creation of this book was and is very much appreciated.

GLOSSARY

accurize, accurizing: the process of altering a stock firearm to improve its accuracy.

action: the physical mechanism that manipulates cartridges and/or seals the breech. The term refers to the method in which cartridges are loaded, locked, and extracted from the mechanism. Actions are generally categorized by the type of mechanism used. A firearm action is technically not present on muzzleloaders as all loading is done by hand. The mechanism that fires a muzzleloader is called the lock.

aftermarket: a part that is not made by the original product manufacturer.

allied equipment: also known as ancillary equipment. This would include holsters, magazine pouches, speedloaders, etc.

ammunition or ammo: gunpowder and artillery. Since the design of the cartridge, the meaning has been transferred to the assembly of a projectile and its propellant in a single package.

appearing target: a target not visible until activated or revealed.

bandolier or bandoleer: a pocketed belt for holding ammunition and cartridges. It was usually slung over the chest. Bandoliers are now rare because most military arms use magazines, which are not well-suited to being stored in such a manner. They are, however, still commonly used with shotguns, as individual 12 gauge shells can easily be stored in traditionally designed bandoliers.

barrel: a tube, usually metal, through which a controlled explosion or rapid expansion of gases are released in order to propel a projectile out of the end at a high velocity.

berm: a raised structure of sand or soil that is used as a backstop to stop projectiles. It's also used to separate shooting bays or stages and COF's from each other.

black powder also called gunpowder: a mixture of sulfur, charcoal, and potassium nitrate. It burns rapidly, producing a volume of hot gas made up of carbon dioxide, water, and nitrogen, and a solid residue of potassium sulfide. Because of its burning properties and the amount of heat and gas volume that it generates, gunpowder has been widely used as a propellant in firearms and as a pyrotechnic composition in fireworks. Modern firearms do not use the traditional black powder described here, but instead use smokeless powder.

boundary line: a physical ground reference line in a course of fire, beyond which the competitor is not allowed to cross.

bullet: the solid projectile part of the cartridge intended to strike the target.

caliber/calibre: in small arms, the internal diameter of a firearm's barrel or a cartridge's bullet, usually expressed in millimeters or hundredths of an inch; in measuring rifled barrels this may be measured across the lands (such as .303 British) or grooves (such as .308 Winchester) or; a specific cartridge for which a firearm is chambered, such as .44 magnum. In artillery, the length of the barrel expressed in terms of the internal diameter.

cartridge: the assembly consisting of a bullet, gunpowder, shell casing, and primer. When counting, it is referred to as a "round."

cartridge case: the brass portion of the loaded round which contains all of the other components.

centerfire: a cartridge in which the primer is located in the center of the cartridge case head. Unlike rimfire cartridges, the primer is a separate and replaceable component. The centerfire cartridge has replaced the rimfire in all but the smallest cartridge sizes. Except for low-powered .22 and .17 caliber cartridges, and a handful of antiques, all modern pistol, rifle, and shotgun ammunition are centerfire.

chamber: the portion of the barrel or firing cylinder in which the cartridge is inserted prior to being fired. Rifles and pistols generally have a single chamber in their barrels, while revolvers have multiple chambers in their cylinders and no chamber in their barrel.

chambering: inserting a round into the chamber, either manually or through the action of the weapon.

cold range: a firing range where all firearms must be unloaded until actually on the firing line and ready to be fired by the shooter/competitor under direct supervision by the range officer.

compensator: a device attached to the end of a firearm, usually a handgun, that redirects the escaping powder gasses coming out of the end of the muzzle upward, to counteract the effects of recoil.

course of fire: (COF) an expression used interchangeably with stage.

cross draw: when the competitor draws the firearm across the body, from the weak side of the competitor using the strong hand.

chronograph: a device which measures the speed of a bullet by using skyscreens. The Oehler M35P is an example of a consumer grade chronograph.

disappearing target: a target which, when activated and after completing its movement, is no longer available for engagement.

dry fire: the practice of "firing" a firearm without ammunition. That is, to pull the trigger and allow the hammer or striker to drop on an empty chamber.

dummy: a round of ammunition that is completely inert, i.e., contains no primer, propellant, or explosive charge. It is used to check weapon function, and for crew training. Unlike a blank it contains no charge at all.

ejector: the part of the firearm that causes the fired cartridge to be ejected from the firearm.

eye relief: for optics such as binoculars or a rifle scope, eye relief is the distance from the eyepiece to the viewers eye which matches the eyepiece exit pupil to the eye's entrance pupil. Short eye relief requires the observer to press his or her eye close to the eyepiece in order to see an unvignetted image. For a shooter, eye relief is an important safety consideration. An optic with too short an eye relief can cause a skin cut at the contact point between the optic and the eyebrow of the shooter due to recoil.

expanding bullet: an expanding bullet is a bullet designed to expand on impact, increasing in diameter to limit penetration and/or produce a larger diameter wound. The two typical designs are the hollow point bullet and the soft point bullet.

extractor: a part in a firearm that serves to remove brass cases of fired ammunition from the chamber after the ammunition has been fired. When the gun's action cycles, the extractor lifts or removes the spent brass casing from the firing chamber.

false start: where the shooter attempts to initiate a stage or COF prior to the start signal.

fault line: a physical ground reference line which delineates the stage or course of fire. Foot faults are caused by the competitor overstepping this line.

fouling: the accumulation of unwanted material on solid surfaces. The fouling material can consist of powder, lubrication residue, or bullet material such as lead or copper. This fouling must be removed from match grade firearms for best accuracy.

frangible: a bullet that is designed to disintegrate into tiny particles upon impact to minimize penetration for reasons of range safety, to limit environmental impact, or to limit the danger behind the intended target. Examples are the Glaser Safety Slug and the breaching round.

grain: is a unit of measurement of mass that is based upon the mass of a single seed of a typical cereal. Used in firearms to denote the amount of powder in a cartridge or the weight of a bullet. Traditionally it was based on the weight of a grain of wheat or barley, but since 1958, the grain (gr) measure has been redefined using the International System of Units as precisely 64.79891 mg. There are 7,000 grains per avoirdupois pound in the Imperial and U.S. customary units.

grip safety: a safety mechanism, usually a lever on the rear of a pistol grip, that automatically unlocks the trigger mechanism of a firearm as pressure is applied by the shooter's hand.

gunpowder, also called black powder: is a mixture of sulfur, charcoal, and potassium nitrate. It burns rapidly, producing a volume of hot gas made up of carbon dioxide, water, and nitrogen, and a solid residue of potassium sulfide. Because of its burning properties and the amount of heat and gas volume that it generates, gunpowder has been widely used as a propellant in firearms and as a pyrotechnic composition in fireworks. The term gunpowder also refers broadly to any propellant powder. Modern firearms do not use the traditional gunpowder (black powder) described here, but instead use smokeless powder.

hammer bite: the action of an external hammer pinching or poking the web of the operator's shooting hand between the thumb and fore-finger when the gun is fired. Some handguns prone to this are the M1911 pistol and the Browning Hi-Power.

hang fire: an unexpected delay between the triggering of a firearm and the ignition of the propellant. This failure was common in firearm actions that relied on open primer pans, due to the poor or inconsistent quality of the powder. Modern weapons are susceptible, particularly if the ammunition has been stored in an environment outside of the design specifications.

half-cock: the position of the hammer where the hammer is partially but not completely cocked. Many firearms, particularly older firearms, had a notch cut into the hammer allowing half-cock, as this position would neither allow the gun to fire nor permit the hammer-mounted firing pin to rest on a live percussion cap or cartridge. The purpose of the half-cock position has variously been used both for loading a firearm, and as a safety-mechanism.

hammer: the function of the hammer is to strike the firing pin in a firearm, which in turn detonates the impact-sensitive cartridge primer. The hammer of a firearm was given its name for both resemblance and functional similarity to the common tool.

headspace: the distance measured from the part of the chamber that stops forward motion of the cartridge (the datum reference) to the face of the bolt. Used as a verb, headspace refers to the interference created between this part of the chamber and the feature of the cartridge that achieves the correct positioning.

headstamp: a headstamp is the markings on the bottom of a cartridge case designed for a firearm. It usually tells who manufactured the case. If it is a civilian case it often also tells the caliber, if it is military, the year of manufacture is often added.

holographic weapon sight: a nonmagnifying gun sight that allows the user to look through a glass optical window and see a cross hair reticle image superimposed at a distance on the field of view. The hologram of the reticle is built into the window and is illuminated by a laser diode.

HBWC: acronym for hollow base wad cutter, a type of target bullet, usually .38 Spl.

IMR powder or Improved Military Rifle: a series of tubular nitrocellulose smokeless powders evolved from World War I through World War II for loading military and commercial ammunition and sold to private citizens for reloading rifle ammunition for hunting and target shooting.

internal ballistics: a subfield of ballistics, that is the study of a projectile's behavior from the time its propellant's igniter is initiated until it exits the gun barrel. The study of internal ballistics is important to designers and users of firearms of all types, from small-bore Olympic rifles and pistols, to high-tech artillery.

iron sights: are a system of aligned markers used to assist in the aiming of a device such as a firearm, crossbow, or telescope, and exclude the use of optics as in a scope. Iron sights are typically composed of two component sights, formed by metal blades: a rear sight mounted perpendicular to the line of sight and consisting of some form of notch (open sight) or aperture (closed sight); and a front sight that is a post, bead, or ring.

jacket: a metal, usually copper, wrapped around a lead core to form a bullet.

jeweling: a cosmetic process to enhance the looks of firearm parts, such as the bolt. The look is created with an abrasive brush and compound that roughs the surface of the metal in a circular pattern.

keyhole or keyholing: refers to the shape of the hole left in a paper target by a bullet fired down a gun barrel which has a diameter larger than the bullet or which fails to properly stabilize the bullet. A bullet fired in this manner tends to wobble or tumble as it moves through the air and leaves a "keyhole" shaped hole in a paper target instead of a round one.

kick: the backward momentum of a gun when it is discharged. In technical terms, the recoil caused by the gun exactly balances the forward momentum of the projectile, according to Newton's third law, that every action has an equal and opposite reaction. (often called kickback or simply recoil)

loading: the insertion of ammunition into the firearm.

match official: a person that has an official duty at a match, but is not qualified as, nor acting as a range officer.

movement: the act of changing position, either by moving the feet, or going from standing to kneeling.

must: mandatory, as in "the shooter must perform a mandatory reload after engaging target #3."

no-shoot: a target(s) that, if struck by a fired bullet, will incur a penalty.

not applicable: a rule that does not apply to the particular match or level.

OFM: original firearms manufacturer.

pepper popper: a type of steel plate which falls down when struck by a bullet.

primer: that part of the cartridge that detonates when struck by the striker or firing pin, and detonates, igniting the powder charge, and sending the bullet down the barrel.

prototype: a firearm that is built as a "proof of concept" or test model, not available to the general public.

radial tears: tears in the paper target radiating out from the bullet hole.

range official (RO): that person who is performing range officer duties.

reloading: the act of replenishing ammunition into the firearm. Also, the act of remanufacturing cartridges using a reloading press along with empty cartridge cases and assembling them with new components so that the reloading cartridge can be refired.

reshoot: a competitors attempt to shoot the course of fire or stage again, authorized by the range officer.

shooting box: usually a square shooting area laid out for the competitor using fault lines.

should: something in the stage that is not required but is highly recommended.

sight picture: aiming at a target prior to starting the stage, without actually firing at it. Also, when the shooter superimposes the front and rear sights onto a target.

snap cap: a type of dummy, or non-firing cartridge.

squib: when a cartridge fires but the bullet doesn't exit the barrel and is lodged in the barrel. Also, squib load, squib round. Can be very dangerous if the shooter doesn't realize the bullet is lodged in the barrel and fires another round on top of the stuck bullet.

stance: the position of the shooter's body. (Arms crossed, or arms and hands in the air)

standard exercise: Courses of fire consisting of two or more separately timed component strings.

string: a separately timed component of a Standard Exercise. In Steel matches, a stage is shot with five, separate five shot strings. A match may consist of 4-9 separate stages.

start position: the stance, shooting position, and location prescribed by a COF prior to the issuance of the start signal.

static targets: targets that do not move, and are not activated.

strong hand: the hand that the competitor uses to draw the handgun from the holster.

sweeping: the act of pointing the muzzle of the handgun across any part of the shooter's body or any other person's body.

target(s): any type of scoring target, or non-scoring (no-shoot) target

tie-down rig: a type of holster with lower straps around the bottom of the holster which attached around the thigh to secure the holster.

unloading: the act of removing all ammunition from the firearm.

view: a visual vantage point around a stage or otherwise at a location. (Could be a window port or side of a barricade or a door in a wall)

weak hand: the hand opposite to the hand that draws the pistol from the holster. (The hand opposite to the strong hand)

will: mandatory

ABOUT THE AUTHOR

STEVE SIEBERTS has been a competitive shooter, gunsmith and firearms writer and editor for over 40 years. He was a member of the original Southwest Pistol League in the mid-70s, shot bullseye with the U.S. Army Marksmanship Unit summer team in 1982 and 1984, and was a permanent member of the U.S. Army Marksmanship Training Unit #1 at Ft Meade, MD, from 1982-83. Steve achieved the NRA 2600 award in 1983 and also received his Distinguished Pistol Shot Badge that same year, and then received his President's Hundred Tab in 1984. He was a Paratrooper and a Small Arms Technician with the 82nd Airborne Division for 3½ years and the 8th Infantry Division, (FRG) for 18 months, and has attended five gunsmithing schools, including the Colorado School of Trades, the Army National Match Gunsmithing course at Rock Island Arsenal, and an NRA Riflesnithing Course given by Robert Hart of Hart Rifle Barrels. He has also attended eight factory Armorer's courses, two Army sniper schools, and two courses on ballistics, including the Ballistics Course put on by Dr,. Ken Oehler at his facility in Fredricksburg, TX.

Steve was the Chief Gunsmith for a classified Department of Defense contractor responsible for the building, testing, evaluation and prototype development of small arms systems for U.S. Special Operations forces for over ten years, specializing in building and testing tactical 1911 handguns and precision bolt action rifles. He has been an IPSC competitor on and off since the 70s, and currently shoots IDPA at his local range. Steve has written for many publications over the years, including Shooter's Bible, SWAT, American Handgunner, Guns and Weapons for Law Enforcement, was the Contributing Editor for The Varmint Hunter Magazine and is the former Editor of Concealed Carry Handguns Magazine, Pocket Guns Magazine and the 2015 and 2016 Gun World Buyer's Guide, and is currently the Gunsmithing Editor at Gun World Magazine at Engaged Media, Inc where he writes a monthly column on gunsmithing tips and projects. Steve currently works full time as an Instructional Developer and Videographer, and lives in the South with his wonderful wife of 26 years, his two beautiful and amazing children, and three dopey dogs. In his spare time he enjoys the three B's of life: barbeque, bourbon and watching baseball, not necessarily in that order.

CONTACTS

SHOOTING ORGANIZATIONS

**U.S. Practical Shooting Association/Steel
   Challenge/3-Gun**
872 North Hill Rd.
Burlington, WA, 98233
Voice: 1.360.855.2245
office@uspsa.org
www.uspsa.org

International Defensive Pistol Association
2232 CR 719
Berryville AR. 72616
Phone: (870) 545-3886
Fax: (870) 545-3894
info@idpa.com
www.idpa.ocom

National Rifle Association
Competition Division
http://competitions.nra.org/

Single Action Shooting Society
215 Cowboy Way
Edgewood, New Mexico 87015
Phone: (505) 843-1320
Fax: (877) 770-8687
amber@sassnet.com
www.sassnet.com

**International Handgun Metallic Silhouette
   Association, Inc.**
PO Box 22356
Cheyenne WY 82003
Contact numbers:
801-733-8423 Phone
801-733-8424 Fax
Civilian Marksmanship Program
www.thecmp.org

Glock Shooting Sports Foundation
gssf@glock.us
6000 Highlands Pkwy
Smyrna, GA 30082
Phone: 770.437.4718
Fax: 770.437.4719
https://us.glock.com/team/gssf

FIREARMS

Springfield Armory®
420 West Main Street
Geneseo, IL 61254
www.springfield-armory.com

GLOCK, Inc.
6000 Highlands Parkway
Smyrna, GA 30082 USA
Phone: 770-432-1202
FAX: 770-433-8719
www.us.glock.com

CZ-USA
P.O. Box 171073
Kansas City, KS 66117-0073
Toll-free: 1-800-955-4486
Phone: (913) 321-1811
Fax: (913) 321-2251

Sturm, Ruger & Co., Inc.
411 Sunapee Street
Newport, NH 03773
Telephone: 336-949-5200 / Fax: 603-863-6165
www.ruger.com

Colt's Manufacturing Company LLC
P.O. Box 1868
Hartford, CT 06144 USA
Tel: 800-962-COLT (2658) * Mon-Fri
   9am to 5pm EST
Fax: (860) 244-1379
www.colt.com

Stoeger Industries / Uberti
901 Eighth Street
Pocomoke, MD 21851
Phone: (301) 283-6981 (option 2) or
   (800) 264-4962 (option 2)
www.uberti.com

Smith & Wesson
2100 Roosevelt Avenue
Springfield, MA 01104
1-800-331-0852 (USA) Mon-Fri 8:00AM-8:00PM
   Eastern Time
1-413-781-8300 (International) Mon-Fri
   8:00AM-5:00PM Eastern Time
www.smith-wesson.com

Kimber Mfg. Inc.
555 Taxter Road, Suite 235
Elmsford, NY 10523
Toll-Free: (888) 243-4522
International Calls: (406) 758-2222
Hours: M–F, 9:30 a.m.– 6 p.m. Eastern
www.kimberamerica.com

STI International, Inc
114 Halmar Cove Georgetown, TX 78628
Phone: 512.819.0656
Fax: 512.819.0465
info@stiguns.com
www.stiguns.com

Caspian Arms Ltd.
75 Cal Foster Dr.
Wolcott, VT05680
Office Hours: Monday-Friday 9AM - 5PM EST
Phone Number: 1-802-472-6454
Fax Number: 1-802-472-6709
sales@caspianarms.com
www.caspianarms.com

Freedom Arms
314 Highway 239
Freedom, Wyoming 83120 USA
307-883-2468
www.freedomarms.com

Thompson/Center
2100 Roosevelt Ave.
Springfield, MA 01104
www.tcarms.com

Wichita Arms, Inc.
969 E 620 Ave
Mulberry, KS 66756
Phone: (620) 249-3959
Fax: (316) 347-4885
info@wichitaarms.com
Store Hours: Monday - Friday 9:00am to 4:00pm
www.wichitaarms.com

HOLSTERS

Safariland, Inc.
Ontario HQ
3120 E. Mission Blvd.
Ontario, CA 91761
(800) 347-1200

Blade-Tech Industries
5530 184th St E
Puyallup, WA 98375
877.331.5793
253.655.8059
www.blade-tech.com

Kirkpatrick Leather Company
Laredo, TX 78040 | 1910 San Bernardo
Phone 956-723-6893 / Fax (956) 725-0672
www.kirkpatrickleather.com

Alien Gear Holsters
827 W. Prairie Ave Hayden,
Idaho 83835 Phone:
(208) 215-2046 Monday - Friday: 5am - 5pm
    PST Saturday & Sunday: 7am - 5pm PST
support@aliengearholsters.com.
http://aliengearholsters.com/contacts

OPTICS

AIMPOINT
14103 Mariah Court
Chantilly, VA 20151-2113 USA
Toll-free USA only: +1 877 246-7646
Phone: +1 703 263-9795
Fax: +1 703 263-9463
www.us.aimpoint.com

C-MORE Systems
PO Box 340
Warrenton, VA 20188
888-265-8266
540-347-4683
540-347-4684

sales@cmore.com
www.cmore.com

LEUPOLD & STEVENS
14400 NW Greenbrier Parkway
Beaverton, OR 97006-5790 USA
1-800-LEUPOLD
www.leupold.com

ACCESSORIES

Hornady Manufacturing Company
3625 West Old Potash Hwy
Grand Island, NE 68803 USA
Phone: 1-800-338-3220
Phone: 308-382-1390
Fax: 308-382-5761
www.hornady.com

Brownells Inc.
200 South Front Street
Montezuma, Iowa 50171 USA
www.brownells.com

Redding reloading
1089 Starr Road
Cortland, NY 13045
Phone (607) 753-3331
FAX (607) 756-8445
www.redding-reloading.com

Dillon Precision Products, Inc.
8009 East Dillon's Way
Scottsdale, AZ 85260 U.S.A.
Call Toll Free 800-223-4570 or 480-948-8009
Fax 480-998-2786
www.dillonprecision.com

BLACKHAWK!
9200 Cody
Overland Park, KS 66214
TECHNICAL SERVICE
Phone: 1.800.379.1732
ts@blackhawk.com
www.blackhawk.com

Ransom International
8301 E Pecos Drive # D,
Prescott Valley, AZ 86314
(928)778-7899 Fax (928)778-7993
www.ransomrest.com

Oehler Research, Inc.
P.O. Box 9135
Austin, Texas 78766
(512) 327-6900 | FAX (512) 327-6903
Toll Free (800) 531-5125
www.oehler-research.com

Bluegrass Sportsmen's League
2500 Handy's Bend Road
Wilmore, KY 40390-8029
859-858-4060
www.bgslinc.com